Asa Bullard

Fifty Years with the Sabbath Schools

Asa Bullard

Fifty Years with the Sabbath Schools

ISBN/EAN: 9783743325043

Manufactured in Europe, USA, Canada, Australia, Japa

Cover: Foto ©ninafisch / pixelio.de

Manufactured and distributed by brebook publishing software (www.brebook.com)

Asa Bullard

Fifty Years with the Sabbath Schools

FIFTY YEARS

WITH THE

SABBATH SCHOOLS.

BY

REV. ASA BULLARD, A. M.,

AUTHOR OF "CHILDREN'S ALBUM OF PICTURES AND STORIES,"
"CHILDREN'S BOOK FOR SABBATH HOURS,"
"SUNNY BANK STORIES,"
ETC.

BOSTON:
LOCKWOOD, BROOKS AND COMPANY.
1876.

Copyright,
LOCKWOOD, BROOKS & CO.
1876.

Press of Rockwell & Churchill.
Stereotyped at the Boston Stereotype Foundry,
19 Spring Lane.

TO THE

NUMEROUS FAMILIES AND FRIENDS

WHOSE CORDIAL GREETINGS, KIND HOSPITALITIES, AND HEARTY
CO-OPERATION HAVE BEEN EXTENDED TO THE
AUTHOR DURING THESE

Fifty Years with the Sabbath Schools,

AND TO

ALL CO-LABORERS IN THE SABBATH SCHOOL WORK,

AND IN THE MORAL AND
RELIGIOUS INSTRUCTION OF THE YOUNG,

THIS VOLUME

IS RESPECTFULLY DEDICATED.

INTRODUCTORY.

An experience of fifty years in any work entitles a man to speak. The impressions which are in the mind after so long service, cannot fail to be instructive. Although very much has been written in connection with Sabbath schools, very little has been said of their history, — what was their origin in this country, what has been their course, what have they accomplished, what are their resources at the present time? These are inquiries of great interest. He who shall answer them intelligently must, almost of necessity, have lived and advanced with them.

It will be acknowledged on every hand that the author of this book has rare qualifications for the work he has done. His personal career is nearly coeval and parallel with Sabbath schools in this land. He has had his life among them. A great part of them he has been. He will be associated with them as long as his name is remembered. He has been active in promoting their interests, has had a true sympathy with their design and methods, has seen their strength and weakness, and has gained by a large experience a vantage ground for instructing the people.

Whoever reads this book, whether he be minister, superintendent, teacher, librarian, parent, child, will find that which will serve him well. In the prominent position now accorded to the Sabbath school, and the inestimable work committed to its charge, will be found good reason for drawing wisdom from the past, for listening to the elders, for widening knowledge and deepening devotion. To this end this book is commended to all who hold any relation to the subjects of which it treats.

ALEXANDER McKENZIE.

CAMBRIDGE, 1876.

PREFACE.

ELIHU says, "Days should speak, and multitude of years should teach wisdom." And it is thought that some of the observations and experiences of fifty years with the Sabbath schools, in regard to their conduct and progress, gathered into permanent form, might be of interest and profit to the friends of this institution at the present day.

This volume is not intended to be an autobiography of the author, only so far as relates to his connection with Sabbath schools. Nor is it intended to be a full and complete history of the rise and progress of this institution.

All that is attempted is to give some brief sketches of the earlier schools, the modes of conducting them, and some of the changes that have taken place, and to present such incidents and illustrations that have fallen under his observation, in regard to the various departments and agencies of the Sabbath school work, as will be likely to aid and quicken all who are in any way interested in the right training of the young, or in promoting the more earnest study of the word of God.

A. B.

Sunnybank, Cambridge, 1876.

CONTENTS.

CHAPTER		PAGE
I.	PERSONAL CONNECTION AND LABORS WITH THE INSTITUTION.	11
II.	SKETCH OF THE RISE AND PROGRESS OF SABBATH SCHOOLS.	29
III.	MODES OF CONDUCTING SABBATH SCHOOLS.	49
IV.	REVIVAL OF THE STUDY OF THE CATECHISM.	75
V.	RELATION OF PARENTS TO THE SABBATH SCHOOL.	81
VI.	LABORS OF PASTORS.	99
VII.	RELATION OF THE CHURCH TO THE SABBATH SCHOOL.	103
VIII.	SUPERINTENDENTS AND TEACHERS.	112
IX.	RELIGIOUS INFLUENCE OF THE SABBATH SCHOOL.	147
X.	THE LIBRARY.	158
XI.	ADULT CLASSES IN THE SABBATH SCHOOL.	180
XII.	INFANT DEPARTMENT.	195
XIII.	WOMAN'S MISSION IN THE SABBATH SCHOOL.	202
XIV.	MISSION SABBATH SCHOOLS.	207
XV.	GATHERING IN NEW SCHOLARS.	215
XVI.	THE SABBATH SCHOOL CONCERT.	223
XVII.	BENEVOLENCE AMONG THE YOUNG.	235

XVIII.	Juvenile Music.	. 241
XIX.	Teaching the Children Temperance. . .	. 246
XX.	Sabbath School Conventions, Celebrations, and Picnics.	. 259
XXI.	Evils resulting from Sabbath Schools. . .	. 268
XXII.	The Family.	. 278
XXIII.	Sabbath Schools an Auxiliary to the Church.	. 318

FIFTY YEARS

WITH

THE SABBATH SCHOOLS.

I.

PERSONAL CONNECTION AND LABORS WITH THE INSTITUTION.

THE author's first connection with the Sabbath school was in Sutton, Mass. This school, his now sainted mother used to say, commenced with only three scholars — his older brother and sister and himself. The people generally, and even the minister, at that time were a little doubtful whether it was right to keep school Sabbath-day, and did not at first allow their children to join it. At length, as it was seen that the lady who had the charge of it was doing no injury to her three scholars, but was rather interesting them in committing verses of the Bible and hymns to memory, one child after another was permitted to enter the school, so that ere long there were several pews well filled with attentive and interested scholars. Then the school was transferred to a large school-house near by, and organized regularly with a superintendent and other officers and teachers.

This must have been in 1817 or 1818.

Since then, for nearly sixty years, he has always been

connected with this institution as a scholar, teacher, superintendent, or in a public capacity, and more than forty-five years in public labors connected with Sabbath schools.

During his preparatory and collegiate course of study in Amherst, Mass., of five or six years, ending September, 1828, he was a teacher or superintendent. For most of the four years in college he conducted a Sabbath school or Bible class among the colored people, in a private dwelling about a mile from college.

A year after graduating was spent in teaching a school for fitting boys for college in Augusta, Me. The following is an account of his Sabbath school labors during that year.

Soon after commencing his school, at the request of the pastor of the Congregational church, the late Rev. Benjamin Tappan, D. D., he prepared and read to the people an address on the subject of Sabbath schools. In a short time he took measures to form a Bible class on the Sabbath for colored people. There were only six or eight of that class of persons in the place, but so much interest was awakened that they came from two to six miles, and he soon had a class of twenty-five or thirty.

The following account of the origin and history of this class was published in the "Sabbath School Treasury," of Boston, in October, 1829:—

"About twelve months since I took up my residence for a year in Augusta, Me. After the exercises of the first Sabbath I sat down in rather a melancholy mood, and began to think of my Sabbaths spent in Massachusetts. On no public exercise of the Sabbath did my mind rest with such intense interest as on that of my colored class. The recollection that the many pleasant seasons spent in that class were now at an end not a little increased my sadness. But the inquiry soon arose in my mind, May there not be some of that neglected people in this place? If so, can they not be collected into a class? On learning that there were two or three small families, consisting in all of some six or eight souls, I resolved to search them out. Accordingly the next week I called at one of their dwellings and found a very intelligent-looking woman, who listened with much apparent interest to the explanation of my object, and said she could not read, but she should like to learn, so that she might read her Bible. This readiness to enter into my plans greatly encouraged me to hope that a class could be collected with but little difficulty.

"As I approached the next dwelling, near by, I heard the loud laugh and the voice of merriment. This damped my early hopes. I stopped, turned about, and well-nigh resolved to abandon my object, at least for that time. But a moment's reflection influenced me to seize the present opportunity, and go forward. I entered with some reluctance, and there found six or eight colored persons, some from other towns, who had collected together to spend their Sabbath evening in amusement.

"It would be rather difficult for a person not familiar with such scenes to conceive the variety of emotions which the presence of a stranger, especially on such an errand, produced among them. At first they manifested an astonishment bordering on consternation. But, as the object of my visit was explained, and the advantages of spending a part of the Sabbath in the study of the Bible mentioned, together with the interest manifested by a class of colored persons in Massachusetts, the first excitement subsided, and some began to show great interest; some appeared indifferent, and some half-concealed a smile of derision.

"After more conversation they concluded to consider the

subject and decide in reference to it at my next call. During the week I called again, and found the subject of my compensation the only thing concerning which they had further inquiries to make. Being informed that the only compensation expected or wished for was their attendance and improvement, they readily accepted my proposals, and appointed the next Sabbath for organization.

"On the next Sabbath I found some six or seven assembled, awaiting my arrival. Having implored the aid of the Divine Spirit, without which all our efforts are inefficient, they were requested to read a chapter in the Bible. Some could read with considerable ease, some very little, and some none at all.

"I felt that the success of this experiment depended in a great measure upon the impression made at the first meeting; and it was so ordered that the impression was most favorable. A very lively interest was evidently awakened among several of the class, who soon visited many of the colored people living two and even six miles distant, and told them all about their class, and invited their attendance.

"On the following Sabbath our number was somewhat enlarged, and the interest increased. One middle-aged female, who barely knew her alphabet, had purchased a Testament, and began to spell out some of the small words. She continued to improve every week, and was soon able to read with the class with some ease. Not unfrequently she would repeat five or ten verses of Scripture which she had learned with much painstaking during the week.

"One girl, eighteen or twenty years of age, who was quite intelligent, was of great service in hearing some of the children read and recite their lessons. She usually recited herself from fifteen to fifty verses every Sabbath. Another little girl of nine recited ten, sometimes forty, verses with great propriety.

"Almost every week would show some increase of interest, sometimes of numbers. During the latter part of autumn the class varied in number from twelve to twenty, some of whom came a distance of six miles, most of them with their new Bibles or Testaments.

"About this time one of the class suggested the expediency of meeting a part of the time at an adjoining town, for the better accommodation of members living at a distance, at the same time manifesting his interest by generously offering to procure a carriage for my conveyance. This suggestion led to the organization of another class in that town, under the care of several resident young men. My class was somewhat diminished by the formation of this new one, but continued to have an average number of twelve or fourteen.

"The interest of the class, which decreased a little during the intense cold of winter, revived again in the spring, and continued to increase through the summer. At some meetings a very deep solemnity pervaded the class, and personal conversation in some instances discovered a tenderness of conscience, which encouraged the hope that the Lord, who 'hath made of one blood all the nations of men, for to dwell on all the face of the earth,' intended to prepare some of these poor souls for his heavenly kingdom.

"A girl about twenty years of age, who, having long striven hard, in opposition to many natural obstacles, to learn to read, having made but little or no progress, one day burst into tears, and said, 'I do want to learn to read my Bible.'

"Another girl, about the same age, who had made considerable progress in her efforts to read, said, with eyes full of tears, 'O, how I want to be able to sit down and read one chapter in my Bible! But I am almost discouraged, and sometimes think I will give it up.' After a little encouragement she said, 'I will begin once more and try harder, for I do want to read my Bible.'

"The woman mentioned above, who had begun to read with the class, appeared exceedingly interested ever after the class was organized. She refused to work out on Wednesday, for she wished to spend that day at home, so as to devote a part of it to her lessons for the Bible class. She often showed much sorrow for sin, and expressed strong desires to become a Christian. This class, which I have now left, I commend to the prayers of those who love the souls of all men, and to the protection of the God of all grace, praying with earnestness that I may meet each member of it in the kingdom of glory."

At nine o'clock, Sabbath morning, he had a class of the boys of his school in the Sabbath school at the church. He then rode three miles and held a public service in a large school-house in the North Parish, as it was called, reading a printed sermon. He soon organized a Sabbath school, which he superintended in this school-house, at the close of the morning service; then in the afternoon he conducted a Bible service, which became so crowded that the house and entry were full, and many gathered on the outside about the windows. Then at five o'clock in the afternoon he held his Bible class for colored people in the village.

A revival of great interest commenced soon after he began his various services at the school-house, which resulted, in a year or two, in the organization of a church of about sixty members. All his half-holidays he spent, after the revival commenced, in visiting among the people of his little parish.

In the Annual Report of the Maine Sabbath School Union for 1832, the Board of Managers thus speak of the school here referred to: —

"In the North Parish of Augusta the Sabbath school

embraces almost the entire number of adults and children who usually meet together for worship. The whole history of this church is identified with the history of Sabbath school operations among them. The exercises of the school have constituted their choicest means of grace and salvation ; and, perhaps, in no place have the privileges of Sabbath school instruction been, or can be, more affectionately cherished. Within the year, eleven have been converted from three classes, and nine of these are adults who have never, before the last spring, been connected with a Sabbath school."

During his two years, beginning September, 1829, in the Theological Seminary, at Andover, Mass., he was connected with the Sabbath school in the Old South Congregational church in the village; the first year as teacher of a class of mothers, and the second as associate superintendent with the late Rev. Thomas Brainard, D. D., of Philadelphia.

That school, at that time, was probably the largest in the state. On one Sabbath there were present six hundred and seven persons, including those of all ages, from three to about ninety.

One vacation, during this course at Andover, the writer was employed, under the appointment of the Massachusetts Sabbath School Union, which was composed of the Congregational and Baptist churches of the state, in visiting and addressing eighteen of the churches in the northern part of Worcester county, in regard to the interests of Sabbath schools; and one vacation he was employed by the friends of this institution in Kennebec county, Maine, in promoting this cause among the churches in that county.

About this time quite an impulse was given to the

cause of Sabbath schools extensively. In 1829 a Sabbath school and Bible class association was formed among the students of the Theological Seminary at Andover, and a similar one was also formed the same year in the theological department of Yale College, in New Haven. The objects of these societies were to collect and diffuse information concerning Bible classes and Sabbath schools, and to ascertain the best mode of conducting and extending them.

The association at Andover held frequent meetings for discussion on various practical subjects connected with the management of Sabbath schools. There were several committees; one of correspondence, whose duty it was to correspond with clergymen and others, in all parts of this and foreign lands, in regard to the interests of this institution; one on review, whose duty it was to examine and recommend books for the library; and another on publication, with which the writer was connected, whose duty it was to prepare articles from the communications received by the committee of correspondence, &c., for the press.

The association published twelve or fifteen articles in the "Sabbath School Treasury" for 1830–31 on subjects like the following: "How can ministers of the gospel best promote the interests of Sabbath schools?" "Mutual instruction;" "What is your mode of teaching?" "How can Sabbath schools be made to benefit remote parts of the town?" "Methods of replenishing the library," &c.

From some of the letters to this association, and some of our communications for the press, we have given extracts in the following pages, as they help to present a correct idea of the state of Sabbath schools at that early period, and of the manner of conducting them.

The students in this seminary, at a meeting, June 12th, the year previous to the establishment of the association, exhibited the interest they felt in this cause by passing the following resolution: —

"*Resolved*, That we will endeavor to make ourselves acquainted with the best system of Sabbath-school management and instruction, and to qualify ourselves in all respects, as far as we are able, to lend our influence to this cause; and that we consider ourselves obligated to aid, according to the measure of our ability, in promoting its advancement, wherever God, in his providence, may call us."

And all these students carried the spirit of this resolution with them into the ministry, and they have ever been the warm friends and supporters of this institution.

In 1831, the writer accepted an invitation from the board of managers of the Maine Sabbath School Union, and became its general agent, and labored in that capacity, and as corresponding secretary, for three years. An account of these three years' service may not be out of place here.

At that time the institution of Sabbath schools in what was then called the "District of Maine," was comparatively in its infancy. There were in all only about three hundred schools connected with the union, and not over five hundred in the whole state, containing, perhaps, a total of twenty thousand teachers and scholars.

The action of the union and the friends of the cause, during those three years, is not wanting in interest and instruction to the most zealous Sabbath school workers of the present day.

At the sixth annual meeting of the union, January, 1832, so important did this work appear, that the following resolution was presented, and, after a most earnest advocacy, unanimously and with much enthusiasm, adopted: —

"*Resolved*, That, relying upon divine assistance, we will establish a Sabbath school in every town and school district in the state, where it is practicable and advisable, within a year and a half from this time."

During the discussion of this subject, a member of the board offered, in case the resolution should be carried into effect, to pay one hundred and fifty dollars towards the expense of the undertaking.

It was understood that it was not generally advisable to establish a school in any district where the children could attend any existing school; and it was not considered practicable unless it could be accomplished at a reasonable expense of money and labor.

It was comparatively an easy matter, on a pleasant January evening and in a warm and comfortable house, to pass this resolution, but it was found to be a very different matter to carry it into effect. But this action of the union deeply stirred the hearts of all the friends of the cause in the state; and it is believed there never has been a period when there was a greater amount of Sabbath school work done in Maine than during the year and a half contemplated in that resolution.

Early in the spring the general agent traversed the state in every direction, visited the auxiliary unions, and held meetings to secure in every county and town committees and individuals who would become responsible for the accomplishment of their portion of the work. Nearly the whole state was thus appropriated to committees and individuals. And a vast amount of labor from voluntary and unpaid agents was secured during the year. Young ladies were obtained to teach district schools, with special reference to the establishment of Sabbath schools in the towns and neighborhoods where they taught. Merchants were engaged to converse with their customers from adjacent towns or districts, and persuade them, if possible, to see that the work was accomplished in their respective communities. Juvenile sewing circles were formed to help furnish funds for carrying on the enterprise.

It is interesting, at this distance of time, to look back and see the enthusiasm manifested so extensively in this undertaking. Men and women everywhere entered into it most heartily. Ten gentlemen took seventeen towns, and promised to visit them on the Sabbath, and, so far as it was practicable, establish schools where they were needed. An aged minister, with whitened locks, pledged himself to carry the resolution into effect in seven different towns, in some of which there never had been a school.

The plan he adopted for the establishment of a school in one of these towns was quite novel and interesting. Having consulted with the minister of the place, and appointed a meeting for the purpose, he took his superintendent and several teachers and went to the meeting. After addressing the people on the subject, he assisted in organizing a school into classes, and choosing a superintendent and teachers. Then, with his superintendent and teachers, he gave the people a practical illustration of his manner of teaching and conducting a Sabbath school. This was, over forty years ago, precisely like the "Sabbath School Exercise" at our conventions of the present day. A few weeks after this, two other schools were in operation, and arrangements were made to organize two more.

At the close of a meeting in another place, while several gentlemen were consulting together on this work, a young woman offered to assume the responsibility of establishing and conducting a Sabbath school in a certain district in an adjoining town, where she expected to teach the public school. "But if I should not," said she, "it is only four miles and a half, and I can walk out on Saturday, spend the Sabbath in the Sabbath school, and then return on Monday."

She taught the public school as she expected, and also established and sustained a Sabbath school through the season almost unaided by any one.

"There is such a neighborhood," said a man, "where there must be a Sabbath school. I don't know whom we can get to go out there. I don't know as there is any one : but I will see that the work is done." As he finished this remark, a woman, perhaps fifty years of age, said, "Why won't you let me go to that neighborhood ? "

One of the managers of a county union proposed at their meeting for consultation that an agent should be employed six months to assist them in redeeming their pledge. He also informed them where no small part of the necessary funds could be obtained. "There are fifteen or sixteen young ladies," said he, "who have been, or are now, connected with my class in the Sabbath school, and have all become hopefully pious.

Two months since they formed themselves into a sewing society, to meet once in two weeks. They have already in their treasury about thirty dollars, and they say they will increase it to seventy-five or one hundred dollars, and give it towards defraying the expense of an agent in this county, if the board will employ one. They have also pledged themselves to redeem one hour from sleep every morning, to work for the cause of Sabbath schools."

In another county, instead of employing an agent, the pastors of the Congregational churches made an arrangement in the spring for a general exchange, when all were to present the subject of Sabbath schools to each other's people. In addition to this, each minister was to spend a few days with the brother with whom he exchanged; and they were to go into all parts of the parish, where it was needful, and hold meetings on the subject, to establish, revive, or encourage Sabbath schools, as the case might require. The effect of this labor was most happy, both upon the ministers and upon the people. The former, from the very fact that they labored in the cause, became more deeply interested in it, while the latter naturally concluded that an object which had taken such a strong hold upon the feelings of their ministers, must be an important one, deserving their hearty coöperation. These are but a few specimens of the zeal with which men and women all over the state entered into this noble work.

At the next annual meeting it was reported that a great amount of work had been performed, and one hundred new schools had been organized; but more remained to be done to carry out the resolution than could be accomplished by the general agent alone.

Early in the spring, therefore, he visited many of our colleges, theological and other seminaries, and clergymen, and secured the services in this work of eighteen students and eight or ten ministers, from one or two to seven weeks each. So that, at the anniversary in 1834, it was reported that the objects of the resolution, passed in 1832, had been substantially accomplished. During that year one hundred and eighty-nine new schools were organized, making the whole number connected with the union nine hundred and twenty-nine, containing a membership of over thirty-eight thousand.

During the three years of this agency about three hundred new schools were organized, under the direction of the general agent. Some of those schools, for want of the fostering care of the church, in a few months became extinct, but many of them are now among the most interesting and efficient schools in the state. And there are many men and women, who took part in that work, who now look back upon it with no small degree of satisfaction. And there were many laborers in those days — more than two score years ago — in Maine, who would compare favorably with the most zealous and successful Sabbath school laborers of the present day in any part of the country.

In order to give more influence and greater facility to the agent, in his labors among the churches, he was licensed, by an association of ministers, at Augusta, October 25, 1831; and was ordained as an evangelist, in connection with the annual meeting of the union, January 13, 1832. The exercises were peculiar for such an occasion, inasmuch as they were all more or less directly connected with the special work of the candidate for ordination. The following account of the services was communicated to the "Sabbath School Instructor," published in Portland, by the union: —

"Ordained, in Portland, on the 13th instant, Rev. Asa Bullard, as an Evangelist. Introductory prayer by Rev. Adam Wilson, of Portland. [Mr. Wilson was the editor of a Baptist paper, and a member of the board of managers of the union.] Sermon by Rev. Benjamin Tappan, of Augusta; text, Deut. xxxi. 12, 13. Consecrating prayer by Rev. Jotham Sewall, of Chesterville. Charge by Rev. Dr. Tyler, of Portland. Right hand of fellowship by Rev. Prof. Alvin Bond, of Bangor. Address by Rev. Daniel D. Tappan, of Alfred. Concluding prayer by Rev. Mr. Butler. of the Baptist church, North Yarmouth.

"The exercises of the occasion were appropriate, and of a peculiarly interesting character. The sermon exhibited, in a happy and impressive manner, the importance of biblical instruction. Among other topics the preacher dwelt upon the Sabbath school institution, as combining the most successful means for diffusing a knowledge of the Bible, and preoccupying the minds of the rising generation in favor of the sacred truths and pure morality of the Gospel."

On resigning his connection with the Maine Sabbath School Union, the board expressed, in an official form, their appreciation of his labors.

Immediately after his resignation, he was invited to become the secretary and general agent of the Massachusetts Sabbath School Society, now called the Congregational Publishing Society, upon which service he entered March 1, 1834.

Having completed a period of forty-two years of labor in connection with this society, a brief review of this period, in its relations to the secretary of the society, may be interesting and suggestive.

There is not a person now connected with the officers of the society or the board of managers who was connected with either of them when the writer entered upon his office forty-two years ago.

There have been during this period five presidents, three of whom have deceased, forty vice-presidents, eight of whom have died, eighty-three members of the board of managers, of whom thirty-two are not living. One agent of the depository and two treasurers have also passed away.

In his work as general agent for forty-five years, including his three years in Maine, the writer has made about thirty-four hundred visits in nearly one thousand different towns and parishes, preached or given addresses seven thousand one hundred and forty-five times, and travelled about two hundred and forty-five thousand miles. With the exception of two western towns, all this has been in comparatively short journeys, mostly in New England and Canada. He has attended every year more or less public meetings, state and county conferences and associations of churches, Sabbath school conventions, festivals, &c., in different parts of the country. In connection with these visits he probably addressed between one million eight hundred thousand and two millions of persons, perhaps more than six hundred thousand different persons, and a large portion of them many times.

In his connection with this society he edited every number of the society's monthly periodical, the "Sabbath School Visitor," for ten years; was assistant editor of the "Congregational Visitor" for three years, and he edited every number of its weekly periodical, the "Well-Spring," for thirty-one years, from its commencement, January 1, 1844, and has since aided in editing it.

He was the corresponding and recording secretary of the society, of the board of managers, and of the Sabbath school publishing department, and several years of the theological publishing department also; he prepared all but five or six of the annual reports of the society, and all of the quarterly reports of the Sabbath school committee, and the committee on agencies for the same period. He wrote numerous circulars, letters to Sabbath schools and juvenile societies, and other public documents; and also wrote or compiled about forty of its 18mo books, containing over four thousand pages, thirty-six 32mo books, containing eight hundred pages, and numerous cards, and performed whatever other labors he could make of service to the society in its work in behalf of Sabbath schools.

At the end of forty-one years a new secretary was chosen, and the writer was chosen honorary secretary, and relieved from a portion of his accustomed duties.

The secretary, during the long period of his service, was seldom absent for personal recreation more than a few days at a time, and never so as to remit his care of the "Well-Spring" for a single number, or the performance of any of his duties connected with the society.

During the forty-two years here referred to the society issued, not including the fifty or more theological works and various tracts of the late Congregational Board of Publication, before it was united in this society, about thirty-four hundred different publications, containing in all about one hundred and eighty thousand pages of new matter. Of these publications over two thousand were bound volumes. This estimate does not include the eleven volumes of the "Sabbath School Visitor," the five volumes of the "Congregational Visitor," nor the thirty-two volumes of the "Well-Spring." Nor does it include the forty-two annual reports, nor the numerous catalogues, circulars, and other special documents that were published.

The amount of business connected with the depository during this period was at least two million five hundred thousand dollars, and the amount of charitable contributions that the society disbursed, mostly in books and papers, to aid in organizing and maintaining Sabbath schools in every part of the country, at least two hundred thousand dollars.

II.

SKETCH OF THE RISE AND PROGRESS OF SABBATH SCHOOLS.

It is well known that Robert Raikes, of Gloucester, England, is generally acknowledged as the founder of Sabbath schools. His first school was started in 1781, when he was forty-six years of age.

"The beginning of this scheme," he says, in a letter dated November 25, 1783, "was entirely owing to accident. Some business leading me, one morning, into the suburbs of the city, where the lowest of the people (who are principally employed in the pin manufactory) chiefly reside, I was struck with concern at seeing a group of children, wretchedly ragged, at play in the street. I asked an inhabitant whether these children belonged to that part of the town, and lamented their misery and idleness. 'Ah, sir,' said the woman to whom I was speaking, 'could you take a view of this part of the town on a Sunday you would be shocked, indeed; for then the street is filled with multitudes of these wretches, who, released on that day from employment, spend their time in noise and riot, playing at chuck, cursing and swearing in a manner so horrid as to convey to any serious mind an idea of hell rather than any other place.'

"This conversation suggested to me that it would be at least a harmless attempt, if it were productive of no good, should some little plan be formed to check this deplorable profanation of the Sabbath. I then inquired of the woman if there were any decent, well-disposed women in the neighborhood who kept schools for teaching to read. I presently was directed to four. To them I applied, and made an agreement with them to receive as many children as I should send upon a Sunday, whom they were to instruct in reading and in the church catechism. For this I engaged to pay them each a shilling for their day's employment.

"This was the commencement of the plan."

A union society, established at Stockport, near Manchester, in 1784, had a school of about five thousand scholars. In one building there were over four thousand under the same roof, divided among eighty-six rooms. There were over three hundred teachers, and all excepting five of these had been scholars. What is remarkable is, that over two thousand of the scholars were past sixteen years of age, and more of them were boys than girls, and more of the teachers males than females. Besides instruction in the Scriptures, they taught writing and elementary book-keeping, with no book used excepting the Bible. A great portion of the scholars were operatives in the factories, and had no other means of education.

There were individuals many years before this, in various places, who instructed children on the Sabbath; but Robert Raikes began what is now so generally adopted in all Christian lands, the system of Sabbath schools. At first they were designed especially for the children of the poor and neglected.

The Rev. Dr. Rauch, in a letter on German characteristics, published in the "Home Missionary" for January, 1836, speaks of the existence of Sabbath schools nearly a century before their establishment by Robert Raikes.

"As early as the year 1695," he says, "we find the Sunday schools already introduced into Wurtemberg, the object of which was to make the scholars, every morning before service, recite psalms, verses of the Bible, and parts of the catechism. In the year 1739 it was made the duty of all ministers to have Sunday and holy-day schools established, which differed from those mentioned above in some particulars. All unmarried persons were required, from the time of their confirmation till their twentieth or twenty-eighth year, to attend, bring their Bibles, catechisms, and hymn-books with them, repeat their whole course of religious instruction, and enlarge upon it. These exercises were as interesting to the congregation as useful to the youth, and are fully retained till the present day."

Nicholas Ferrar was born in London in 1591. In 1625 he established his family at Little Gidding, a retired part of Huntingdonshire. Here, in his family and neighborhood, we find, two hundred and fifty-one years ago, what was in truth a Sabbath school.

In returning from divine service in the morning, Mr. Ferrar's elder nieces, and some others appointed for that duty, heard the children repeat the psalms which they had learned the week before. Mr. F., desiring the religious improvement of all around him, offered such children as would come to his house Sabbath morning a penny for every psalm they would commit to memory perfectly, and also a dinner. Sometimes there were present forty or fifty at once. He gave a Psalter to every one who came. The psalm-children, as they were called, used frequently to recite portions of what they had learned before, in addition to what they had committed that week, so as to fix them more strongly in their memories.

"The influence of this Sabbath school," says the biographer, "was such that the neighboring ministers declared a mighty change was wrought, not only on the children, but on the men and women at home; for the parents would naturally hear their children repeating their sacred lessons, whereas, heretofore their tongues had been exercised in singing lewd or profane songs, or, at least, idle ballads. Now the streets and doors resounded with the sacred poetry of David's harp. Thus it is that little children, in multitudes of instances, become the instructors of their parents, and this is one of the greatest encouragements which we have in the work of Sabbath schools."

In the early history of our own country, great interest was manifested in the moral and religious instruction of the young in the family, the church, and the public school.

Cotton Mather, in his life of the Rev. John Eliot, says of him, "He always had a mighty concern upon his mind for the little children. 'Twas an affectionate stroke in one of the little papers he published for them; sure Christ is not willing to lose his lambs; and I have come to remember with what a hearty, fervent, zealous application he addressed himself, when, in the name of the neighboring pastors and churches, he gave me the right hand of their fellowship at my ordination, and said, 'Brother, art thou a lover of the Lord Jesus Christ? Then, pray, Feed his lambs.'" *

* Magnalia, third book, art. 4th, p. 186.

Ministers very generally were in the habit of catechising the children of their respective parishes on a week day, sometimes in the public schools or on the Sabbath. Of Mr. Brock, of Reding, it was said, at his funeral, June 19, 1688, he was "a worthy, good minister, generally lamented; was very laborious in catechising and instructing youth."* And even the General Court of Massachusetts took this subject under consideration.

In 1642, a law was passed by this court which required the selectmen to see "that all masters of families do, once a week at least, catechise their children and servants in the grounds and principles of religion; and if any be unable to do so much, that then, at least, they procure such children and apprentices to learn some short orthodox catechism without book, that they may be able to answer unto the questions that shall be propounded to them out of such catechism, by their parents or masters, or any of the selectmen, when they shall call them to a trial of what they have learned in that kind."†

A law similar to the above was also in force in Connecticut.‡ Evils, however, having arisen from the neglect of some, if not all the provisions of the above law, in some places, the court again interposed.

"March 9, 1669 or '70. The governor and council advised the clergymen of all the towns 'to catechise and instruct all people (especially youth) in the sound principles of the Christian religion, and that not only in public, but privately, from house to house, or at least three, four, or more families meeting together, as time

---

* Sewall's Journal. † Colony Laws, chap. xxii.
‡ Trumbull's His. Cons. R. I., chap. xiii.

and strength may permit; taking to your assistance such godly and grave persons as to you may seem expedient.' " * This "advice" and "orders" were frequently renewed as occasion required. "November 8, 1675. According to notice from General Court, Mr. Higginson revives his attention to the children of his congregation. He proposed to catechise them every second week, in the fifth and sixth days, as formerly." †

"The Selectmen mette the 5: day of Octob. 1674; and agreed on the 15: day of this instant mo. to goe throo the Town and examin the familys about catechizing." ‡

Nor did the care of our pious ancestors to maintain catechetical instruction subside in their posterity, till comparatively a recent period. "1808, May 19. Voted, that the sacred Scriptures and the Assembly's Catechism be in future introduced into all our schools." §

There are many persons now living, who were born in New England, who can remember when catechising was common, not only by ministers, but in the family and at the public schools.

At the first settlement of New England, there was no catechism which the settlers entirely approved; and, in 1641, the General Court ordered "that the ministers should agree upon a form of catechism, which should be printed for general use." ‖ Several ministers wrote and published catechisms in their individual capacity. Rev. Mr. Cotton, of Boston, published one of his own

---

* Felt's Annals of Salem, p. 236.   † Felt's Annals of Salem, p. 251.
‡ Woburn Record, selectmen; day book, vol. i. p.166.
§ Lexington church record, p. 145, supposed to be a transcript from the Town Records.
‖ Emerson's First Church, Boston, p. 71.

composing, entitled, "Milk for Babes;" and this was used in other congregations besides his own. "1660, September 10th. It was voted, that Mr. Cotton's catechism should be used in families for teaching children, so that they might be prepared for public catechising in the congregation."* Rev. Mr. Fiske, first pastor of the church of Chelmsford, at the earnest solicitation of his people, composed and published a catechism, 1657, entitled, "Watering of the Olive Plants in Christ's Kingdom, or, a Short Catechism for the Entrance of our Chelmsford Children; enlarged by a threefold Appendix," which was "designed for youth of maturer years." †

But the Westminster Shorter Catechism was introduced into New England soon after its publication, in 1647, and came at length to be almost universally used.

The gradual subsidence of interest in the catechising of the young in the family, the church, and the public school, it is believed, was among the causes which led to the introduction of the system of Sabbath school instruction. We cannot think that Sabbath schools were the means of driving catechisms into the shade, as some have suggested.

There were isolated schools organized early in this country. The first one known, was established by Ludwig Thacher, in the town of Ephrata, Lancaster County, Pennsylvania, as early as the middle of the last century, some thirty or forty years previous to those established by Raikes, and it was conducted by him for more than thirty years.

In 1783, Bishop Asbury, it is claimed, organized a

---

* Felt's Annals of Salem, p. 307.   † Allen's History of Chelmsford, p. 123.

school of this kind in Hanover, Virginia. The First-day, or Sunday school Society was organized in the city of Philadelphia, on the 11th of January, 1791, and the first school opened by it was in March, 1791. In 1800 there had been admitted to the several schools of this society more than two thousand scholars. But oral religious instruction was not given in these schools. The instruction was confined to reading and writing, after 1793, from the Bible.

The Newburyport "Herald," of January 12, 1791, in giving an account of the establishment of this first Sabbath school in Philadelphia, adds this comment: "Pity their benevolence did not extend so far as to afford them tuition on days when it is lawful to follow such pursuits, and not thereby lay a foundation for the profanation of the Sabbath."

Truly, times and opinions change, but truth, never. Now the parents who keep their children away from the Sabbath school are the ones who are supposed to "profane" the Sabbath.

A Sabbath school was started in Paterson, N. J., in 1794, by Sarah Colt, a little girl of eleven years of age.

At the suggestion of Samuel Slater, Esq., a student of Brown University established a school in Pawtucket, R. I., in 1797; and one was opened in Hudson, N. Y., in 1803; and one in Pittsburg, Penn., on the 22d of August, 1809.*

The first Sabbath school in New England, for the sole purpose of the religious instruction of children, so far as is now known, was established in Bath, N. H.,

---

* Pray's History of Sunday Schools.

in 1805. Shortly before, the Rev. David Sutherland, — who had been engaged in early efforts to found Sabbath schools in Scotland, his native country, — was settled as pastor of the church in Bath, and at once started a Sabbath school in the principal village, which he conducted with various success, and with very little aid from others, for thirteen years. In 1817 a new spirit was awakened, and other schools were opened in different parts of the town.*

In 1850 the writer prepared a brief history of the rise and progress of Sabbath schools in the Congregational denomination in Massachusetts, which was published by the Massachusetts Sabbath School Society, and from which we gather the following items: —

The first Sabbath school, so far as we are able to learn, in this state, and probably in New England, intended for moral and religious instruction, was established in Beverly, in 1810. This school was commenced by two young ladies, Joanna Prince and Hannah Hill. The latter died in 1838. The former is still living, at Brunswick, Me., the respected lady of Ebenezer Everett, Esq. She is a member of Rev. Dr. Adams's church, and is now (1850) a teacher in his Sabbath school, forty years from the time she established the school in Beverly.† Miss Prince was teaching a day school in a room of her mother's house. She and Miss Hill opened a Sabbath school in her school-room. This school was held in the morning, and after the afternoon service. About thirty scholars attended the first season, and manifested great enthusiasm. Some of the members were very

---

* Sketch of the Rise of Sabbath Schools, p. 138.
† Mrs. Everett died September 5, 1859, having served as a Sabbath school teacher about half a century.

zealous in learning to read, while others had long Scripture lessons to recite from memory. The ladies continued their school, all by themselves, with great success, for three years. The second season they hired a larger room. After the third year the enterprise was taken up by others, and a general school was established, in which all the societies united. Jealousies soon sprung up, and separate parish schools were established.

The founders of this school were both of them Orthodox Congregationalists.

The first school in Boston was established in 1812, by Miss Lydia Adams. While on a visit to Beverly, in October of that year, — as we learn from herself, — she heard of the school in that place, and, although she did not see it, she was at once impressed with the importance of a similar one in Boston, and on her return immediately commenced the work. "She was then teaching a week-day charity school, and was supported by the ladies of the West Parish — Dr. Lowell's. This school was continued until the year 1822, when, the parish Sunday school having been established, her pupils, from that time, became members of that for religious instruction."* The plan of the school, the founder of it regards as exclusively her own, though the pastor gave it his sanction and hearty coöperation. This lady united with the Orthodox church in Jaffrey, New Hampshire, in 1805, and she ever maintained the faith she then professed. For many years she was known in this city, by many of the prominent members of the Orthodox churches, as a

---

* Pray's History of Sunday Schools, &c., page 210.

truly evangelical, devoted Christian. So that the honor of establishing the first two Sabbath schools in this commonwealth, instead of belonging, as is indirectly claimed in Pray's "History of Sunday Schools," to the Unitarian denomination, is, beyond all controversy, due to Orthodox Congregationalists, the true descendants of the Puritans, who first planted the gospel upon these shores.

The late Charles Walley, Esq., of Boston, having heard of the enterprise of this lady, sent her a donation of books for her school, consisting of six Bibles, twelve New Testaments, twelve Watts's "Shorter Catechisms," twelve Watts's "Divine Songs for Children," and twelve "Hymns for Infant Minds;" in all, fifty-four volumes. This donation constituted the first Sabbath school library in Boston.

A Sabbath school was commenced in Brunswick, Me., in 1812. In the winter of the same year a Sabbath school was formed in Salem, under the patronage of a company of ladies belonging to the society of the Rev. Dr. Hopkins, predecessor of the Rev. Dr. Emerson. The pupils were placed under the tuition of a teacher of a school of young ladies.* The same year a school was established in connection with the Tabernacle church.

A Sabbath school was established in Newburyport, in 1814, by three young ladies, two of whom became wives of clergymen.

The young ladies secured the use of the Rev. Dr. Spring's vestry for their purposes, and, without aid or coöperation from the churches, began their benevolent

---

* Correspondent of New York Observer, March 23, 1850.

undertaking. The first year the number of pupils did not exceed one hundred. In four years it had grown into favor, and numbered eight hundred.

The school began after public service in the afternoon, and occupied more than three hours. The whole instruction was given by these young ladies, and principally by two of them.

In 1815, the school in Dr. Spring's vestry was intrusted to some members of his society; and two of the young ladies, originators of the school, commenced another in Joppa, a more destitute part of the town. In 1816, one of the young ladies started another school at Kennebunkport, Me.*

The first school in Franklin, Conn., was established in 1815, and in a few years it contained a very large portion of people of the parish, of all ages.

The first Sabbath school established in Charlestown, was in connection with the First Congregational church, under the pastoral care of Rev. Dr. Morse, in the autumn of 1816.†

Among the Sabbath schools next established in Massachusetts, in connection with the Orthodox Congregational churches and societies, were those established under the auspices of the Boston Society for the Moral and Religious Instruction of the Poor. That society was organized in 1816, and its first Sabbath school was established in 1817. In a few years there were, in the city of Boston, fourteen schools under the special care of that society.‡

---

* Editor of [N. H.] Parents' Monitor.
† Report of Winthrop Sabbath school, Charlestown, 1850.
‡ Seventeenth Annual Report of The Boston Society for the Moral and Religious Instruction of the Poor.

A Sabbath school was opened in Concord, Mass., in 1810, by Miss Sarah Ripley, daughter of Rev. Dr. Ripley. She gathered a few children upon Sabbath afternoons, after church, at her father's house, and taught them the Scriptures and catechism. After this school had continued four or five years, through the warm season, three pious young ladies opened a school in a room at a house in the centre of the town; but the people generally did not give their influence to the project, and a regular Sabbath school was not organized till June, 1818.*

Rev. Samuel Goddard, in a letter to the Sabbath School and Bible Association at Andover, dated Norwich, Vt., January 12, 1830, says:—

"It is now about twenty years since I was first settled in the ministry in one of the new towns in the north part of this state. They had never before had a minister, and the youth and children were growing up in ignorance, and the Bible had been neglected by the parents.

"I had never seen and rarely heard of a Sabbath school. I, however, attempted to engage the children to study the Scriptures, and collected a few together in what I called a 'Bible school.' At first I could obtain only the children of two or three families. For several years I could not persuade an individual to assist in the instruction; but the school increased, and one after another was induced to assist in instructing. In a few years there were teachers enough, and the children of every family but one in town were members of the Sabbath school, and I have seen a child of that family sorry because her father would not permit her to attend.

"Although I had never heard of a Bible class, I invited

* Sketch of the Rise of Sabbath Schools, p. 139.

my neighbors, old and young, to collect together once a week, on winter evenings, to attend to the Scriptures. A chapter was given out one week for the next. When we met, the chapter was read and then taken up, verse by verse, compared with other Scriptures, explanations and illustrations were made, and the truths enforced on the consciences. These exercises excited interest in the Scriptures.

"After I left that people, who were very poorly able to support the gospel, they were much disheartened, and ready to despair of ever seeing another minister settled among them. But these Sabbath school children were not satisfied. Their anxiety to have the Sabbath school and their solicitations with their parents were the very efficient means in establishing again the preached gospel among them; and many of these scholars are now hopefully in the kingdom of Christ."

Although the precise date of this Sabbath school and Bible class movement is not here given, it was evidently among the earlier ones in New England; and the name given, "Bible school," is almost identical with the modern name, "Bible service."

At this time there seems to have been awakened quite a general interest in the subject of doing more for the children, and in interesting persons of all ages in the Bible. The report of the Sabbath school movement in England had doubtless led ministers and the churches to inquiries on the subject.

In 1814, in addition to the school established in Newburyport, one was organized in New York by two young ladies; one in Wilmington, Delaware, and one in Cambridgeport.

Several schools were founded in 1815: one in connection with Christ Church, Boston; one in the Northern Liberties of Philadelphia, and one in Newark, N. J.

In 1816 a Sabbath school was instituted in Chillicothe, O., in Westboro', Mass., in Cambridge, in Greensborough and Hardwick, Vt., in Carlisle, Penn., in the Third, Second, and First Baptist churches, Boston, in Northampton, Mass., New London, Conn., in the First church in Charlestown, and in Framingham. After this, schools were organized rapidly in various parts of the land.

The thirtieth Annual Report of the Sabbath school in Newburyport gives the following account of the early history of this school: —

"In 1814 three young ladies established the first Sabbath school in this city, in the old chapel that formerly belonged to this church. This they continued for one year, without aid or assistance from any of the churches. The largest number they had did not exceed one hundred.

"In 1815 members of this society took charge of the school, and continued it for two years. In 1817 the Newburyport Sabbath school was formed, or, as is more probable, the school established in this place removed to the court-house, and associated with it other societies. There were present at the first meeting of the Newburyport school thirty teachers and three hundred and fifty scholars. This school was continued thirteen years, to 1830, and, from the records we have of it, seems to have been very successfully conducted; and through the exertions of its teachers and friends many were brought to receive religious instruction who otherwise would have known nothing of divine things.

"In 1827 there were connected with this school eight hundred scholars and teachers, and we find it recorded that there were present at one time five hundred and twenty-three scholars and seventy-two teachers. All this was done in the infancy of the Sabbath school movement in this country, this school being among the first that were established. There were no Sabbath school societies, papers, libraries, text-books, or Sabbath school music; in short, scarcely nothing of which we now have showered upon us so abundantly.

"This was effected, and the interest kept up, in a great measure, by a well-ordered weekly teachers' meeting. These meetings appear to have been very interesting, and they were punctually attended by the teachers. On three successive meetings there were present sixty-six, sixty-five, and eighty-four."

Among the early doings of the teachers' meeting, as given in this report, are the following:—

"*Voted*, That the 'Evangelical and Familiar Catechism for Sunday Schools in New York,' abridged from the Rev. Joseph Emerson's, and 'The Assembly's Shorter Catechism,' be taught in this school. Also, as some provision is made for black children, at the African school, in their vicinity, and as their presence at this school might prevent the attendance of some white children, it was *Voted*, 'That for the present no blacks be admitted.' This last vote, however, was reconsidered at the next meeting, and it was voted 'that the blacks be admitted.'

"The subjects of opening the school with singing, requiring the scholars to give the text and leading ideas of the sermons, assisting in the formation of other schools, interesting the scholars in committing the Scriptures to memory, were acted on at these teachers' meetings.

"One girl, ten years of age, Abigail Follensbee, in a little less than six months committed to memory the Book of Matthew and the one hundred and nineteenth Psalm, containing one thousand one hundred and ninety-nine verses, together with twenty-two texts, consisting of fifty-four verses, twenty hymns, forty-four Scripture proofs, and one tract; also the principal part of the 'Assembly's Shorter Catechism.' The Annual Report of the twenty-second of August, 1818, gives the number of verses committed to memory the first four months of the season as something near one hundred thousand."

" In the summer of 1815," — according to an account given by Rev. Alexander McKenzie, in his volume of "Lectures on the History of the First Church in Cambridge,"* "a Sabbath school was opened at the meeting-house, with the design of promoting the moral and religious improvement of children and youth. The school was taught during three summers by Miss Mary Munro and Miss Hannah Tenney. Then five other young ladies came to their assistance; and Mr. James D. Farnsworth, master of the grammar school, tendered his services for the instruction of the boys. More than eighty children of both sexes received instruction at the Sabbath school. They were taught to read and to commit to memory select portions of the Bible, catechisms, hymns, and prayers, and to answer Cummings's questions on the New Testament. Books and tracts were early provided for their use."

In 1817 the General Association of Congregational Churches in Massachusetts recommended the establishment of schools for the pious education of children and youth.

At the semi-centennial anniversary of the Sabbath school in West Boylston, the pastor, Rev. James H.

* P. 180.

Fitts, gave an historical address, from which it appears that the first school in that place, for strictly religious instruction, was established in 1818. It met, at first, in an unfinished room in a private house, which had been fitted up for holding meetings. The extemporized seats consisted of rough boards, resting on chairs arranged throughout the room. There were about twenty scholars. Soon the school adjourned to meet in the "old centre school-house."

The first mention of Sabbath schools in this country, in the "Boston Recorder," so far as we can find, was in vol. xi., for 1817, in an article by Thomas Vose, Secretary of the Boston Society for the Moral and Religious Instruction of the Poor. It spoke of the interest that had been excited by the establishment of Sabbath schools in towns among the poor; and mentioned that "the anniversary of the society would be held on Wednesday, in the afternoon, at the Old South Church, where the children of their Sabbath school would be present, and a sermon, composed for the occasion, would be preached by the Rev. Mr. Huntington, and a contribution would be taken to aid in defraying the expenses incidental to this important object." *

In the same volume of the "Recorder," p. 110, there is published a brief account of the origin, progress, and improvement of the Sabbath school system of education, taken from the "Sunday School Guide," by J. A. James, published in England, and republished in New York.

And on p. 177 of the same volume, there is a long editorial article defending Sabbath schools from some

---

* Boston Recorder, vol. xi. p. 173.

of the objections that were urged against them, as that they are a novelty; are unnecessary; that they will interfere with the sanctity of the Sabbath; deprive children of their only time for relaxation, &c.

The semi-centennial anniversary of the school established in Beverly, in 1810, was celebrated in that town in 1860 with appropriate and very interesting services. And similar anniversaries of most of the earlier schools, in various parts of New England and of the country, have also been celebrated, and historical sketches of them, full of instructive incidents and reminiscences, have been published.

It is interesting, in this centennial year of our country, 1876, to contrast the present condition of the Sabbath school work, even in the single state of Massachusetts, with its "day of small things" sixty-six years ago. Then there was but a single school of two teachers and thirty scholars. Now there are in the state, probably, more than three hundred and fifty thousand scholars, and from fifty to sixty thousand teachers engaged in giving or receiving instruction in the Word of Life! Sixty-six years ago the Sabbath school cause was but a little rill, like a silver thread, flowing down the mountain-side, that a child with his hand or foot could have stopped. But through these years it has gone on increasing in size and rapidity; it has widened and deepened; its waters have accumulated and swelled, till it now rolls on, a mighty Amazon!

If we compare the Sabbath school literature of the present day with that of sixty-six years ago, the same striking contrast is seen. Then the "New England Primer" was almost the only book published specially for the young. Now, every denomination has its own juvenile literature, comprising from three or four hundred to several thousand volumes each.

Looking at this wonderful progress for these past almost threescore years and ten, and then looking forward through a similar period to come, our minds almost stagger at the prospect. What progress may we not anticipate in connection with the Sabbath school enterprise! Instead of a new and untried enterprise, with but few teachers, few helps, and no experience, we now have a sacramental host — many of them with years of experience, and all of them trained in the Sabbath school work, with the accumulated wisdom of the past, and a great variety of other helps — and the hundreds of thousands of scholars, all receiving that instruction which will fit large numbers of them in turn to become themselves teachers. What, then, may not the friends of Sabbath schools in our churches hope, with the divine blessing, to accomplish in the future?

In 1825, the Massachusetts Sabbath School Union, at first composed of the different evangelical denominations, was formed, "to promote the opening of new and the increase and prosperity of old Sabbath schools, within the limits of this state; to form depositories for supplying the schools with suitable books on the lowest terms possible; to stimulate and encourage each other in the moral and religious instruction of children and others," &c.

On the 31st of May, 1832, the Massachusetts Sabbath School Society, composed only of the Congregational denomination, was formed for similar purposes.

In 1870, the name was changed to Congregational Publishing Society.

III.

MODES OF CONDUCTING SABBATH SCHOOLS.

The general mode of conducting Sabbath schools, almost from their first establishment to the present time, has been somewhat uniform, while the details in different schools have been various. And there have been frequent changes even in the same schools — though changes have not always been improvements — in the attempts that have been made to secure greater efficiency. Then, again, old modes have been revived.

The past history of this institution has taught us the importance of variety in our plans of promoting the cause. A certain plan may be adopted which, for a time, will be very useful in creating an increased interest and zeal in the work. By and by this plan may seem to have lost especial power to interest, and may be superseded by some new plan, and so on. In a few years some of these obsolete plans may be revived, and with the same happy results as at first, or as would attend a new plan. They are new to most of those who revive them.

It is interesting to look back and see how many of the exercises and various modes of conducting Sabbath schools twenty-five and thirty years ago have within the past few years been introduced, and some of them as though they were now adopted for the first time.

Among the plans adopted in many of the earlier schools, and that are now extensively in use, were the following: Opening or closing the school with singing by the scholars and teachers; repeating together the Lord's Prayer; reading the Scriptures alternately; the Sabbath school concert, which, even as far back as when it was held Monday evening, was represented, as is now the case, as being the most interesting meeting held; teachers' meeting; class records and monthly or quarterly reports by the teachers, to be read at the concerts; anniversaries and various celebrations; contributions in the school for benevolent purposes; temperance societies among the young; various measures for getting in new scholars; mission schools; the blackboard even; conventions, &c.; — so that we can almost say, in regard to this institution, as in regard to other things, "There is nothing new under the sun."

Of course, with all the experience of more than a generation, and with all the talent, wisdom, and piety of so many able men directed to this subject, there have been improvements, in reference to many things, in the present conduct of our schools.

There were some plans that were adopted extensively in the earlier schools, that might be introduced with the improvements which the age would suggest, to great advantage at the present day. For example, correspondence of schools with each other; the letters to be read at the concert; reciprocal visits by committees, between different schools, at the schools and the concerts; celebrations on the Fourth of July; a committee of vigilance to bring into the school any in the entry, and around the church, &c. These and many other plans that have been adopted from time to time in conducting Sabbath schools, will be more fully considered in the sequel.

At the first, the chief exercise of most schools in this country consisted mainly in hearing the children repeat verses of Scripture and hymns. There were not generally any lessons assigned. The scholars learned such verses, and as many, as they chose; and not unfrequently whole chapters were recited. In a class of six or eight, it would sometimes occur that so many chapters had been committed to memory, that not more than one half or two thirds of the members would have time during the session to recite. There was no time for explanations or any remarks.

The excellence of a school seemed to consist in the amount committed to memory. Rewards were given to stimulate the scholars in this work. A ticket, on which was written or printed "Merit," was given in some schools for every ten verses; when ten tickets were obtained, or one hundred verses had been recited, a tract was given; and when five tracts were obtained, then a book was the reward. And the first book we ever received in this way was "Henry and his Bearer," one of the earlier books published for the use of Sabbath schools.

After a few years, the friends of this institution, or, as they are now called, "the workers," began to think that, instead of crowding the minds of the young with whole chapters of the Bible, a better way would be to give out a certain number of verses, from six to ten, as a lesson to be committed to memory, and studied, so that the scholars would be able to answer the questions their teachers might ask them on the subject.

The first "Annual Report of the Maine Sabbath

School Union " for 1827 says : " The practice of hearing long lessons, and estimating the merit of the scholar by the quantity committed to memory, has been discarded to a considerable extent; and many advantages have been found to result from limited recitation, accompanied with full and easy explanations from the teachers. It is evident that to understand and remember the lesson, rather than to display his own part, should be the object of the learner. All that is committed to memory, without being understood, — although it may, after being long hidden and unprofitable, be recalled in after life to great advantage, — seems, on the whole, to be little better than lost. At the best, much valuable time is unnecessarily consumed, the mind of the child is oppressed with a useless burden, and a pernicious habit of superficial reading and study contracted, which will ever after prove a source of inconvenience. The classes should be small, and the lesson confined to a few verses ; and the same lesson should generally be assigned to the whole school, and always to the members of the same class. Then the teachers should converse with each scholar, to see, as far as possible, that he understands the lesson, and comprehends the manner in which it ought to affect him."

This plan of a limited number of verses was then very generally adopted by the schools. But it was found, after a short time, that many of the teachers could do but little more than hear the scholars repeat these few verses, as they used to repeat their chapters. They were not able to ask questions and interest the scholars by any instructions connected with the lesson. And then, too, many of the scholars did not understand how to study the verses they had committed to memory. If the verse were, "Come unto me, all ye that labor and are heavy laden, and I will give you rest," they did not know how to analyze it; to take up the different clauses and inquire what their meaning was. They would not, perhaps, ask themselves, "Who says this?" "Is this a command or an invitation?" "What is it to 'labor and be heavy laden'?" "What is it to come to Christ?" "What is the 'rest' he promises to give?" This state of things led many to see the need of some helps and questions to be prepared by persons especially qualified for this work, on the lessons, both to aid the scholars in studying the lessons and the teachers in imparting instruction. And this led to the preparation of question books, which for many years, till the publication of the "Uniform Lesson Papers," most of the schools, at least in New England, have used; and, indeed, most of them still prefer question books, though on the uniform lessons, to the lesson papers.

The superintendent of the Congregational Sabbath school, in Portsmouth, N. H., the late Rev. Prof. Peabody, of Dartmouth College, in a letter to the committee of correspondence of the Sabbath School and Bible Class Association of Andover Theological Seminary, dated December 25, 1829, thus speaks of the mode of conducting that school: —

"First, prayer by the superintendent, all the children standing in one and the same attitude, and, at the close, audibly joining in the Lord's Prayer. Then the class recitations. Then the superintendent relates some anecdote, or remarks on some Scripture truth or some remarkable providence.

"Since requiring the children to join in the Lord's Prayer,

the superintendent has usually occupied ten or fifteen minutes in illustrating and enforcing practically the several parts of it.

"The school is closed by singing, in which all are desired to unite. Our plan has thus far succeeded admirably."

Rev. Frederick E. Cannon, of Ludlow, Vt., in a letter to the above committee, dated December 19, 1829, thus describes his mode of conducting his school at that early day. In the spring of that year he united his Bible classes with the Sabbath school for the purpose of giving character and importance to the school. He says:—

"Of the two hundred and fifty persons, old and young, who had given their names as willing to attend, twelve classes were made, besides about one hundred adults, which I reserved for myself. One of the twelve classes was made up of about thirty young ladies, and another of about twenty young men. All the classes take the same lesson of twelve verses. As early as the middle of each week I endeavor to have my preparation made for the school on the ensuing Sabbath; and the preparation consists of a series of forty or fifty carefully written questions upon the lesson in course, and all the answers. Between this time and the Sabbath, the teachers are in the habit of obtaining the questions, and transcribing them for the benefit of their several classes. This method is adopted to render their preparation more thorough than it would be by a mere exposition of the lesson to them at a meeting appointed for the purpose.

"On the Sabbath immediately after the morning service, the classes and teachers are at their places, when a rap is heard from the superintendent, calling all to the attitude of prayer for the opening of the school. Then the business of the school commences. I devote myself entirely to my class, and the assistant superintendent takes a general oversight of the school. At the close of the exercises in the several classes, the librarian will have made all necessary arrangements of the books for the day, and I then turn to the whole school and give a plain, familiar, and practical exposition of the lesson, interspersing it with a variety of questions to the children, generally chosen from the list of questions used with the adults. And it is in no small degree interesting to see with what promptness and eagerness the questions are answered by the children from all parts of the house.

"After this I require the children to give some account of the morning text and sermon, and to direct me to the psalm or hymn given out on the previous Sabbath to be sung at this time by the school. After the hymn is read, the superintendent's rap is again heard, and we all rise and sing, old trembling voices mingling with the voices of youth and children in the song of Zion. This is the closing scene, except a short prayer; and it is like heaven."

Rev. Samuel Goddard, in a letter to the above association, dated Norwich, Vt., January 18, 1830, writes:—

"The method which, on the whole, appears to me the best of any we have tried since I have been with this people the past eight years, is the one pursued by us the past season. We have had our Bible classes and Sabbath school all together in the meeting-house during the intermission of public service, except several small schools in the outer parts of the town, where it is so far that the children could not come. We all, except some small children, take the same portion of Scripture. Questions are asked and remarks made by the teachers. After the classes have gone through, the pastor addresses the whole school a few minutes on some prominent truth in the lesson.

"We introduce the exercises with singing and a short

prayer, and close with prayer and singing the Doxology. This method has excited more interest, and called in greater numbers, than any other which we have tried. Parents and old people, some over seventy years of age, encourage the children and youth by their attendance. Two thirds of the worshipping assembly are engaged in the Bible classes and Sabbath school. We have, in all, over three hundred connected with both departments. Some of the children have pretty constantly walked four or five miles.

"Our Bible classes and Sabbath school are the concern of the church. The church attends to their interests, and appoints the superintendent and teachers. It is the business of the pastor, though not the superintendent, to be as really the pastor of the Sabbath school and Bible classes as of the church."

The late Charles Stoddard, Esq., of Boston, in a letter to the above association, dated December 22, 1829, thus describes his mode of conducting the Fort Hill school, which was established in 1820. This school, like most of the schools, especially in the cities and larger towns, for some years held two sessions a day. It used only the Bible for a text-book. He says: —

"In the morning, when the school meets, precisely at eight and a half, one stroke of the bell brings the faces of the scholars towards the superintendent, who folds his hands, which is to them a signal to do the same. He then makes a short introductory address, in simple language, and at its close holds up a book, at noticing which the scholars all rise and close their eyes for prayer. This is very short and simple. No one is permitted to enter the school during this exercise, and everything is still.

"The teachers then hear their scholars recite their lesson,

which is committed to memory at home, and spend the remainder of the time in asking and answering questions, and exhorting their scholars, until the bell strikes and the book is held up again, which is a signal for the scholars to rise and fold their hands for singing. They are then dismissed and go out single file, headed by their teachers.

"We act upon the nerves of the scholars, in our government, by signs, raising a book, &c., to call the school to order. This, I am persuaded, is the true secret of government. I have seen some superintendents almost break their knuckles in rapping the school into order, and strain their lungs by expressions such as these: 'We cannot have such a noise!' 'The children must be more quiet!' &c. Such scolding tones produce no good effect, but are worse than useless. All you want is to gain their attention by one stroke of the bell, and then, if there are a hundred children present, and no teachers, they can all be made perfectly quiet without uttering a word.

"In the afternoon, the introductory address is omitted. After prayer, the time is occupied by the teachers in explaining the lesson for the following Sabbath. The library books are given out to those who are punctual and have good lessons and conduct.

"On the first Sabbath of the month we question the scholars audibly, to which audible answers are given, and we vary the exercises from time to time."

In —— school, one subject only is presented on the same Sabbath. A motto, in large characters, is hung up in a conspicuous part of the school, where all can see, consisting of the prominent verse or sentiment in the lesson of the day.

This, it will be seen, is much like the golden text upon the blackboard at the present day.

Questions are proposed monthly to the scholars, and all who are capable are desired to bring written answers from the Bible. For example: "How can you prove that it is the duty of parents to correct disobedient children?" These answers are corrected by the superintendent and returned to the scholars. This exercise became quite general in that school.

Rev. Daniel A. Clark, in a letter to the Sabbath School and Bible Class Association, referred to above, dated Bennington, Vt., March 24, 1830, gives an account of his Bible class and Sabbath school labors at that early day, that is so interesting and suggestive that it deserves to be made known. He says:—

"I commenced a Bible class among the youth of my charge in 1816, while yet there was no name that had reached my ear appropriate to such an institution. I drew out a system of questions on the text to be examined, which were copied and used by the class, composed of fifty of my youth, all of whom engaged to be present at every exercise. The questions were intended to make the youth exercise some thought. The class were greatly interested in the study.

"At a public examination, a large audience, filling the house, was held in silent suspense two and a half hours, while my class answered these questions.

"I have had a Bible class in one shape and another ever since.

"At present [1830] I have what I call, for want of a better name, a 'bibliary,' embracing my whole parish, old and young, male and female. I attend upon their instruction in the intermission of divine service on the Lord's day. I name a week beforehand the portion of Scripture, and on Monday morning prepare on the passage a set of questions drawing out the history of the parts. Then a set of reflections, &c., which I give out to be copied and used by the people. They soon multiply the copies till, before the Sabbath comes, there is a copy in every family in the parish.

"Soon as I have dismissed the congregation in the morning, all who will stay arrange themselves in pews, with some sprightly, active man at the head of each pew. These are called sponsors. To them I put the questions, and they put them to their respective classes. After a moment's pause, for them to get an answer, I ask any one of the sponsors for the answer. He rises and gives me, audibly, the best answer he can get from his class. The same question is, of course, agitated in every class through the house; each child and youth, man and woman, has, in turn, opportunity to answer the sponsor, and each sponsor opportunity to answer me, no one knowing from whom I shall demand an answer.

"I have suffered this bibliary to swallow up, at present, Bible class and Sabbath school, except that there are several district Sabbath schools at five o'clock; and I am perfectly satisfied that I have never yet hit upon a plan so useful. More attend upon biblical instruction on this plan. All are interested through the week, as well as during the hour of recitation. Young men have come in that never could be urged to the work before."

The Sabbath school in Pawlet, Vt., in 1830, had two hundred and eleven scholars, divided into two divisions: those from fourteen to eighty-eight years of age in one division, and the infant class composing the other. This school, from the first, used the "Sabbath School Guide." Those above twenty-five years of age were taught in a class by themselves by the pastor. The school was held Sabbath noon, and was kept up summer and winter.

The pastor occupied ten or fifteen minutes before the

school closed in questioning the whole school in their respective lessons, aiming in his inquiries to elicit a train of thought which the teachers would not be likely to have taught them, and yet so simple as to secure twenty answers at once to each inquiry. The pastor says:—

"Our quarter-day occurs on the Sabbath. In the morning a sermon is preached to the children on a subject and in a style calculated to interest and profit them. In the afternoon, after singing and prayer, a report is read, giving a succinct account of the state of the school during the last quarter, and some principle is discussed which is intimately connected with the prosperity of the school and the good of the children; objections to Sabbath school operations are met, and greater interest is enjoined on parents and guardians in behalf of the school and the institution generally. The scholars are then examined on the lessons over which they have passed during the quarter, and opportunity given to friends of Sabbath schools to make remarks.

"The system was new to all of us, and at first it did not excite interest; some were even opposed to this method of spending the Sabbath; but now we have few Sabbaths of more general or deeper interest during the year than our quarter-days.

"We are in the habit of receiving and dismissing scholars with some ceremony.

"The scholar, if willing, on entering the school, accompanies the teacher to the superintendent's stand, who addresses a few words of counsel and encouragement to the new scholar, gives him concisely the rules of the school, and prays for him. This service is attended to at the close of the school in presence of all the members.

"When any one is about to leave the school, he is presented as before, and after receiving advice and an affectionate farewell, in the name of the school a certificate is given, signifying that he has attended our school, and is, consequently, recommended to the special regard and oversight of all friends of the institution. As you may imagine, this is an impressive service, and draws the cords of attachment too close to leave the members of our school very widely apart."

At a meeting of the Andover Sabbath School and Bible Class Association, in 1830, the subject considered was the mode of teaching. Each member gave an account of his own mode. From these accounts the committee of publication, of which we were a member, prepared the following facts, which were published in the "Sabbath School Treasury:"—

"*Method of teaching children under twelve years of age.* — I have a class of boys about twelve years old, who use the 'Union Questions.' I first endeavor to ascertain whether they have studied the lesson; for if they have not treasured at least some part of it in their memory, they are poorly prepared to derive benefit from my instructions. To ascertain this point, I require each one to repeat a verse or two of the lesson from the Bible. I then proceed to ask those questions, which are printed in large type, pausing upon each question to ascertain how far the scholar understands what he has recited. For this purpose I take up some of the questions in small type, and suggest such incidental circumstances as will exercise his powers of mind, and elicit his views on the subject. The answers will often be correct, in a limited or modified sense, in which case I admit their correctness with the necessary qualifications. If the answer be wholly incorrect, I put the question in another shape, or let it go to the next, or call upon any one in the class to answer it who can. If no one is able to do it, then, and not otherwise, I answer it myself, and explain the difficulty by familiar illustrations, until I am sure that they all understand it. The practical application of the lesson requires much prudence, and cannot, I am sure, be rightly made without a deep tone of pious feeling in my own heart. A formal appeal at the close of every recitation, I observe, is not so useful as to apply the truth at any part of the lesson, when such an application can naturally be made. To attempt it indiscriminately on every verse becomes tiresome to the class, if not disgusting. I have found, also, that much is depending on the manner of applying divine truth, and endeavor to be so various in my manner that the class shall not be able to anticipate my remarks. Sometimes it seems best to make an appeal to the whole class; sometimes to address the individual who is reciting; and at other times to apply the truth to some supposed person, of a similar character and in like circumstances. I have often observed that the interest of the class is in a great measure graduated by the interest which I feel myself; and nothing tends more powerfully to keep my feelings in a proper state than to consider these immortal souls as committed to my care for one great and definite object — their conversion to God. In addition to the above exercise, I require from each pupil some account of the book which he returned to the library.

"This, while it serves to form habits of attentive reading on their part, also affords me an excellent opportunity to introduce and urge the subject of personal piety.

"*Method of teaching young persons from twenty to twenty-five years old.* — I have under my instruction a class of young ladies from twenty to twenty-five years of age, in the first number of 'Fisk and Abbott's Bible Class Book.' I usually divide the time allotted to the recitation into two equal portions, and proceed in the following manner: The first half is devoted to a critical examination of the lesson, according to the directions found in the beginning of the

'Bible Class Book,' with such variations, however, as seem necessary to keep the attention of the class. To effect this fundamental object, as well as to render the exercise more profitable to them, I encourage the utmost freedom of inquiry, and on some subjects endeavor to lead them into a discussion among themselves. I dwell particularly upon the different traits of character exhibited in the lesson, and the tendencies of such and such courses of conduct. I make the Bible its own interpreter as far as possible; and whenever a promise is made, a threatening denounced, or a prophecy uttered, I always require my scholars to tell me where, and when, and how it was fulfilled. When we have gone through the lesson in this manner, the first half of our time has usually expired. The remaining half is spent in remarking upon the lesson as a whole, showing its connection with what precedes it, and noticing a few prominent points as landmarks, to aid in obtaining a connected view of sacred history. If testimony can be had from profane authors, illustrative of any part of the lesson, it is introduced. I always reserve some prominent, interesting particular for the last, and dwell upon it at considerable length. For example, in the call of Abraham I would select the offering up of Isaac, and endeavor to impress on the minds of my scholars an idea of faith and obedience by describing minutely the probable feelings of Abraham in all the trying circumstances of that event, his regard for the divine authority urging him against the strongest current of natural affection. In addition to the regular lesson I give out to the class each Sabbath one book of the Old Testament, in chronological order, and request them to ascertain when and by whom it was written, and to give an account of its author and contents. This usually costs me much labor and time; but the interest and profit of the exercise to myself and the class more than compensates for all the toil. I formerly learned by experience the disastrous effects of closing my instructions, even a few moments only, before the time expired, and consequently I now endeavor to be broken off by the rap of the superintendent in the midst of some interesting remarks. I meet my class one evening during the week, at which time we also have a Bible exercise, and familiar conversation on Bible subjects.

"*General method of teaching persons from thirty to eighty years of age.*—The venerable appearance of my class continually suggests to me the importance of avoiding everything dictatorial in my manner of teaching. We use no book but the Bible. Sometimes I select a chapter myself for examination, at other times I request them to do it. Though it belongs to me to conduct the exercise, still I always place myself along with them as an inquirer after 'what saith the Scriptures?' We proceed in the following manner: I read a verse, or request one of them to do it, and then we all enter into a familiar conversation about its meaning. At first I had to ask nearly all the questions myself, and to do most of the talking. I convinced my class, at length, that this was not the most profitable method, and now they ask nearly all the questions themselves. If any one is dissatisfied with the answer or explanation, he has full liberty to state his reasons, and to give his own views. When opposite opinions are advanced, I attempt to harmonize them. If I fail in this attempt, as is sometimes the case, I never think it best to enter into a long discussion, but generally sum up the evidence for each opinion and the difficulties attending it, and leave each member of the class to form his own opinion.

"Plain illustrations and simple language are no less important in teaching old persons than in teaching children. I have often found it profitable to direct their attention to recent occurrences in God's providence for illustration of the Bible. Appeals can be made to the experience of old persons much oftener and with more advantage than to the young."

Twenty-five or thirty years ago the superintendent of the Sabbath school in Dedham writes: —

"Of late we have resorted to the blackboard. A liberal-minded teacher, aided by the superintendent, procured one, six feet by four. We now use it almost every Sabbath. When the other duties begin to grow rather irksome, we call the attention of the teachers and pupils to something else. Sometimes we teach the geography of the lesson, as the situation of Capernaum or Nazareth, or the Sea of Galilee, or Mount Carmel. Sometimes we mark out a city, as Jerusalem, or make a map of some river, as the Jordan. At other times, for the sake of variety, we make a map of some missionary station, as Constantinople, or Beyroot, or Ooromiah. In this way we often spend ten or fifteen minutes, not only very pleasantly, but also very profitably."

In some schools, the older scholars, in addition to the usual exercises, have read biographical sketches of Scripture characters which they have written. Then, again, they have written answers to the more difficult questions in a small book prepared for the purpose.

Some one class has been publicly examined on the lesson, so that parents, and all others present, might see what attention had been given to it.

Constancy and punctuality in attendance, for bringing in new scholars, &c., have often been stimulated by the offer of certificates, or other rewards.

In 1831 a Sabbath school adopted the method of having all the recitations made in a whisper. Nothing ever undertaken before, it was said, so much improved the school. Order and solemnity, it was thought, cannot be so effectually secured in any other way.

But few of the Sabbath schools, the first fifteen or twenty years after their introduction into this country, were continued through the winter. The subject was very earnestly discussed in all the religious papers and in addresses. It was clearly shown that the winter months were even more favorable for study than the warmer seasons. Now there are but few schools anywhere that are suspended during any part of the year, except for a short summer vacation. This is a comparatively recent practice in some schools, and is by many regarded as a practice of doubtful utility.

REWARDS OF MERIT.

The Congregational school in Portsmouth, N. H., in 1829, had the following system of rewards. The teachers were furnished with class bills, on which they kept an exact account of the conduct of every scholar in the class, including punctual attendance, correct recitations, proper deportment, &c. At the end of each quarter, a general report, made out from these bills, was given to the superintendent. By this report he was able, at once, to know who were the good and who the bad scholars in every class. The names of the most punctual and exemplary scholars were read before the school. At the end of the first and third quarters, bills of credit were awarded to the exemplary scholars in each class, making punctuality one of the principal grounds of the award; and at the end of the second and fourth quarters, rewards consisting of suitable books, one or more, were presented to those classes whose members, in general, had been exemplary in their conduct, punctual in their attendance, &c. These books were presented on condition that, after being read by all the members of the class, they should be deposited in the library of the school, with a card on the cover bearing the names of those scholars on whose account they were presented.

This mode of rewarding, as it addresses itself to classes rather than individuals, it was said, seems less calculated to excite invidious emulation than any other. Besides, it answers two purposes at once : that of rewarding merit, and at the same time that of constantly replenishing the library, which then numbered three hundred volumes.*

There was one feature, in the early history of the First Parish Sabbath School, in Charlestown, that would seem strange to us at the present day. At the first meeting of the Board of Managers, it was voted to print one thousand tickets, to be given as rewards for punctual attendance, good behavior, &c. The reward tickets represented a money value. If constantly punctual and well-behaved, the value for the fifty-two Sabbaths would amount to twenty-six cents. This, however, was payable quarterly in books or clothing. Disorderly behavior in school or church, or neglect in bringing their books, caused a forfeiture of tickets.

At the annual meeting in 1822, the value of the tickets was reduced, twenty marks being valued at only one mill. This was payable in money. This tariff of prices was, we think, well calculated to check that "evil eye" that "hasteth to be rich;" for, with this reduced value, if always punctual, a child might in two years receive one cent; and the money thus received the children were expected to give for the education of heathen youth!

---

* Letter of D. Peabody to S. S. and B. C. Asso., at Andover.

One of the rules of the school required cleanliness, as well as strict attention to the commands of the teacher. Another designated the punishment for a lack of punctual attendance at school or church, for loss of books, &c. Then follow rules for conduct of scholars when out of school. Becoming deportment at home was enjoined; spending their time on the Sabbath in the study of their books was required; thus showing that, in the estimation of the founders, it was a privilege to become a member of the Sabbath school.

In the "Sunday School Repository" for 1818, under the head of "Internal Regulations of Sunday Schools," blue and red tickets are recommended for "Rewards." Six blue tickets, given for the correct recitation of thirty-six verses of Scripture, should be equal to one red one, and one red one equal to half a cent in value: the tickets to be redeemed, every three months, with religious books and tracts suitable to the capacities of children. Under the head of "Penalties," teachers absent at roll-call should forfeit twelve and a half cents each. If unavoidably prevented from attending, they must provide a substitute, or forfeit twenty-five cents. For not reporting the reason of the absence of their scholars, twelve and a half cents. Superintendents, fines double.*

Some of the pupils in the Sabbath school at West Boylston, which was established in 1818, recited from one to two hundred verses and hymns per week. From the first, premiums, consisting of valuable books and tracts, were given to scholars in proportion to the lessons recited. Some of the books were the "Dairy-

---

* Semi-centennial Celebration of the First Parish Sabbath School, Charlestown, pp. 60–62.

man's Daughter;" "Two Lambs;" "Life of Ruby Foster;" "Walks of Usefulness;" "The Robber's Daughter, or the Sunday School Convert: a Narrative founded on Fact;" "Alfred Galba, or History of Two Brothers, supposed to be written by themselves."*

QUESTION BOOKS.

Question books and catechisms were introduced into some schools quite early. The school connected with the First Church in Cambridge, which was organized in 1815, from the beginning used Cummings's "Questions on the New Testament," and various catechisms. The school in Framingham, which was formed in 1816, used Emerson's catechism, and Cummings's questions; the "Assembly's Shorter Catechism," and Wilbur's "Biblical Catechism;" Baldwin's catechism; and "Doctrinal and Historical Catechisms."

The "Christian Mirror," of Portland, Me., published a series of selected lessons for Sabbath schools for several years, beginning 1827. To accommodate those who might wish them, copies were struck off on cards, or separate papers.*

Judson's "Question Book" was published in 1827 or 1828, by the American Sabbath School Union. The Massachusetts Sabbath School Union published "Fiske and Abbott's Bible Class Book, for the use of Sabbath Schools and Bible Classes," in 1829. In 1836, the Massachusetts Sabbath School Society began the publication of a series of "Biblical Catechisms for Infant Sabbath Schools;" and the same year it published a question book on Romans. It was prepared with

---

* Semi-centennial Anniversary of the Sabbath School of West Boylston.
† Boston Recorder, 1829, p. 65.

great care and labor. It was divided into two parts: the first for the younger classes, and the second for the older classes. The author, the late Harvey Newcomb, resided in Pittsburg, Penn.; and the whole of this large volume was sent by mail, in letters, written in large folio sheets, two columns on a page; the postage being twenty-five cents a letter.

Soon after the publication of this book on Romans, the society published "Newcomb's First Question Book," in two volumes, on *topics*. Since then, the society has published about one hundred question books and catechisms; and all other Sabbath school publishing associations, and many private publishing houses, have issued a great variety of text-books for the use of Sabbath schools.

Within a few years, the "Uniform Lessons," now called the "International Lessons," have been very generally adopted by the schools of nearly all denominations throughout the country. The subject of uniform lessons for all our Sabbath schools, it is said, was first proposed in 1865 or 1866, by the Chicago Sunday School Union, through the "Sunday School Teacher," a periodical published under its direction. The first schedule of lessons was agreed upon for 1872. And Mr. B. F. Jacobs, a member of that union, is claimed to be the father of the idea of a national uniformity of lessons. These lessons have now become international.

It is stated, on what is regarded as good authority, that these lessons have been adopted by the Presbyterian, Methodist, Baptist, Congregational, Episcopalian, Lutheran, Moravian, and some Universalist churches in our own country; and that they are being published and used in Great Britain, France, Germany, Norway, Sweden, Austria, Switzerland, Turkey, Northern India, Burmah, China, Japan, Australia, Fiji Islands, Sandwich Islands, Siam, and the language of the Choctaw Indians.

Most of the different denominations have prepared their own lesson papers, or question books, and their distinctive annotations. And the various religious newspapers are also publishing the lessons, from week to week, with appropriate illustrations and comments.

Some have objected to the use of question books at all. They have said they make the teacher's work too easy. Many leaned upon them too much; that they merely ask the questions, without making any effort to enforce the truth contained in the lesson, allowing the scholars to read the answers.

In answer to this, it may be said that very much depends upon the teacher, whether the exercises of the class, with or without the use of such a help, is interesting and beneficial. A teacher who would make such an exercise interesting without a question book, would not fail to do so with one. The question book contains the Scripture lesson; and it need be no hinderance to the teacher's freedom. He could use questions, little or much, as he chose. But a portion of our teachers find the question book a great help to them; and to some teachers it is indispensable. They would be unable to take charge of a class, and make the exercises tolerably interesting, without it.

A question book used as every teacher should use it, cannot be an injury; and those who use it improperly would do still worse in attempting to teach a class without any such aid. And then the question book is intended especially to help the scholars in their study of the lesson, like many of the catechetical text-books on the various branches of study in our public schools and higher seminaries of learning. The younger scholars, without such a course of lessons, with questions and answers and references, would do nothing but commit the text to memory, and this much all scholars should do with a question book. They would not know how to study the lesson beyond committing it to memory. They would not, without such a guide, search the Scriptures for parallel passages, and to ascertain how one passage sheds light upon another. This the question book, with its references, would teach them. And having studied the lesson with this help of the question book, they would be prepared to answer any appropriate and intelligible questions the teacher might ask in regard to the passage under consideration, whether they were in the question book or not. Intelligent and well-informed teachers in such cases might, if they chose, dispense themselves with the use of the question book. The scholars, having studied the passage and learned its general meaning in this way, would of course understand the teacher's questions and explanations, whether he used the question book or not. For most younger scholars, therefore, the question book, with a suitable teacher, cannot be otherwise than useful. And at the present time, those who formerly objected to question books are freely using, more or less, the lesson papers, with their explanations, questions, and references, or the question books on the international lessons.

A judicious clergyman in 1830 said: " Where questions are used, an experienced and capable teacher will not feel confined to them, but will omit and add as he pleases, and make various remarks of his own as he goes along."

The great defect in regard to the lessons in our Sabbath schools is, and ever has been, with or without a question book, that both teachers and scholars do not give the lessons the amount of study that is necessary to secure interest and profit from the exercise of the class. How can a Sabbath school deserve the name of school, if there be no earnest study on the part of the teacher and the taught? How can it, without this study, be of any real, practical benefit to any one? If superintendents feel obliged to say, as one certainly did say, " I really suppose there are some classes present in which neither the teachers nor the scholars yet know where the lesson for to-day is!" how can there be any interest?

Let the teachers set an example of an earnest preparation of the lesson, and then insist on a similar preparation on the part of the scholars, and this important defect would be removed. No scholar should be allowed to read the answers to his questions in the Sabbath school, any more than he is in his lessons in geography or history in the public school. Then reciting a Sabbath school lesson would mean something. Till such a course of study and recitation is insisted upon, it is surely unfair to throw the blame for any want of interest in the exercises upon the question book. It should be understood that nothing can compensate for the want of study in the Sabbath school. No amount of external interest that may be secured by other means — singing, festivals, concerts, with whatever attractions, measures to bring in new scholars,

&c., — can be an equivalent for thorough, earnest study of the lesson. The study of God's Word is one of the primary objects of the Sabbath school. Without this, — where the scholars are advanced enough to study, — the holding of such a school on the Lord's day would be a desecration of the Sabbath. A meeting for religious exercises, of singing, prayer, and exhortation, with the children on the Sabbath, may be appropriate; but a school on that day, week after week, without any study of the Bible, or books founded on the Bible, would be inappropriate to the sacred hours.

IV.

REVIVAL OF THE STUDY OF THE CATECHISM.

For a long time previous to 1835, the use of the "Assembly's Shorter Catechism" and the "New England Primer" were almost unknown to the young. In the early part of that year, a series of articles, each consisting of one question and answer of the catechism, with the proof-texts, explanations, and an anecdote to illustrate it, was published in the "Sabbath School Visitor," the monthly periodical of the Massachusetts Sabbath School Society.

After the publication of two or three articles, there began to be received letters, inquiring, "What has become of the shorter catechism?" "Why has the catechism been banished from our families and schools?" &c.

About that time a clergyman inquired, "Why does not the society publish a cheap edition of the catechism?" As an inducement to the society to do it, he offered to take five hundred copies. In less than two weeks an edition of five thousand copies was published. In a short time some of the religious periodicals and ecclesiastical associations began to speak on the subject, and to recommend the restoration of this banished or neglected manual.

The following resolution was adopted by a Sabbath School Convention held in Hallowell, Me., in 1836:—

"*Resolved,* That the convention cordially recommend the use of the 'Westminster Assembly's Shorter Catechism' in Sabbath schools."

Rev. Mr. J., one of the leading ministers of the state, in presenting this resolution, said it would not have been necessary thirty years ago. A change has taken place; we do all by explanation now, nothing by thought; not so in former ages, when there were giant minds. Now all is on the surface, and fades away from the mind almost as soon as received. Something to administer to gratification is sought, something merely to excite. Now is the time to meet the evil by training the rising generation to think, and not to be merely passive recipients. He referred to his early life when the catechism was taught in families. Is it so now? How comes it that it is not so? He knew there were objections to this system of truth. Some may be for making a compromise. But with whom? The enemies of truth? Truth must be sought after, not relinquished. The catechism holds up a bird's-eye view of doctrines, and exceeds every other book but the Bible. There is mind running through it; it overflows with mind, and piety too.

If desiring posthumous fame, he would rather be the author of the "Assembly's Catechism" than any other book, besides the Bible; and ought not this catechism to be introduced into our Sabbath schools? Two editions of the catechism were soon after published by private houses. One weekly religious paper published a brief commentary on every question and answer, one each week.

Then the society published an edition with proof-texts and explanations; then a larger work, called "Exercises on the Shorter Catechism;" and in 1836 the "New England Primer." Several editions of the primer were afterwards issued by individual publishers.

This little book — the "children's book" of past generations — found a very ready demand. For ten or fifteen years the study of the catechism was revived in the families and Sabbath schools of the Congregational denomination very generally throughout New England. From fifty to one hundred or more children, in some parishes, committed the catechism accurately to memory, and received the reward of a Testament, Bible, or a handsome certificate that had been published, which had been offered.

Among the many interesting incidents connected with the revived study of the catechism in the Sabbath school, is the following: —

The superintendent of the Sabbath school at West Springfield offered to give every scholar who would commit it perfectly to memory, — not partly commit it, but commit it perfectly, — a beautiful little pocket Bible, with gilt edges and a tuck. He was willing to pay out of his own pocket five or ten dollars to encourage the children in this work.

About six months after this, we were invited to spend a Sabbath there, and witness the result of the superintendent's offer.

At the third service, at five o'clock, on a pleasant Sabbath afternoon in June, all assembled at the church. It appeared that one hundred and five scholars had committed the catechism, of whom about seventy-five were present; so that, instead of costing the good superintendent five or ten dollars, the prospect was that it would cost him between seventy-five and one hundred dollars. However, he got his Bibles bound very cheaply, though very beautifully, so that it actually cost him only about sixty dollars to redeem his pledge. And any one could see that he would not have had it one dollar less, he was so delighted with the result.

After the introductory services, the pastor took the catechism, and in just thirty minutes every question was asked and every answer given. And there were only six mistakes of any kind that we could detect. Every one was surprised at the promptness and accuracy with which it was recited.

A lady offered a Bible to every member of a Sabbath school who would commit the catechism to memory. She had to give ninety-five Bibles to redeem her pledge. She then offered a valuable present to every one who would commit the catechism, questions and answers, and proof-texts, and five young ladies obtained the prizes.

In some cases the catechism was used at the quarterly meetings of maternal associations, and at the Sabbath school concert; and it was made in many cases the subject of remarks, by the pastor and brethren, at the weekly church meeting, and at the third service on the Sabbath; and very great interest was excited in this exercise.

In many cases arrangements were made to have the "New England Primer" placed in every family in the parish or in the town. And in some instances, as the children and youth who were engaged in the work of distribution, went from house to house with the primer, this little book was welcomed almost with tears of joy by fathers and mothers, as the cherished friend of their childhood and youth.

The late Charles A. Spring, of Rock Island, Ill., who was interested in the "New England Primer" when a boy, after his conversion, about the time the primer was republished in 1836, engaged in introducing it into that state; and he distributed personally about ten thousand copies.

Within fifteen years from the time the study of the catechism was revived, probably more than half a million copies of it, in various forms, were published and sold.

Many regarded the general introduction of this excellent compendium of religious truth into our Sabbath schools, and the restoration of the primer to the fireside, as events full of promise to the church and the cause of Christ.

"This little manual has been," in the language of a correspondent of a secular newspaper, "one of the greatest blessings to New England that God, in his wisdom and goodness, ever bestowed on a race of sinners. What numberless individuals and families thence drew their first instruction in reading, and had their minds imbued with a taste for knowledge, and their hearts inspired with moral and religious principles by studying its pages!"

In regard to the importance of catechetical instruction, the late Rev. Dr. Lyman Beecher, in one of his occasional sermons, says: "It was adopted universally by the primitive Christians; was preached by the Waldenses as their safeguard against the seductions of the Papists; was resorted to by the churches of the Reformation, and continued by the churches of New England;

and has uniformly been followed by the revival or decline of religion as it has been persisted in or neglected. It is preëminently important that there be in the church symbols of evangelical doctrine associated with the earliest recollections of her children.

"The sure consequence of leaving children to grow up without religious instruction will be irreligion and prejudice against the truth. Whenever, therefore, our doctrinal catechisms are laid aside, a breach wide as the sea is opened for the enemy to come in."

The value of laying up the catechism in early life is illustrated by the following incident: —

An intelligent lady, sixty years old, during a severe sickness, was unable to fix her mind on any subject for a long time. At length the catechism, which she learned in early life, came fresh to her recollection, and she remembered it fully. Here she found a subject on which her mind could rest. Here was a brief compend of the great doctrines of the Bible, those doctrines which constitute the foundation of all our hopes, upon which she was able to meditate with much profit and pleasure.

All the evangelical denominations have their respective catechisms for this purpose, the "Assembly's Shorter Catechism" being the one more generally used in the Congregational churches and the various branches of the Presbyterian church.

V.

RELATION OF PARENTS TO THE SABBATH SCHOOL.

THE interest children feel in the Sabbath school, and the benefit they derive from it, depend very much on their parents. The children usually bring to the school the family likeness. If they do not look like their parents, they show the influence of home training. If all the arrangements of the family, on Saturday evening and Sabbath morning, are such as to prevent or not to aid the children in the preparation of their lessons, and in a punctual attendance at the school, it will be seen in their frequent absences, late arrivals, and imperfect lessons, and their general indifference to the school. Punctual attendance and well-studied lessons greatly encourage the hearts and strengthen the hands of teachers. They are an assurance of parental coöperation and sympathy. This assurance teachers ought to have. It is justly their due. And in reference to this matter there is a special duty resting on the father.

The lessons of the Sabbath school ought, in part at least, to be prepared during the week, and both parents, as opportunity may present or occasion require, may encourage and aid their children in this work.

But in many cases, it is to be feared, nearly the

whole of this preparation is deferred till Sabbath morning, when the mother's time is fully occupied with various family duties. Not so with the father. If a layman, — and especially a mechanic or merchant, instead of a farmer with the care of his flocks and herds, — his time is almost entirely at his command, and a portion of it he can, and ought to, employ in preparing his children for the exercises of the Sabbath school. How can he spend an hour more pleasantly to his children, or profitably to himself, than by sitting down with them and aiding in the preparation of their lesson? As he encourages them to make their inquiries, and familiarly explains their difficulties, what an interest will kindle in their eyes and glow in their countenances! What an opportunity is here presented, in answering some questions, or explaining some fact, to enforce truth on the heart and conscience!

Every Christian parent acknowledges the duty of giving his children religious instruction. How does the exercise here proposed facilitate the performance of this duty? When can the father find an occasion so favorable, in all respects, to sit down and instruct his children, as on the morning and evening of the holy Sabbath? No worldly cares are then pressing his mind, and no domestic labors call for his attention. Why, then, should not the father regard it as peculiarly his duty to see that the children's Sabbath lessons are well prepared? Why should this labor, as is often the case, be left wholly to the mother? It should not. It is the father's duty: a duty he owes to his companion, to his children, to the teachers, and to himself. Will not every parent give this subject a serious consideration?

RELATION OF PARENTS TO THE SABBATH SCHOOL.

Perhaps we cannot better give the result of our experience and observation in regard to the relation and duties of parents to the Sabbath school than we did, some years ago, in the following "Superintendent's Letter to Parents."

Respected Friends:— Permit me, in behalf of the teachers, to address you in regard to our Sabbath school.

We take it for granted that you are interested in the spiritual and eternal welfare of your children. You believe that their highest happiness depends, instrumentally, on their moral and religious training.

We take it for granted, likewise, that you are, with us, interested in the institution of Sabbath schools. You regard it as an institution rich in promises of good to the young; an institution whose special office is to help take care of the children, to aid in their moral and religious education. Through its influence thousands of the young have obtained great benefit to their minds, morals, and hearts, and have been, at least, *aided* in becoming the children of God. As evidence that you do regard the Sabbath school favorably, you have committed your own children to our institution.

But, respected friends, we wish it here distinctly understood that it is no part of our object, as Sabbath school teachers, to assume any of your responsibilities, or in any degree to lessen your obligations in regard to the training of your children. Our only object is to aid you in this work, to add our efforts to your faithful labors for their salvation.

You are no doubt aware that it is often said that the Sabbath school is made a substitute for parental instruction; that many parents favor this institution, and bring their children under its influence for the very purpose of relieving themselves of the responsibility of attending to their religious instruction at home.

Now we cannot believe this is true to anything like the extent that some suppose. Very few parents, who neglect the religious instruction of their children now, would attend to it were the Sabbath school abolished.

Still we fear it is true, in regard to a large portion of the young, that the Sabbath school is their only source of personal religious instruction, except so far as they receive it from the ministry. They either have no parents, or they have such parents as concern not themselves with the religious education of their children. In their dwellings there is no closet or altar of prayer, no Bible read, no parental example or instruction that will lead the children in the way of truth and holiness. Sabbath school or no Sabbath school, it is all the same to them.

To these multitudes of the young we do, indeed, wish to perform, as far as may be, the kind offices of pious parents. We would take them by the hand and lead them, with all the earnestness and love of parental piety, to the Saviour.

How awful will be the account those parents must hereafter give, who, while they have been carefully nourishing the body and the mind of their children, have neglected the soul! But while we wish, in the Sabbath school, to supply their lack of religious instruction to their children, we do not, we dare not, even in such cases, assume any of their responsibility in this matter. We cannot appear as their substitutes at the Judgment. They must answer themselves for the right training of their children.

But it is said that pious parents sometimes transfer their responsibilities in regard to the religious instruction of their children to Sabbath school teachers. So far as this is attempted, it is a most unnatural evil. "Shall our children be turned away from their father's table and sent to find bread at the hand of strangers?" Alas, for such cruelty! God has laid duties on parents which they can neither throw off nor delegate to others.

The obligation of parents to attend personally to the spiritual interests of their children is founded upon that immutable relation that subsists between parents and children; and no circumstances which do not annihilate this relation can destroy or diminish its force. So long as the ties which bind parents and children together exist, so long must the obligation rest upon parents to "bring up their children in the nurture and admonition of the Lord." This obligation cannot be transferred to another. So far from it, new responsibilities are laid upon them from the very circumstance that their children are intrusted to the care of the Sabbath school teacher. They must now not only instruct their children themselves, but they must also look after the seed sown by the teacher, that it may not be lost, but bring forth fruit to the glory of God.

It is not merely for the good of the children that God has placed this work in the hands of parents; it is also for the personal good of parents themselves. Nothing will more surely promote a parent's own growth in grace than the daily prayers and instructions which deep parental solicitude will call forth.

All this good the parents lose when they transfer the religious education of their children to the Sabbath school teacher.

While we would thus earnestly warn you against looking upon the Sabbath school as a substitute for parental instruction, we would encourage you to regard it as a most important auxiliary. And we pledge you our prayers and labors, in coöperation with yours, in training your children for usefulness and for heaven.

You will find, we trust, that our Sabbath school will aid you in the intellectual improvement of your children.

Although this is not our great object, yet "the instructions in the Sabbath school are wonderfully adapted to quicken, enlarge, and strengthen all the intellectual faculties." There are no fields of knowledge that can be thrown open to the human mind so rich, and varied, and interesting, as those spread out before us in the Scriptures. And there is nothing so well adapted to arouse and stimulate to diligence in exploring those fields as that same wonderful book itself, which is our book of instruction in the Sabbath school.

You will find this instruction an auxiliary to parental government.

You consider it, we doubt not, of immense consequence that young children early possess the spirit and form the habit of subordination and cheerful obedience. You feel that the temper which will lead to cheerful obedience to parental authority is the temper of the Bible. This you wish to teach your children, and any assistance in this work you would thankfully receive. Here is the very place where we come in as your fellow-helpers. In the Sabbath school your children have this instruction and discipline. "Every week they subject their will to the will of their teachers; submit to restraint and government. They are subdued; they are chained down by the law of kindness and the bonds of love."

But the principal object of the Sabbath school is to aid you in training up your children for heaven.

This, we trust, is the great end of all your solicitude and effort in regard to them. You feel that your family has been constituted, and you placed at its head, to hold the affections of your children and sway over them an unbounded influence, so that you may guide them home to God.

To aid you in this most interesting work we cheerfully proffer our services. We will do all we can to assist you in cultivating the consciences and the hearts of your children, that they may be fitted for the duties of life and for the rewards of the faithful in heaven.

And now, respected friends, you will allow us, your fellow-helpers, freely to suggest a few things which we regard as essential on your part, to render our labors, and the whole influence of the Sabbath school, in the highest degree interesting and profitable to your children.

In the first place, then, we look to you for the constant and punctual attendance of your children.

To secure the benefits of the school, your children must, of course, attend, and attend constantly and punctually. We have no authority and no power, excepting that of persuasion and love, and the general interest the school may awaken, to secure their attendance. For this we must look to you. And shall we not receive your coöperation in this matter? Will you not arrange all your domestic affairs on the Sabbath with reference to their constant and punctual attendance? All such arrangements will magnify, in their view, the value of this institution. Let no slight cause, no trivial excuse which the indolence or caprice of your children may plead, be a sufficient reason for their absence. The constant and seasonable attendance of their parents at church will have a powerful influence on their minds in regard to their attendance at school.

The importance to the young of a habit of punctuality in meeting all their duties and engagements you acknowledge.

We hope you think with us that no one is ever too old or too wise to study the Word of God, and to study it in the Sabbath school; and that you will teach this distinctly to your children. It pains us to see so many of our older youth and young people, and even the children of professedly pious parents, withdrawing from the Sabbath school. We are confident this would not often occur were parents faithful in regard to this subject.

While your children are under age, you are answerable for the instruction they receive; and consequently you have the right to direct them in regard to that instruction.

The manner in which the attendance of older children and youth can be secured is described in the sequel.

In the second place, we must look to you to see that your children's lessons are properly prepared.

In order that a school may be of any practical service to the scholars, there must be study, earnest, thorough study. This is as needful in regard to the Sabbath school as any other. Perhaps there is no one thing in our Sabbath schools more discouraging at the present time than the superficial manner in which the lessons, in many instances, are prepared. Indeed, with many scholars, it is to be feared, there is no preparation, not even an examination of the lessons before they reach the class. They seem not to understand that the Sabbath school is not the place to study, that it should all be done at home. The business at the school is to recite what has before been studied, and to listen to the explanations and remarks of the teacher. Without such a preparation of the lessons, the Sabbath school can be of but little benefit. And for such a preparation we must look to the parents. Shall we look in vain?

There is scarcely anything that so disheartens the teachers in their work as irregular attendance and neglected lessons on the part of the scholars. They see evidence in this that the parents feel no interest in all their labors. They are compelled to exclaim, "We are toiling and praying for the spiritual welfare of their children, and what do they care for it?"

On the other hand, the constant and regular attendance of their scholars, with well-prepared lessons, cheers and encourages the teachers. It shows that they have the sympathy and coöperation of their parents at home.

What exercise could you find more pleasant and profitable for an hour Saturday evening, or Sabbath morning, than to sit down with your children and go over the lessons, explaining the more difficult parts, and encouraging them to learn and reflect upon their meaning? We are certain such an exercise would be pleasant to most children. Their attention at the outset would be arrested, and their interest excited, by the very circumstance that they are to enjoy the society and instruction of their dear father or mother. The mind and heart of each would thus be all open to receive the full power of every truth you might address to them.

Then, parents, you should examine your children after the school, and ascertain what kind of instruction they have received, — how this or that truth or duty was explained by the teachers. If your child is learning a trade, or attending the public school, you often make inquiries as to his progress, and whether any wrong instruction is given. But what is a mistake or error in regard to mere human science, or business, compared with wrong instruction in divine truth and the great matter of salvation?

The Sabbath school will often furnish you with favorable opportunities for personal religious conversation with your children. How often, as they come to you with their inquiries respecting the lesson, does their deportment invite such conversation! What favorable opportunities are these for sowing the good seed! Here some highly practical truth or duty occurs in the lesson; what is more natural than that you should seize hold of that truth or duty, and make a practical application of it? A word, under such circumstances, may prove "a word in season," — a word of life and salvation to them. Should you not hail and eagerly improve every such occasion, when you can so naturally, and without weariness to your children, direct their thoughts to the subject of their personal salvation?

This view of the Sabbath school, inasmuch as it increases your opportunities of doing good to your children, increases, instead of lessens, your responsibility. And this very fact will endear the Sabbath school to the faithful parent. He will not care how momentous the responsibilities that press upon him, so long as he can hear his Saviour saying to him, "As thy day, so shall thy strength be. My grace is sufficient for thee."

May we not, then, expect your special coöperation in securing a thorough preparation of the lessons, and in exciting an interest in them?

Again, you can help give much interest and efficiency to our Sabbath school by your own constant presence at the concert.

In many places the Sabbath school concert is the most interesting meeting of the month. It is regarded as the children's meeting. They perform that delightful part of the service, the singing. The pastor and the superintendent make special preparation to give interest to the meeting. The teachers are all there, together with many Christian friends, to unite their fervent supplications for the selectest blessings of heaven upon the young.

And will not you be there, to unite in all these services and to witness these exhibitions of interest in the welfare of your own children; to hear the kind words that will be spoken to them, and the earnest prayers that will be offered for them; and to listen to their sweet songs of praise? All heaven, we doubt not, is interested in these scenes. Angels bend their wings and listen to these infant notes of praise. And shall not every father and mother be there to listen too?

What place is there like the Sabbath school concert to awaken mutual interest between parents, teachers, and children? A teacher is requested to pray. With all the fervor of a Christian heart, he pleads with God for blessings upon the young. Will not such a prayer draw forth the affections of the parents towards that teacher?

Then a father prays. He prays especially for those who are so faithfully laboring for his children. O, how such a prayer encourages the hearts of the teachers; and what new interest it awakens among them in their labors!

And then, how can you more certainly interest the young than by exhibitions of such mutual interest, on the part of parents and teachers both, in their behalf? We trust, parents, that your hearts, and ours, and the hearts of your children, will ever be cheered by your presence at the concert.

If you would help to make the Sabbath school in the highest degree a blessing to your children, we would suggest that you should become personally connected with the school.

We are aware that various circumstances — such as infirmity, domestic cares and duties, especially where there are small children, &c., — are often given as reasons for not uniting with the Sabbath school. But we think that all should regard themselves, in some relation, as members to this institution. This all owe to themselves, to the young, and to the whole community. Let every one, of whatever age, be connected with the school, as superintendents, teachers, pupils, or, at least, as an occasional visitor. Let your names be enrolled as members; and then, as Providence shall enable you, attend in some of these relations. In this way you would help create a public sentiment in reference to the school, so that every individual in the society, of whatever age or standing, would feel that his or her connection with the school would be reputable.

We often hear young people, and even youth, saying they are too old to attend the Sabbath school! But who ever heard them saying this in regard to public worship? Let parents manifest an interest in the Sabbath school, as they do in public worship — by their attendance — and their children will never think of being too old to attend. The truth of this can be shown by numerous cases. We know of instances where whole families of children have grown up, with their parents, in the Sabbath school. Even the older ones — some now of age, some in college, some in business — still accompany their parents to Sabbath school as in their childhood. The question of leaving the school is one they have never entertained for a moment, if it has ever occurred to them. They would not leave it if they could. They would be as restless, as much lost, on the Sabbath, without the Sabbath school, as they would without public worship. This is all the result of parental example.

There are also numerous instances, where the indifference of even professedly Christian parents is giving us just the opposite result. At the age of twelve or thirteen, all their children become too smart for the Sabbath school. A teacher asked a lad why he had left the school. His answer was, "You don't catch me at that business again." It was ascertained that he had heard his professedly pious parents speak very lightly of the Sabbath school. They had also said, "The children may attend or not, as they wish; we shall not interfere with them about it." How long before such indifference to public worship would lead all their children to forsake the house of God?

Let it be remembered, then, that the question, whether or not our young people shall be retained in the Sabbath school, depends upon the example and influence of their parents.

Once more, permit us to entreat you, by every means in your power, to coöperate with the teachers in their work.

If there are any two classes of laborers in the kingdom of Christ, whose situation and duties seem to point them out peculiarly as fellow-laborers, they are parents and Sabbath school teachers. The field in which they labor is one; and the object for which they are laboring is one. Why then should they not join heart and hand, and labor together? The same difficulties and discouragements meet them both; why, then, should they not unite their strength to resist or overcome them? The same precious promises are held out to them both; the same bright hopes inspire them; and the same glorious reward awaits them both, if they are faithful; why, then, should they not walk together, cheering and gladdening each other's hearts by mutual counsel and encouragement?

Parents, be fellow-laborers with the teachers of your children. Encourage them in their work by your prayers, your affectionate counsel, and your hearty coöperation. Let them see you constantly imploring the blessing of God upon their instructions, and watering with your tears the seed they have sown in the hearts of your children. Then will they take courage to go on in their labor of love; then will they join their prayers and mingle their tears with yours; and together with you will they rejoice over your dear offspring turning unto God, if by your mutual labors and prayers this unspeakable blessing shall be brought down from above.

But how it must discourage and distress the faithful teacher to see all his efforts lost, or nearly so, because parents do not coöperate with him!

To counteract the influence of teachers, it is not necessary that parents should go so far as to oppose Sabbath schools. It is not necessary that they should tell their children that this or that thing which their teachers taught them is not true. No. Let parents manifest before their children merely an indifference to the cause of Sabbath schools, or an indifference to the commands of the Bible,— in a word, let them only fail to commend to their children, by their precepts and example, the great truths of the Scriptures which are taught in the Sabbath school, and teachers will have sad reason to fear that they are laboring in vain.

The teacher meets his class on the Sabbath. His very countenance, like that of Moses, shows that he has just come from holy communion with God. Under the influence of this love to souls, which he has fanned to a flame in his closet, he enters upon his pleasing but responsible duties. Even the smallest child sees affection and anxiety beaming in the teacher's eye. All know that they are the objects of this affection and anxiety. Now, who does not see that this teacher, so far as he himself is concerned, has the most flattering prospects of doing good?

Cheered with these prospects, at length he begins to press home upon the hearts of his dear children the duty of loving God " now in the days of their youth." One, and another, and another of his class begin to show that truth is reaching their hearts — they weep. He becomes more and more earnest and affectionate; but, alas! there is one member of his class that remains unmoved. Truth falls upon his ear just as it does upon the others, but, unlike the others, he can keep it from his heart. When the teacher tells him he must love God, he immediately says to himself, if not to the teacher, " Why, my father and mother love me; but they never told me I must love God. They would have told me if I ought to love him." In this way the truth is repelled from the heart. And the efforts of the teacher with that scholar are almost as hopeless as they would be if his parents were heathen.

And oh, how often, too, do even Christian parents, by their coldness in the performance of religious duties, or by their neglect of them, counteract, in the same way, the influence of the Sabbath school!

And parents, be especially watchful, if you would not counteract the influence of the teachers, how you speak of them before your children. Their influence for good, as well as that of a pastor, is ruined, unless they are respected and esteemed by those for whose good they labor. And one disparaging remark from a parent, in regard to the person, character, manners, ability, instruction, &c., of a teacher or minister, may destroy all the respect and esteem which the children have been cherishing for him. Are parents aware of the spiritual injury they do their own children, when they speak lightly, or in any way disparagingly, before them, of their teachers or ministers?

Permit us, respected friends, briefly to recapitulate, and say, you cannot too deeply feel that the great object of the Sabbath school is the religious instruction and salvation of your children. For the accomplishment of this object there must be, on your part, an earnest, constant, and practical interest in the institution. There is no class of persons whom it so deeply concerns. It seeks the good of your own offspring. If you, then, are not interested in its existence and efficiency, who can we expect will be? The friends of this institution have a right to expect the warm sympathy and most earnest coöperation of parents in this work. Indeed, the character and object of the Sabbath school are such, that one would suppose parents would be its principal supporters. They would take the lead in the work, and others come in only as their assistants.

If you do not engage in the work personally as superintendents and teachers, you certainly should manifest an interest in it greater than all others, — by using your influence to secure the constant, punctual, and interested attendance of your children; by seeing that they come with lessons properly studied; and by your own presence at the concert, and, so far as may be, at the school; and by giving the teachers your cheerful and hearty coöperation in every way possible.

We renewedly pledge you our most earnest endeavors, by labor and prayer, to aid you in training up your beloved children to be useful on earth, and at last to meet you and us in the kingdom of heaven.

In behalf of the Teachers,
Yours, ⸺⸺ ⸺⸺

VI.

LABORS OF PASTORS.

Pastors, with all their other numerous and responsible duties, cannot generally, and especially on the Sabbath, perform much direct labor in connection with the Sabbath school. This is the peculiarly appropriate field of labor for private Christians. Pastors may be expected to take a general supervision of the school; but the teaching and the immediate superintendence of the school may well be attended to by private Christians. Circumstances have induced some pastors to take the sole superintendence of their schools, and oftener to perform the labor of teachers in their schools. Some of these testify that they never passed their Sabbaths so profitably and pleasantly as when thus connected with the Sabbath school. Yet it is doubted whether there are many pastors who can consistently perform this labor. By throwing the burden of this work upon the private members of the church, not a little of their moral power, which otherwise might be lost to Zion, is thus brought into operation, and at the same time a larger amount of the pastor's energies may be directed to that department more properly ministerial. Another consideration is that a greater number of persons are thus engaged in the work, and they can labor to greater advantage.

But though the pastor cannot perform much labor directly in the school, yet he may in many ways indirectly do more to give interest and efficiency to it than any other individual, and that, too, without greatly increasing the amount of his labors.

In every parochial visit he may exert a secret but most happy influence on the prosperity of his school. His occasional prayers, also, and short addresses in the school and at the concert, and his word of encouragement, counsel, or admonition, whenever he may feel able to tarry a moment, and pass from one smiling group to another, will kindle a glow of interest in every heart. Even his occasional presence, though he speak not a word, and do nothing more than pass through the school, dispensing here and there his expressions of interest and affection, will exert an important influence.

"Do you care," inquired a father of his little daughter, as they returned from the Sabbath school, "do you care about having the minister visit the school, unless he talks to the scholars?"

"O, yes, sir," said she, with the greatest enthusiasm, "because he looks on us so pleasantly." There is an eloquence in the approving, affectionate look of an interested pastor that will often move the heart of the young more effectually than any eloquence of words.

"Mr. L——," said a mother to her minister, "my little James will never forget you as long as he lives. He often says, 'Mother, the minister, when he was going out of meeting, put his hand on my head.'"

Children notice these little attentions at church and in the Sabbath school; and no minister can take the trouble to put his hand on the head of a child without gaining a warm and permanent place in that child's young heart. These apparently trifling attentions may procure the minister many a true friend to stand by him in the hour of adversity and in the decline of life.

We have known but few, if any, pastors who regard this sort of supervision of the Sabbath school, and such an attention to its interest and its welfare, as an interference with their other duties, or as too great an addition to their other labors. On the other hand, most regard the institution as their auxiliary, and watch over it and use it accordingly. The case can hardly be conceived where a minister's duties and labors are so numerous and fatiguing as to demand or even justify an entire neglect of this institution. As a faithful pastor he must see that the lambs as well as the sheep of his flock are fed, and that if he choose to commit them in part to other hands, still the responsibility of seeing that they are fed, and fed, too, with the sincere milk of the word, rests upon him.

One pastor, at least,—and one who ranked among those most abundant in their labors in the pulpit, at the social meeting, and from house to house,—used to meet his school every Sabbath, when at home, and spend the whole time of its session in various labors to promote its efficiency. And his testimony in this respect was, that he was better fitted in body, mind, and heart for his other duties in consequence. It afforded variety to the labors of the day, and was to him really a season of rest. This, however, might not, and probably would not, be the experience of every pastor; nor, however gratifying it might be to the school, should it be expected of every pastor that he should imitate such an example.

There is hardly any way in which a pastor can, indirectly, exert so great an influence on his school as through the teachers' meeting. A short season spent with the teachers, once in one or two weeks, in explaining to them the lesson for the school, could hardly be employed more profitably.

By attending the teachers' meeting, the pastor greatly increases the power of his ministry. The teachers become the instruments with which he works. Teachers, it has been well said, are the pastor's colleagues to the extent of their ability. He electrotypes himself, as it were, upon them, and through them becomes himself a teacher in every class in the school. His remarks and illustrations of truth will be repeated by them in every class. He becomes himself acquainted with the lessons, so that his prayers for the school, and his own teachings from the pulpit, his remarks at the school and the concerts, and his personal addresses to the members of his school, as he meets them in their homes or by the way, will be more appropriate and practical.

A large proportion of the pastors at the present day are doing more or less for the prosperity of their respective Sabbath schools. Some open the school every Sabbath, or occasionally, with prayer and a short address; some spend the whole season the school is in session in various labors for its prosperity; others take charge of a class of young people; some preach once or twice every year on the subject of Sabbath schools; others preach frequently on some portion of the lessons; some always attend the teachers' meeting and the concert, and some few take the entire superintendence of their school.

VII.

RELATION OF THE CHURCH TO THE SABBATH SCHOOL.

The Sabbath school is the child of the church, and to the church it should ever look for its support and instruction. It is called the nursery of the church. From this nursery the church is to obtain many of her most vigorous, thrifty, fruitful plants.

An institution, then, so intimately connected with the growth of the church should be vigorously sustained. Its general management and support should be under the care of the church.

Many of the churches are organized professedly into Sabbath school societies, as stated heretofore, and have their schools under their control. The superintendents are church officers. They are chosen, like other officers and committees, at the annual church meeting. Usually the teachers are requested to nominate the superintendent; and then the church, if the nomination is regarded a suitable one, confirms the action of the teachers. In some cases, not only the superintendents, but all the officers and teachers are appointed at the annual meeting of the church. A committee is also appointed, who, with the pastor, have the general supervision of the school for the year. This committee visit the school in rotation, one each Sabbath: they are consulted in regard to all new or special measures, examine the class papers, &c. They hold quarterly meetings for consultation. This committee, in some cases, is a board of counsellors, with whom the superintendent may, at all times, confer.

The church, by this committee, is consulted in regard to the course of lessons to be used, and in the purchase of the books for the library. And then the church, as should be the case, furnishes the means for the increase of the library and to meet all the expenses of the school. In too many cases this expense is all left to fall upon the teachers, who are doing all the work.

The church is God's ordained, divinely appointed institution for all moral and religious instruction and reformation.

No Sabbath school, or any other organization, should come between the professing disciples of Christ and the church. No other organization or institution — except the family, which is also divinely appointed — can have prior or superior claims upon them. To no other should they feel under such obligations to give their toils and prayers as to the church. She should be preferred above their chief joy. We cannot enlist in the Sabbath school work, or any other system of means for building up the kingdom of Christ, irrespective of the church. All these should be the outgrowth of the church. The church combines in herself every possible means for doing the work. She can put in operation and direct all the machinery needed for its accomplishment.

What is the church established for, in any given location, if not to labor, not only in seeking the spiritual growth of her own members, but also for Christ in seeking the salvation of all, old and youth, within her reach? The Sabbath school she will cherish as a very important auxiliary in this work, or rather as one of her own agencies, which she has called into existence, through which to do the work. It and all other plans of doing Christian work are to be under the direction of the church, — they are but different modes in which the church herself is carrying on her great mission in the world. All should be conducted so as not to interfere with the highest efficiency of the church, but rather to give scope for all her activities. As no weapon formed against the church shall prosper, so no plan that may be devised to take the place of the church and do its work can prosper.

Such being the relation of the church to the Sabbath school, and the instruction of this institution being adapted to all of every age, of course all the members of the church, so far as circumstances will permit, should give it the encouragement and support of their presence as teachers or scholars. No one is too old to study the Scriptures. No one can have finished his education in the Bible. No one has yet penetrated all the rich mines of the Word of God.

As to the particular relation the pastor sustains to the Sabbath school, it may be said, he is the moderator of all meetings of the church. The general supervision of all plans adopted by the church for the moral and religious improvement of the people, is his prerogative — not less of the Sabbath school, than of the meetings of the church for prayer and conference. His relations to the Sabbath school and all the various meetings of the church, are such, that he may at any time feel a perfect liberty to be present, and make such suggestions, and give such advice, counsel, and exhortation, as he shall think the best interests of the school and the people require.

There ought not to be — in a parish Sabbath school especially — the most distant appearance of interests distinct from those of the pastor, the church, and society. Such a school, organized and conducted independently of the ministry and the church, may be managed so as to exert the most baneful influence on the usefulness of the pastor, and the prosperity of the church and congregation. The superintendent and his cabinet of teachers, bound together, as they usually are, by strong sympathy and fellow-feeling, — should they become disaffected, or for any reason disposed, — might make the Sabbath school anything but a blessing, — a kingdom within a kingdom, — an engine of the greatest mischief.

We do not say that such has ever been the case. But we have known a few instances where pastors have been not a little embarrassed, and have felt their influence much crippled and abridged, by such an organization of the Sabbath school as has shut them out from that general oversight and supervision which properly belongs to them, and deprived them of the cheerful and harmonious coöperation of their superintendents.

This difficulty is avoided where the churches, as is now extensively the case, take this institution under their own care, organizing themselves in some instances into Sabbath school societies, with the pastors of course for the presidents or moderators, electing their superintendents and teachers, and adopting such a course of instruction and such plans to give interest and efficiency to the schools, as their wisdom may suggest.

A clergyman, in one of our cities, in 1830 wrote: "The class under my care has been organized about eighteen months. Between twenty and thirty young ladies, from sixteen to twenty-five years of age, were connected with it. Since the class commenced, two thirds of the whole number have become pious. I do not feel as if any more need be said to show the utility of ministers becoming Sabbath school teachers. Should it be said another might fill their place as well and even better, I would answer, no other person could have collected the class of young ladies under my care. They would have felt too wise and old to be Sabbath school scholars, but from the fact that their pastor was their teacher. I can truly say, if I ever felt I was honored, it is when I am seated as a Sabbath school teacher. Some may intimate that it must be too laborious for me, with my other duties on the Sabbath. Paul did more in one day than I do in a month! I need say no more."

The late Rev. Dr. Hawes, of Hartford, Conn., in a letter to the Sabbath School and Bible Association, in Andover Theological Seminary, dated March 16, 1830, writes : —

"I can assure my brethren who are preparing for the ministry, that no part of their future duties will be more important and more interesting than instructing the young in Bible classes and Sabbath schools."

He thus describes his own labors among his young people : —

"From the first of my ministry here, I have endeavored to engage the confidence of my young people, and especially of young men. In attempting to draw them around me for instruction, I have had recourse to various expedients. Soon after I came here, I formed a class of my most intelligent young people for the purpose of studying Porter's 'Evidences of Christianity.' Subsequently I collected a circle of my first young ladies to recite Paley's 'Moral Philosophy.' This I found very useful, as it gave me access to some minds that I could not well reach in any other way. I have also made use of Weeks's catechism, and afterwards of Wilbur's, and last of all, the Bible, which is by far the best class-book I have yet found.

"My method of teaching is very simple. Nearly three years ago I requested my young people over twelve years of age, who were desirous of uniting in a Bible class, to give me their names. A class of about two hundred was soon formed. I met them once in two weeks, and began with Matthew. I generally gave out a chapter, or a part of a chapter, as the case might be, and requested them to study it in the most thorough manner they were able. At the meeting I questioned any I chose. And here the great point, I have thought, to be arrived at, is familiarity. I have endeavored to make the meetings as social as possible, giving myself great latitude, both as to the topics discussed and the manner of discussing them. I have wished to make the exercise a rallying point for my young people. I have, therefore, studied to interest them by varying my addresses and remarks so as to keep up their attention, and send them away with subjects to think of and talk about. In this way I find no difficulty in calling them together.

"I meet the class now once a week. The place of meeting will seat nearly five hundred persons, and for more than two years it has been constantly filled, often thronged, and sometimes hundreds have gone away. I have been exceedingly interested in the exercise myself, and every week, I have reason to believe, the interest of those who attend has been increasing. I open and close the meeting with a short prayer, sometimes sing, and usually spend just one hour in the service. This is important. Long meetings weary. The class know my rule, and they are always in their seats within five minutes of the time, and then I always begin.

"If I may judge from my own limited experience, I would say that the great secret of conducting Bible classes is in making them interesting. Do this, and all obstacles are removed. There is no difficulty in getting young persons together if you can only interest them. To effect this, we must be familiar, social, not abstract, not critical, not always serious, solemn, not always driving at the heart and conscience. Choose your time, then strike, and strike hard."

Rev. Fred. E. Cannon, of Ludlow, Vt., in a letter to the above association, dated December 19, 1829, writes:

"I would express it as my full conviction that a large share of ministerial labor can in no way be better bestowed than in Bible class and Sabbath school efforts. If I have accomplished any good to the souls of men in this place, the past year especially, I believe it has been principally through this medium. I believe, also, that a very essential service would be done to this cause if some person would publish a system of high intellectual and critical questions upon the Scriptures, adapted to assist the minds of thinking men in Bible classes. I have in vain sought for such a system, and, for want of it, I have been driven to the herculean task of making my own. Such a work is a great desideratum, and perhaps the gentlemen of your association may devise some method of placing it in the hands of the churches."

Since 1829, numerous books have been prepared in accordance with this suggestion. Among others, the "Pastor's Bible Class Question Book," published by the Massachusetts Sabbath School Society, in 1850, was extensively used by pastors in their instructions to Bible classes, and especially classes of converts.

Rev. Moses Miller, of Heath, Mass., who organized a Sabbath school in his parish in 1815, which was the first one in Franklin county, and who had previously, for several years, conducted Bible classes in the different districts of this town, recommended, in 1829, that the school should, as far as practical, have the same lesson, and the preacher should select the themes of his discourse from the lesson, and expound, as far as he can consistently with variety, selecting either the most difficult or prominent texts in the lesson.

In a few years after his settlement in 1803, he became interested in the instruction of the young, and he commenced teaching the children Emerson's catechisms during the intermission of public worship. Soon after he commenced teaching a class of youth in Wilbur's catechism during the week, and immediately after formed a Bible class; then Bible classes in the different districts for persons of all ages; then a Bible class for the young during the intermission of worship, — thus alternately instructing the youth and children on the Sabbath. In the weekly Bible classes in the school districts, parents and children met and were questioned upon the lesson given out on the Sabbath previous. He longed to see the whole congregation studying the Bible, especially during the intermission on the Sabbath, instead of engaging, as he feared was the case, in vain conversation. He entered warmly into every plan connected with the Sabbath school after it was established, and in a few years he had the pleasure of seeing a larger portion of the people in the school than probably in any other school in the land.

VIII.

SUPERINTENDENTS AND TEACHERS.

A VERY common subject for essays and discussions at conventions and other Sabbath school meetings has ever been, "The Qualifications of Superintendents and Teachers."

These qualifications have often been placed so high and imposing that many of our most devoted and successful superintendents and teachers have shrunk back abashed and discouraged at the solemn array of responsibilities and duties of this work. These qualifications have been simply impracticable in the case of most teachers. None but theological professors could possibly attain to the standard presented.

But we cannot have such professors for superintendents and teachers in all our Sabbath schools. And the only practical question in any given church or place where there is to be a school is, What can we do that will best promote the interests of the school with the materials we have? Who is the best man among us for superintendent, and who are the best men and women among us for teachers? These selected, the next thing is, How can such best qualify themselves for their work? We must remember that a large portion of them are engaged in daily employments that call for their undivided time and thought during most of the hours of their week-days. They have but little time, except on the Sabbath, to prepare themselves for teaching.

Fathers and mothers, who have some experience in the training of their own children, in learning the peculiarities of mind and the various temperaments of the young, and what is the best way to lead them into the paths of truth and piety, other things being equal, may be expected to make the best teachers in the Sabbath school. But it is often the case that young Christians have far better natural qualifications for this important office than many older Christians, even parents. They are more apt to teach, have a special faculty of getting the attention and awakening the interest of the young. They have not yet forgotten, as some older persons often seem to have done, that they were once children themselves. They can recall all the embarrassments and restraints they felt in their associations with older people; how they longed for something bright and cheerful connected with religious instruction.

There may be some even, who are not Christians, whose moral tone of character is so high, who have such a love for children, such an aptness for communicating instruction, and such a magnetism in drawing the young to them, that they will be much more likely to benefit their pupils than some professors of religion who have none of these qualifications.

Of course we should, ordinarily, make personal piety the first and the most important qualification in a teacher. But we must not forget that in many places, especially in the early days of this institution, there could be no successful Sabbath school if none but professors of religion were to be employed as teachers.

Having selected the best materials the church has for superintendent and teachers, then everything should be done that can be to impress them with the importance and solemnity of their office, and their need of earnest effort to qualify themselves, in the best manner possible, for their work, by reading such books and periodicals as they can obtain on the subject; by the most careful study of the lesson; by a constant attendance of the teachers' meeting; by seeking the aid and advice of their pastor as they have opportunity, and by much prayer for the teaching and aid of the Holy Spirit.

A superintendent, in 1829, was accustomed to devote a large share of his time to making preparation for his Sabbath labors in the school. He usually prepared a course of lectures, explaining, in a simple and interesting manner, the historical parts of the Bible, or the practical parts, connecting together the fragments of history or moral precepts in chronological or natural order.

Another superintendent, about the same time, was accustomed to spend two whole days a week in preparing for his school. But few persons, of course, can command their time in this way. And we must not expect it from the great body of superintendents and teachers.

Some of the most successful superintendents and teachers ever connected with Sabbath schools, — those who have had the honor of leading the largest number of scholars to the Saviour, — have been those who, apparently, have had very small advantages for qualifying themselves for their work. They have been men and women whose daily employments have left them but little time during the week-days for this purpose;

but they have been persons of a plain and simple piety and of earnest prayer. They have been accustomed to study their lessons on their knees, and go from their closets as from the very presence-chamber of the Almighty to their schools and classes, and their faces almost shone with a heavenly radiance, as did the face of Moses when he came down from the Mount of God. They received their qualifications mainly from the teachings of the Holy Spirit. God was with them, and they taught under the divine guidance. Their great end was not merely to please and interest their pupils, but to secure their salvation. For this they labored earnestly in the class, and for this they daily prayed. And the fruit of their labor was a rich harvest of souls. A teacher of a class of thirty-two scholars during six months in 1832 had the pleasure of seeing twenty-eight of those scholars make a public profession of religion.

In a school, the same year, where only four were converted, three of them were from a class whose teacher resolved to "attempt great things."

A teacher, more than thirty years ago, frequently rose before light, in the coldest winter weather, to prepare her heart for the responsible duties of the Sabbath school. In a short time she had evidence that five of her scholars had become reconciled to God.

Another teacher, about the same time, labored for several months with strong confidence that she would see her whole class converted; and some thirteen of them were soon after hopefully converted, and the remaining one was an anxious inquirer.

A scholar expressed a preference for Mr. —— as a teacher, "because," he said, "he always talks to his class till he cries." And this is one example out of many that might be given, to show that scholars generally prefer faithful teachers, and that such, generally, rather than those who are using any special machinery, or introducing novelties, are the ones that interest their scholars and secure their conversion.

A teacher for a long time had been unusually anxious for her class of six little girls. She urged them to attend a protracted meeting in a neighboring parish. On the third day she saw her superintendent, and, taking him by the hand, while the tears of Christian joy were gushing from her eyes, she exclaimed, "Can you believe it? — all my class are rejoicing in hope!"

A teacher, in speaking of some hopeful appearances in a member of his class, said, "I shall not fail to bear him upon my mind in prayer in an especial manner;" and added, "If I can be instrumental in saving one soul from ruin, and preparing it for heaven, how abundantly shall I be rewarded for all the toil and effort I may make in such an enterprise."

A teacher in Maine, in 1831, said: "One Sabbath morning I was engaged in the exercise of family worship. As I came to pray for the Sabbath school, as I always do, the thought flashed upon my mind that I had not been faithful to my class. I became very much affected, and made confession of my wrong, and earnestly prayed that the Lord would forgive me, and help me henceforth to be faithful. I went to the Sabbath school, and, after hearing my class recite their lesson, began to converse with them faithfully. To my astonishment, they were all melted into tears. Several of my scholars were hopefully converted."

How many teachers have been astonished, and had

their hearts made glad, by faithful labors among the members of their classes!

Mrs. R., in the same state, in the summer of 1833, feeling that a Sabbath school was much needed in her neighborhood, began to make inquiries about having one commenced. There had formerly been one, but the teachers did not find it convenient again to enlist in the work.

She felt the delicacy of engaging alone; but, after having sought wisdom and guidance from above, she ventured to commence a school. Sometimes her husband, sometimes her children, and sometimes other females gave their assistance. About forty children were brought under the influence of this school.

She confined her lessons to the Bible, commencing with the gospel of John, and taking one chapter for a Sabbath, but requesting the scholars to commit only ten verses. She studied her lessons upon her knees, with Scott's "Notes and Observations," taking one division each day, till she had completed the chapter. At the school,—which was opened and closed with singing and prayer,—the scholars read the chapter, and she asked questions, and made such remarks as were deemed suitable. In relation to this exercise she remarked:—

"Though this book has long seemed peculiarly interesting to me, yet I never discovered such beauty, such sublimity, and such glory in it before. I hope my scholars made some progress in studying the Bible, but I really believe that I made far more than any of them. It seems to me as though I reaped all the good myself; for while I was waiting about the Temple, and sowing in tears, the Lord visited my own family in mercy, and drew, as it were, my own flesh and bones to himself. Our eldest son, then seventy miles distant, was awakened by the Holy Spirit, and led to turn his feet into the testimonies of the Lord, and to rejoice in God his Saviour. O come, and rejoice with us."

Twenty-five or thirty years ago, a class of fourteen young ladies was formed in a Sabbath school, and they were requested to select their teacher. They chose a lady about sixty years of age, who was herself a scholar in the school, as most of the members of the church were connected with it as scholars or teachers.

For some time this lady declined to take charge of that class, on account of the great responsibility of such a position. Many of the sisters in the church urged her to become the teacher of that interesting class. At length she consented, on the promise of these sisters that they would unite with her in praying for the conversion of the thirteen impenitent members of the class.

The plan of this teacher on assuming the charge of that class was, to select one member, for whom the pious scholar and these sisters in the church were to unite with her in praying. The very next Sabbath, that scholar was rejoicing in hope. She then chose another, and soon that one also was hopefully converted. She then informed the class what she was doing, when another member burst into tears, and exclaimed, "Won't you choose me to pray for this week? Do choose me."

She did choose her, and in a few weeks she too was rejoicing in hope. In about three months, all the members of that class were hopefully converted. We have often related this incident, with the declaration that that teacher was our own dear mother.

These are specimens of what was accomplished many years ago by a common class of teachers, whose principal preparation was simple prayer, thorough study, and deep earnestness for the salvation of those under their care. And they are very instructive to all the friends of this institution, and especially to teachers, at the present day.

After these many years of careful observation, we feel that it is hardly possible to represent too strongly the responsibility that rests upon those who have the moral and religious instruction of the young. In some cases almost the whole of this training, and in many cases an important part of it, must be performed, if performed at all, by Sabbath school teachers; and on them, therefore, rests a large share of this responsibility. The more deeply teachers realize this solemn truth, of course, the more zealously and prayerfully will they engage in their work; and constantly occurring facts show that the results of their labors are nearly in proportion to their prayerfulness and fidelity. If they engage in their work with proper zeal and dependence on God, they may be instrumental, in his hands, of spreading a Christian influence over the whole earth.

That little ragged boy, who by the kind Christian teacher is brought under the influence of the Sabbath school, may prove a spiritual Samson to demolish the temple of many a Dagon.

Most of the young who are hereafter to be converted will doubtless belong to this institution. Teachers are called upon, then, in their labors in this cause, to superintend the early training of most of those who will hereafter constitute the sacramental host, and stand up the fearless champions for the Lord Jesus Christ. To their culture may be intrusted the budding intellect of an Edwards or a Payson, a Hannah More or a Mrs. Huntington. Yes, by their labors a single year they may give a turn and direction to some giant mind, which shall hereafter, like the Reformers, pour a flood of light upon the moral darkness and corruption of the world.

These considerations have led many anxiously to ask,—

WHAT IS TO BE THE CHARACTER OF OUR FUTURE CONVERTS?

The time of the world's conversion, it is believed, depends very much upon the character of the church; and there can be no doubt that the character of the church, in ages to come, will be greatly modified by the training which her future members shall receive in the Sabbath school.

To the hands of teachers, therefore, not only the character of the church, but also the period of the world's conversion, in a fearful manner, are intrusted. The piety of their scholars, if converted, will very much resemble their own. Thus we see one good and probable reason why the scholars of many teachers are not converted. If converted, they would be converted to the standard of piety which they have been accustomed to see in their teachers. As Christians, they would resemble them; and what would be the character of a church, were it to be composed of such members? When would the world be converted, were the great mass of children and youth in our Sabbath schools to become such Christians as many of their teachers are?

This question is asked kindly, and with a strong desire that it may lead all of us who are engaged in the religious training of the young, solemnly to consider the character of our influence. Would it really be a blessing to the church and the world to have all the children and youth under our influence become just such Christians as we are ourselves? If not, can we expect that God will convert them, to become a burden and a hinderance to his cause?

It is true that the only perfect and proper standard of Christian character is in the Bible; and all ought to seek after a likeness to Christ, our only perfect pattern. But we must take the world as we find it. We are all, more or less, creatures of imitation, and are influenced, even in our views of Christian character and Christian duty, in no small measure by those around us, especially by our superiors and instructors.

We see, then, why some teachers, like those already referred to, are so much blessed in their labors for the conversion of their scholars. The great reason, so far as concerns human instrumentality, no doubt is, that those means which God is wont to bless in the conversion of souls are faithfully used, and that earnest, persevering prayer, which God is wont to answer, is offered. But another reason doubtless is, that God sees that the standard of piety exhibited by these teachers, to which their scholars will be likely to be converted, is such as will make their conversion a real blessing to his cause.

It is not strange that the devoted Harlan Page was

blessed in his labors for the salvation of souls. Were there such a standard of personal consecration to God seen in all our teachers as he exhibited, our Sabbath schools would become the spiritual birthplaces of thousands and thousands of precious youth. Then, no youth could be encouraged by the example of his teacher to think himself a Christian unless he were disposed and impelled to engage with all his heart and strength in personal labors for the salvation of others. What a moral power a church of two or three hundred members like Harlan Page would be able to wield against the kingdom of darkness! Think of the power of the whole church of Christ on earth, were all her members like that eminent Christian! Through the instrumentality of such an almost omnipotent influence, how would the period of the world's conversion roll on, and draw nearer and nearer, like the fast rising light of the morning!

THE ORPHAN'S PARENTS.

What object can make a stronger appeal to a Christian heart than a helpless orphan? No Christian can think of the dangers and temptations to which such a child or youth will be exposed without deep emotions; without a prayer to the God of the fatherless that He will raise up friends and spiritual guardians for them.

There are, no doubt, many orphan children connected with our Sabbath schools. Upon the teachers of such there rests a special and most solemn obligation. They are, so far as relates to religious instruction, to become these orphans' parents. For their souls, peculiarly, they are to watch as those that must give account. Perhaps there are no others that care for their souls; certainly there are none who would be more likely to exercise a faithful guardianship over their spiritual, and, so far as possible, their temporal interests, than pious, faithful teachers.

We once heard a father, one who feels a tender interest for orphan children, and who knows, by his own mournful experience, what it is to be left an orphan child, with orphan brothers and sisters looking up to him for protection, — we heard such a father say, "Were I to leave my children fatherless, I know of no one to whose care and guardianship I would intrust them sooner than to a faithful Sabbath school teacher."

Such is the confidence many parents repose in faithful teachers. Such confidence, it may be, many parents now in heaven felt, when on their dying-bed, in those to whose instructions they were then leaving their fatherless and motherless children.

Teachers, have you been faithful to those children? Are you still worthy of that confidence? O, forget not the hopes of those dying parents, and forget not your obligations to their orphan children! If you are faithful and wise in training their children for heaven, with what blessings will those parents hail you when you finish your labors and enter upon your rest!

But, teachers, how much better than orphans, so far as respects their spiritual interests, are all those of your scholars whose parents care not for their souls? Indeed, it may be, in some instances, that their situation is even worse than that of orphans, inasmuch as parental example, and perhaps instruction, are obstructing their way to heaven and leading them on to ruin. For their souls, then, you must watch and pray.

There ever have been large numbers of superintendents and teachers — and we gladly record the statement — who most deeply feel the importance of their work. They are accustomed to look upon their schools and their classes — as all indeed should — as their little parishes; and, like faithful pastors, they feel that they are watching for souls. They feel some of the same responsibility that a pastor does, to be constant and punctual in their attendance, and to come with thorough preparations for their work. They do not forget the disappointment a people would feel to have the pastor absent, or even tardy, or to have him come with no preparation for the pulpit.

Those superintendents and teachers who are most successful in their work occupy as many spare moments as they can through the week in reading and study, with reference to their preparation for the Sabbath. They gather and study out in their minds all the illustrations they can to give variety and interest to their instructions, and which will aid their pupils in understanding their lessons, and in feeling an interest in all the exercises of the school.

Among the many reminiscences in regard to teachers that we have from time to time gathered up, the following, though fragmentary, may be interesting and instructive to some: —

PRAYING FOR A DEFINITE OBJECT.

Mr. —— took charge of a class of young ladies, some of whom were professedly Christians. One day, after a solemn conversation with them, he inquired if any member of the class wished a particular remembrance in prayer that week.

He noticed one young lady, who had appeared quite serious during his remarks, struggling with the deep emotions which this inquiry awakened in her mind. He then addressed her personally, and asked if she wished to be made the subject of special prayer. She answered in the affirmative. He then told her, that as many of the class as lived sufficiently near would meet that evening for prayer, and that they would bear her case especially on their hearts before God.

The next Sabbath this scholar entered the class with a heart heavily burdened with a sense of sin, having found no peace in believing. The teacher talked faithfully with her, and pointed her to the sinner's only friend and hope. At the close of the exercises he told her that they would again remember her case that evening in their class prayer-meeting.

After the afternoon service, the minister requested several of the church, if they knew of any persons who were in an inquiring state of mind, to invite them to call at his house on the coming Thursday. On that day Mr. —— went to see this inquiring scholar, that he might learn the state of her mind and inform her of the request of her pastor. He had no sooner begun to converse, than he saw her eyes commence to beam. She could not repress the joy of her heart, and she frankly told her teacher what the Lord had done for her soul.

"When did you begin to experience this change in your feelings?" inquired the teacher.

"Last Sabbath evening," was the reply.

"At what time?" And it appeared that it was the very hour when her teacher and the pious members of her class were offering up their united prayers for her salvation.

How strange it is that so many teachers, with all the encouragements held out to them in the word and providence of God, take so little encouragement to pray!

This incident should encourage every teacher to pray — to pray for a definite object; namely, the salvation of particular individuals, and to enlist the united and the secret prayer of his pious scholars in the same object; and it should also encourage him to frequent personal conversation with each scholar, both in the class and at their homes.

SCHOLARS EXPECT FAITHFULNESS.

Teachers will rarely, if ever, alienate the affections of their scholars, or drive them from the school, by a kind, faithful, personal application of religious truth. Many facts have occurred which show that even impenitent, thoughtless children respect and love those teachers best who are the most earnest in endeavors to save their souls. Some of the most thoughtless and giddy scholars have requested the privilege of leaving a teacher, who never did anything but hear the lesson and ask a few general questions, that they might join a class where the teacher was known to make direct appeals to the heart and conscience of each scholar.

This might be illustrated by numerous facts. The following may be taken as a specimen: —

Mr. E—— had a class of seven lads, about fourteen years of age. As none of them gave evidence of piety, their conversion became a special object of his daily desire and prayer, and of his faithful labors in the class. He was accustomed to converse with members individually in regard to his salvation; and all his instructions were highly practical and direct.

So far from fearing that this course of faithfulness would offend his pupils and break up his class, he felt confident that this was the surest way to gain their attention and regard, and secure their willing and interested attendance. And he felt, also, that their good and the glory of God demanded of him this faithfulness.

The class directly in front of Mr. E——'s consisted of seven lads, of about the same age as his own. But the teacher seemed to have no just apprehension of the duties and responsibilities of his station. The exercises of his class consisted merely in asking and answering the questions of the lesson. No explanations or application of the truths it contained were ever given.

One Sabbath this teacher was absent, and the superintendent, after much reasoning and entreaty, persuaded Mr. E—— to leave his own class for one Sabbath, and supply the place of the absent teacher.

Mr. E—— was aware that he was now with a class that had been accustomed to hear but little in regard to their salvation. Some might suppose that the direct, personal, faithful mode of address which he used to his own scholars would offend these. Mr. E—— might possibly have feared it himself; but he resolved that they should not go from a Sabbath school to the judgment-seat of Christ without at least one faithful, affectionate warning. And such he gave them, and with tears.

The next Sabbath came, and such was the effect of these faithful instructions of Mr. E—— upon the minds of those seven boys, that they all wished to unite with his class. And so strong were their desires for this, that the superintendent and their teacher felt that they should be regarded. Mr. E—— accordingly received these seven lads into his own class, increasing the number to fourteen promising youths.

This occurrence imparted a new zeal and earnestness to the labors of Mr. E—— for the salvation of his interesting charge. From Sabbath to Sabbath their attention became more and more fixed, and a growing interest in the subject of personal religion more and more apparent. At length the tear of penitence and the anxious inquiry, "What must I do to be saved?" showed that the Spirit of God was indeed present.

In less than three months from the time these two classes were united, six of Mr. E——'s original scholars, and all the new ones, thirteen out of fourteen, were hopefully converted.

The first fifteen minutes of the concert, after the opening exercises, in one school, were devoted by all the teachers to personal conversation with the scholars of their respective classes, on the subject of their salvation. This was a season of great interest and solemnity. Stillness and attention reigned through the school. And the influence of this exercise was thought to be very salutary.

No one, not even among the older scholars, manifested any unwillingness to engage in this exercise. And it is believed that few, if any scholars in any school would object to such an exercise if the teachers are wise and judicious in addressing them. Many scholars, no doubt, are longing for just such personal conversation with their teachers.

EFFECT OF PERSEVERANCE.

In the town of —— there was no Sabbath school; the church had become very inefficient, and religion was languishing. This state of things excited the benevolent spirit of a young Christian female, Miss Smith. She resolved to attempt the establishment of a Sabbath school as the most hopeful effort she could make for the good of the people.

A Mr. Page was keeping the district school; and, though sceptical in his views, he was much beloved by his pupils. Miss Smith visited him, and explained her plan for a Sabbath school. She told him she had divided the district, one half of which she was going to canvass to see how many scholars could be secured, and she wished him to canvass the other half. He said he would not do it. Miss Smith then told him she would call on Friday and compare papers, and see which had obtained the most scholars. He again said that he could not engage in that work.

On Friday this persevering female called, as she had promised, and informed Mr. Page that she had obtained the names of about thirty scholars; and that she had told them all he was going to superintend the school. He told her that he should not superintend the school, and that he had not visited the section she had assigned to him, and that he should not visit it.

Miss Smith again left him, after having told him that she would call the next day and make arrangements for the school.

The subject of this interview rested on the mind of the teacher through the night. In the morning he rose and said to himself, "I will not be outdone by a female."

He canvassed his district, and obtained twenty-five or thirty scholars, all of whom seemed pleased that he was to superintend the school.

The school was organized the 1st of June. After two Sabbaths, Mr. Page became troubled about prayers in the school, and asked Miss Smith what should be done. She told him he must pray himself. At length he succeeded in persuading a deacon to come into the school and pray.

The mind of Mr. Page soon became deeply impressed with divine truth. On the 4th of July, which was the Sabbath, at an evening meeting he rose and addressed his associates in regard to a contemplated excursion the next day. He told them he could not go, and must not go, for he had a soul to take care of. The effect of his address was almost overwhelming; and it was instrumental in the conversion of eight or ten of his associates. A general revival of religion immediately began, of which some of the leading men of the town became subjects.

Mr. Page soon became hopefully pious himself, and commenced study for the gospel ministry. At the academy, where he studied, he was instrumental by his personal labors with the students in the conversion of several. One of these the next winter engaged in school teaching, and was the means of a revival among his scholars. In a letter to Mr. Page, he said, "Had it not been for the conversation you had with me respecting my soul, I should have been spending this winter in pleasure and amusement, but now I am in the midst of a revival of religion."

Mr. Page's piety was of no ordinary character. He often visited the sick and sorrowful, and was always received by the afflicted as a "son of consolation." His influence at the Theological Seminary, of which he was a member, was very salutary, till his last sickness and triumphant death.

ANOTHER EXAMPLE.

Mr. C—— began to attend the Sabbath school at the age of nineteen, in the year 1817. For three years he seldom, if ever, failed to get a lesson, although he was naturally so dull a scholar, that from two to ten verses a week were all he was able to commit to memory. Sometimes he used to say, "he did not know as it would do him any good to attend the Sabbath school, but he thought he would try to learn some of the Bible."

In a revival in 1821 he became interested in religion. He now found the benefit of his toils in committing to memory every week a few verses of the Scriptures. He became a very active Christian, though he suffered great embarrassment from an uncommon share of diffidence.

In the spring of 1822 he moved into another place, and set up business as a mechanic. He was the only pious young person in the place. There was no meeting, no meeting-house, and only a few professors of religion.

His heart yearned over the young around him who were growing up without religious instruction. He remembered where he had been taught to study and love the word of God. It was not long before he effected the establishment of a Sabbath school, of which he was the only teacher. At length he so far secured the coöperation of one professor as to persuade him to come into the school and pray. The school soon began to awaken, among some, a desire for religious meetings. This desire spread and deepened, till, in the autumn, it began to secure occasional preaching. Nor did it stop here. Arrangements began to be made for the erection of a house of worship. The next season, the house was completed, a minister of the gospel was settled, the rains and the dews of divine grace were bestowed, and a flourishing church was established. Most of the young men in the place were hopefully converted.

We saw a letter from Mr. C——, from which we gathered the following facts respecting his usual labors on the Sabbath. At eight o'clock in the morning he attended a Sabbath school, sometimes one, and sometimes five miles from his home. At noon, he attended the school at the meeting-house. At three o'clock in the afternoon, he attended another school six miles distant. At five o'clock, another eight miles from his home! These schools were the scenes of frequent revivals. Can any teacher, in view of this incident, say he has no influence? Are there greater obstacles in the way of any one becoming eminently useful than were surmounted by Mr. C——?

THE TEACHER'S HIRE.

The parable of the householder, who hired laborers into his vineyard, is very encouraging to the faithful teacher. The great Householder says to every disciple, "Go thou also into the vineyard; and whatsoever is right, that shall ye receive." And what a hire the earnest laborer is sure to receive!

See that little group of youths listening to the words of piety and affection as they fall from that devoted teacher's lips! See, here and there the tear of penitence is silently stealing from eyes that never wept for sin before. Hear the half-stifled but earnest inquiry, "What must I do to be saved?" Hark! Do you hear those seraphic strains? How they rise and swell! What a tide of joy rolls through all the plains of heaven! It is the angels' song of rejoicing over those new-born youths. Teacher, such is thy hire.

See that little girl returning to her miserable home, and more miserable parents. Hear her telling them of the blessed Bible she now loves to study, and of the dear Saviour who is now precious to her soul. See her tears; hear her tender expostulations. How affectionately she entreats those parents to repent and learn to pray. Now she has fallen upon her knees, and her voice, half choked with sobs, is ascending in earnest prayer to God, who hears the young ravens when they cry. This is too much. Those eyes for the first time begin to weep over sin; those hard and icy hearts now begin to warm and soften: they melt. Yes, her parents repent and are forgiven. How great the change! That house, before the abode of wretchedness and woe, has become the dwelling-place of comfort and holy joy. It is a little Bethel, from which goes up the morning and evening incense, and where ascend and descend the angels of God. A holy influence emanates from that converted family; it pervades the neighborhood; and now, where seldom was heard the voice of prayer and praise till it fell from the lips of that little child, you may see the multitude assembling from Sabbath to Sabbath to engage in the worship of the sanctuary. Teacher, what a hire for the prayers and self-denying labors it cost you to establish and sustain a Sabbath school in that neglected neighborhood! Did you anticipate such a hire? Did not the great Master of the vineyard more than fulfil his promise, "Whatsoever is right, that shalt thou receive"?

See that devoted youth, tearing himself from the embraces of his weeping parents and friends, and bidding farewell to the land of his birth and the scenes of his boyhood, to become the almoner of the bread and water of life to the perishing millions in the darkness of heathenism! Look again. There he stands at the judgment-seat of Christ, encircled by a multitude of those whom he has led from darkness into light, who are to be his crown of rejoicing forever. Teacher, that missionary was once that profane and miserable youth whom you persuaded by your repeated and earnest solicitations to join your class in the Sabbath-school! Did you anticipate that you were then taking such a hold on the eternal destinies of multitudes who were sitting in the shades of death? O, did you look for such hire for your toil?

RESPONSIBLE FOR SOULS.

A foreign missionary once said he believed we should be held responsible for the salvation of every soul that we could in any possible way have saved. This statement seems to accord with some very solemn words in the thirty-third chapter of the prophecy of Ezekiel, connected with the responsibility of watchmen.

With this subject in mind, let us look at the following narrative in relation to two Sabbath school teachers:—

Susan was a member of the Sabbath school. She was favored with a very pious, devoted teacher, who always met her class not only with a lesson thoroughly prepared, but also with her own heart prepared and warmed by frequent visits to her closet and earnest intercessions for her pupils. Every scholar could see, by her every expression, that she had come from the very presence-chamber of the Almighty.

She not only endeavored to communicate clearly and forcibly the truths contained in the lessons, but she sought every Sabbath to gain access to the hearts and consciences of her charge, by inquiries, exhortations, warnings and entreaties, addressed to each one personally. She felt that she was set to watch for these souls as one that must give account. The salvation of the dear youth thus committed to her watch and care seemed to her an object of unutterable solemnity and importance; and she labored as though their salvation might depend upon her fidelity. She was not satisfied with what she could do for them during one or two hours on the Sabbath and in her closet, but she often addressed them by letter, in the most solemn, affectionate, and earnest manner, respecting the interests of their souls.

Under the instructions of such a teacher, it is not strange that Susan became deeply anxious about her salvation, and that her parents began to cherish the fond hope that they would soon be able to exclaim, "This our child was dead, and is alive again; and was lost, and is found."

Soon after this the family of which Susan was a member moved to another community, where she came under the instruction of another teacher; but O, how different from the one who had labored so earnestly for her spiritual good! She was professedly a Christian, but she seemed to have no heart for her work, nor the faintest idea of its importance, her own responsibility in the case, or that, in any sense, she was to watch for the souls of her scholars. The possibility of benefiting them for eternity did not appear to have entered her mind. She was probably ignorant of their religious feelings, and did not suspect that one of them had been almost upon the very threshold of heaven.

Susan, whose seriousness had been gradually diminishing ever since she lost the faithful instructions of her former teacher, at length disclosed to her disappointed parents this astonishing fact, that her last teacher had never spoken a word to her respecting the concerns of her soul! All she pretended to do, as a teacher, was merely to propound the questions as she found them in the book or on the lesson paper.

We do not believe that the unfaithfulness of that teacher is any good excuse for Susan to continue an enemy to God, or that she will dare mention it as an excuse at the judgment; but we do believe that this want of fidelity and watchfulness in regard to the souls of her pupils, if unrepented of, will be a subject of most bitter reflection for that teacher when she lies on her dying-bed.

UNCONVERTED TEACHERS.

The following incidents may help to answer the question whether it is ever right to employ teachers who are not Christians.

Among the three hundred Sabbath schools organized in Maine during our agency, two were in the town of W——. The church in this place was almost extinct, being reduced to only one male, and a small number of female members.

Under these circumstances, these two schools were established. In the one at the centre there was but one pious teacher. A lawyer, physician, hotel-keeper, and postmaster were among the male teachers. At the close of the fourth Sabbath, after the scholars had left, the hotel-keeper, with much emotion, said to the teachers, "I don't know what ails me lately; I never felt so in my life. I find I am trying to teach these children what I do not understand myself, and it does seem to me there ought to be some one to pray in this Sabbath school."

All the teachers, it seemed, were in much the same state of mind, without knowing it of each other; and the lawyer said to him, —

"Won't you pray now?"

"No," said he, "I can't pray; I never did pray." But, being urged, he prayed. As he returned home, his wife, seeing that he was in trouble, inquired if he was sick. "Not in my body," said he; "but I am sick in my soul. I find I am trying to teach children the way to Heaven when I do not know the way myself."

That same week, he and his wife were both hopefully converted. It was the commencement of an interesting work of grace, which brought all those teachers, and a large number of the scholars, and others, into the church.

In the earlier days of Sabbath schools, the reports, like the above, of the conversion of teachers, were too numerous, and of a character too deeply interesting, to justify the decision, that teachers not experimentally acquainted with the truth should *never* be employed in Sabbath schools. If pious teachers, well qualified in other respects, can be obtained, they certainly should be in most cases. There are instances, however, when individuals of good moral character, and well fitted for the business in every respect, excepting that of personal piety, can be brought into the school only by appointing them to the office of teachers. It may not be so advantageous for the scholars, but there can be no more hopeful place for an unconverted teacher. He must soon see how perfectly unqualified he is for one important part of his duty. How can he lead a child to Christ if he has never learned the way himself? And how can he withstand the inquiry which will often drop from the lips of some inquisitive child?

Mr. ——, who has died in the triumph of the gospel, received his first impressions from his appointment to teach a class in the Sabbath school. The consideration that he was appointed to instruct others while destitute of religion himself was the means of his awakening.

TEACHERS' VISITS.

Much is said of the importance of teachers visiting their scholars at their homes, and also visiting neglected families. The happy results of such visits among the neglected is favorably illustrated by the following incident: —

A female teacher, while laboring to obtain new scholars for the Sabbath school, visited a house in which there were two families, consisting of parents and children, and three other adult members. These families were extremely uncultivated and heathenish. The men had not attended religious worship for fourteen years, and none of the other members were in the habit of attending. The teacher succeeded in getting two little girls, one of nine years of age and the other younger, to join the

Sabbath school. After six weeks the oldest child was taken sick. Her sickness soon became very distressing and dangerous, and she requested her parents to send for her teacher. They complied with her request, and the teacher came, and talked and prayed with her. She became so much interested in the state of mind exhibited by her afflicted pupil that she often repeated her visits, and at length took other teachers with her that they might see the work of grace which she believed God was carrying on in the heart of this till recently neglected child.

In about three weeks this dear child died, giving her teacher and Christian friends as good evidence as the circumstances of the case would admit that she died in the Lord.

During the sickness of this departed one she often exhorted her parents and uncle to attend meeting on the Sabbath, and no more to take God's name in vain. Her exhortations reached their hearts, and the very next Sabbath after her death all the seven adults, with the remaining children of those two families, were found in the house of God, where they continued regularly to attend, and several of them became personally interested in the subject of religion.

Such are some of the happy results, through the blessing of God, of that teacher's visit to that neglected family.

"They that be wise shall shine as the brightness of the firmament; and they that turn many to righteousness, as the stars forever and ever."

Many years ago we prepared two cards, as pocket companions for superintendents and teachers, with a brief statement of what seemed to us at that time, and what seems to us at the present time, some of the more important duties connected with their office, as follows: —

DUTIES OF THE SUPERINTENDENT.

1. Punctuality, to a minute, in commencing the exercises at the appointed hour. Mr. R——, for seven years, was never absent a Sabbath from his school, and seldom tardy a moment. Mr. C——, for six years, was absent but once.

2. In the opening and closing exercises, whether reading, singing, remarks, or prayer, be very brief.

3. Have the utmost order and decorum through the whole school.

4. Go from class to class with a word of instruction, advice, encouragement, or admonition, to scholars and teachers.

5. The superintendent should make himself perfectly familiar with the lesson.

6. He should become acquainted with the teachers, their characters, qualifications, fidelity, and methods of communicating instruction and illustrating truth.

7. He must be a bright example to his teachers in familiarity, in impartiality of conduct, in love for his work, in piety, in zeal and holy earnestness for the salvation of the scholars.

8. He should learn the names of the scholars, always meet them with exhibitions of affectionate interest, notice all absences, and the next Sabbath go round to each and learn the cause, and keep a record of everything encouraging or otherwise respecting each member of the school.

9. Daily study ways and means, and weekly make

thorough preparations, to give variety to the exercises and secure the highest interest and efficiency of the school. Mr. P—— used to devote two whole days, weekly, to these preparations.

10. Devise plans to enlist the scholars in the cause of missions, temperance, and all the objects of benevolence.

11. He should feel and manifest a deep interest in the teachers' meeting and the concert.

12. A good superintendent will be eminently a person of prayer.

DUTIES OF THE SABBATH SCHOOL TEACHER.

1. Constant and strict punctuality.
2. Thorough acquaintance with the lesson.
3. Regular attendance on the teachers' meeting and the concert.
4. Go from the closet to the class.
5. In teaching, be familiar, affectionate, practical, serious, earnest.
6. Converse personally with each scholar respecting his soul. Merely asking the questions on the lesson will produce but little good.
7. See that your instructions are enforced by your habitual life and conversation.
8. Study the characters of your scholars, their tempers, habits, associations, &c., and adapt instruction accordingly.
9. Visit the scholars at their homes, especially when they have been absent.
10. Often look at the names on the back of this card,* and think of the Judgment. (See Dan. xii. 3. James v. 20.)

* The teacher was directed to put the scholars' names on the back.

11. Bear each scholar on your heart in daily, earnest prayer.

12. Make their salvation the great object of all your instructions.

13. Regard your office as second in importance to none, excepting that of the parent and the pastor.

14. Cultivate a spirit of ardent piety, self-consecration, and a constant dependence on God for success.

Teacher! Momentous consequences may result from your performance or neglect of these duties. Will you not pray over them daily?

THAT CLASS OF BOYS.

In 1847 we met that class of eleven boys, about eight or ten years of age, one Saturday evening at the house of their minister. The minister's wife was their Sabbath school teacher.

These boys were all bright and intelligent, and their countenances were never more radiant than when they met their teacher. They were very constant and punctual at school, with well-prepared lessons. That their lessons were thus prepared will not seem strange when we learn how and where most of the class study them.

One Friday evening, about a year before, just as the teacher of this class was rejoicing at the arrival of some distant friend, she heard a knock at her door. On opening it, there stood two or three of the younger members of her class.

"Well, boys," said she, "what books are those you have with you?"

"Our question books, ma'am," they answered.

"Have you come to have me assist you in getting your lesson?"

"Yes, ma'am," said they, with animated countenances.

"Well, I am very glad; but I have company just come in, so that I do not see as it will be possible for me to assist you this evening. Can't you come to-morrow evening?"

"Yes, ma'am, just as well," they replied.

"Well, you come to-morrow evening, and I will then be very happy to aid you."

As they turned to leave, the teacher saw one or two of her older scholars behind a tree, where they had been waiting to learn what reception the younger ones, whom they had sent before them, met with.

The next evening some five or six of her class came, according to appointment; and ever after that, through the autumn and winter, while the evenings were long, a portion of this class were in the habit of spending an hour Saturday evening with their teacher in the study of their lessons.

The Saturday evening we spent with this family, five of these boys were punctually present at the appointed hour. So great was their interest in their Sabbath school and their teacher that one of these lads had come on foot two miles, and another three miles.

The next day this class were in the sanctuary and the Sabbath school, giving the most careful and interested attention to all that was said and done.

TEACHERS' MEETINGS.

Teachers' meetings, for prayer and mutual study of the lesson, were established quite early in the history of Sabbath schools.

The managers of the Maine Sabbath School Union, in their first annual Report, in 1827, say:—

"Teachers should make special efforts to obtain a minute and extensive knowledge of their lesson, that they may impart it to their pupils. For this purpose they would do well to form themselves into a Bible class, and seek for the assistance of their minister, or, if that cannot be had, the help of their elder brethren and of pious commentators. They should thus anticipate every lesson."

In the early history of the Massachusetts Sabbath School Society, great importance was given to the teachers' meeting. It was regarded by many as a sort of thermometer of the state of a school. There was scarcely any one thing that the friends of this institution insisted on with more urgency.

In the Report of this society, in May, 1834, it was stated that returns had been received from one hundred and seventy-one schools, of which forty-nine reported teachers' meetings.

A superintendent, in his report of his school more than thirty years ago, said:—

"Here is a surprising question: 'Do you hold teachers' meetings?' How long do you think we should have a Sabbath school without a teachers' meeting for social prayer and mutual study of the lesson? Yes, sir; we have a teachers' meeting, and we should as soon think of putting to sea without a sheet-anchor as to attempt to conduct a Sabbath school without such a meeting. It must be hard work, indeed, to sustain any good degree of interest in a school, and presumptuous to expect the blessing of God, without such a meeting."

The chief object of this meeting should not be to study the lesson — to relieve the teachers from faithful antecedent efforts on their own behalf. This should be done, so far as possible, at home, before the meeting; then they should come together at this meeting as a class for mutual instruction, under the pastor or superintendent, and go over the lesson, comparing their views, freely making inquiries, solving any difficulties they may have met with, giving illustrations, and thus acquiring, by this mutual consultation, a more correct and thorough understanding of the lesson, and treasuring up all that is important for use in the instruction of their respective classes. Then, if they have any aptitude to teach, they will be able to interest and benefit their scholars. Even teachers of only moderate abilities and limited education, with this aid for every lesson, may become very useful in the work.

One of the most interesting and spirited teachers' meetings we ever attended was where the lesson had been thoroughly studied at home. There were no books present but the question book, and a few others for reference in the hands of the superintendent. Every teacher answered the questions from memory, as every scholar in the school should be required to do; and all entered enthusiastically into the work of unfolding and elucidating the meaning of every verse. Such a preparation of the lesson would, of course, be observed and felt by every scholar on the Sabbath. Even children are quick to discover any want of preparation on the part of the teacher.

One important influence of the teachers' meeting is that uniformity of instruction is secured. A boy twelve years of age once wrote an anonymous communication to be read at the Sabbath school concert, on the importance of the teachers' meeting; and he illustrated the subject by the fact that he heard three teachers, his own, and the one behind him and the one before him, give each a different answer to the same question; and he thought they ought to meet together to harmonize their views. In another school the question was as to the length of time between the selling of Joseph into Egypt and his standing before Pharaoh. Some teachers gave one answer, the superintendent at the close of the school gave a different one, and the pastor, coming in at the time, gave still another.

Without consultation on the lesson there must be much diversity of opinion, and all that diversity will go to the classes, and who can foretell the evils that may follow? If the teachers disagree, the scholars will also disagree, and be led into doubt and scepticism. But where this meeting is properly maintained, there is such a harmony in the interpretation of the doctrines and precepts of the Bible that the scholars of different classes, when they converse together on the subject, will all understand it alike, and have no ground of dispute.

Among other advantages of the teachers' meetings, they are eminently suited to unite teachers in Christian love, and to encourage and stimulate them to persevere in their labors.

IX.

RELIGIOUS INFLUENCE OF THE SABBATH SCHOOL.

Sabbath schools, almost from their establishment in our country, have been more or less directly instrumental in at least promoting the conversion of souls, especially among the young. There is scarcely any portion of the land where there are not more or less ready to rise up and call this institution "Blessed," and to acknowledge it, with heartfelt gratitude, as the instrument in promoting their salvation.

Revivals have been intimately connected with Sabbath schools; frequently they have originated in them, and sometimes they have been confined almost exclusively within their limits. This sacred inclosure, under the influence of the showers of divine grace, has often appeared verdant as the garden of God, in the midst of surrounding drought and sterility. From fifty to over one hundred members of a single school, in a single season, have been hopefully converted. A large portion of all the accessions to our churches, from year to year, have been from among those who are connected with the Sabbath school.

It has become a common thing, in the report on the state of religion, in all our conferences and associations, to hear it said, that most of the conversions have been among the young, and especially among those connected with the Sabbath school. Pastors very generally regard the members of the Sabbath school as the most hopeful part of their people, in regard to their own labors.

But it should not be supposed that all who are converted in the Sabbath school are converted through the instrumentality of this institution alone. A great variety of influences — parental, where there is right parental instruction, the preaching of the gospel, &c., — have no doubt usually been connected with the influence of this institution, in these conversions. All we need to say in relation to this subject is, that those who are engaged in the study of the Bible in the Sabbath school are much more likely to be converted, through the combined good influences that are brought to bear upon them, than any other class of persons. There is usually more truth in the minds of such, on which the Spirit of God can operate, and they seem more directly within the sphere of the Spirit's influence. This qualification we should ever be ready to make, so as not to overlook the divinely appointed institutions of the family and the ministry.

But, with the above qualification, all that is claimed for the institution of Sabbath schools in the conversion of men, and especially of the young, is no doubt true. It is filling heaven with joy and earth with rejoicing. Multitudes of youth, more or less directly through this influence, have learned their way to the New Jerusalem, and other multitudes are fast treading in their footsteps.

The whole history of the past is an encouragement to all who labor in this institution.

EARLY CONVERSIONS.

Numerous well authenticated facts have compelled many to believe that there may be such a thing as the conversion of a little child. The providence of God has, within the past half century, effected a great change on this subject. Pastors have acknowledged that, when they used to urge their teachers to labor for the speedy conversion of little children, they did not mean such little ones as have since evidently been converted in their Sabbath schools. But even now, though many Christians profess to believe that young children may be converted, still few make vigorous, consistent efforts to secure the blessing.

The conversion of a young child generally awakens in the church but little interest, compared with the same change in a man of forty. And yet the child, if destined to move in the same sphere, will probably accomplish many times more for the redemption of the world, before he arrives at the meridian of life, than the man will ever be able to effect. But when the child has numbered the years of the man, how widely will his enjoyment and influence differ from what they must have been had he lived to this period unreconciled to God, and he now been compelled to expend his best energies in eradicating the evil associations and habits he had previously cherished. Many spend the best portion of their days in nourishing those appetites and passions which are at open war with every Christian excellence!

The opinion that early conversion is impracticable is very pernicious in its influence. It pervades the minds of parents, teachers, and children. It prevents the teacher and the parents from praying and laboring as they ought for the conversion of children. It is very pernicious in its influence on the young. They look at their parents, and say, "My father and mother did not become pious while young; it is only a few years since they united with the people of God. What, then, if we do not become pious now? We undoubtedly shall when we are as old as our parents were when they turned to God." This opinion bars the hearts of the rising generation from immediate repentance, quiets their fears, and urges them on in a course of impenitence.

All well know that there is no period of our existence when we are so susceptible of religious impressions as in childhood. Tender anxieties are felt for the young, and prayer is offered which, in the case of many at least, fails not in any day of life. Moreover, the church is in constant contact with these tender and susceptible minds. She needs not to stretch her hands across an ocean or a continent to reach them. They are nigh her, in her very bosom. And all the hallowed influence she ought to have upon them can be exerted all the while. Not in the sanctuary and Sabbath school only does this contact exist, but in the nursery, in the domestic circle, in the varied forms of social intercourse. The almost infinitely varied and attractive forms in which divine truth is prepared for the youthful mind increases the facilities of their conversion; and more than all, the blessing of God, which is multiplying greatly, among children and youth, the subjects of his holy kingdom. In view of all this, is it not true that there are great encouragements to labor for the salvation of the young?

It is well known, too, that the influence of every day's continuance in sin is to remove the soul farther and farther from God and salvation. Who has not seen the inveteracy of those habits which are formed by protracted impenitence? Who does not know that sin long indulged encases the soul as with a shield of brass? Look at the man who has grown old in forgetfulness of God and the violation of all his commands; see the shafts of truth all broken at his feet! Do not the comparative prospects of success, as well as the interests of the church and the world, call upon us to devote a larger amount of labor for the conversion of the young? And then, how much easier it is for a little child to surrender himself to the Saviour, than for the man of years — of cares, and of many sins — to become "as a little child."

The interest on the subject of the conversion of children has greatly increased since the establishment of Sabbath schools.

Said a pastor in 1842, in communicating the fact that forty-six of the members of the Sabbath school had been hopefully converted within a few months, "Our deacons and church committee are much tried and perplexed to know what to do with so many young Christians."

This subject certainly requires great wisdom and good judgment. The proper course to be pursued, in reference to pious children, depends very much on their previous instruction, their maturity of character, and the various circumstances by which they are surrounded. Some children of seven, and even younger, are much older in knowledge, stability of character, and in all their intellectual, moral, and religious developments, than others of fifteen. Now it would not be judicious to pursue the same course with both these classes of children. As a general remark, however, it may be said, that in the case of all children there should be a suitable season of probation, in which they are to be carefully and faithfully instructed in the truths of the gospel, and in what is implied in making a public profession of religion. Nothing can be more unhappy and dangerous in its influence upon them than the course often pursued, of leaving them six months or a year, or several years, unguarded and uninstructed, as a trial of their religious principles. Scarcely less wise or less fatal would it be to leave a new-born infant without protection and nourishment, as a test of its constitution. No wonder that many of them, by degrees, lose their serious impressions.

As soon as a child or youth begins to exhibit seriousness on the subject of religion, he should at once — especially if not favored with pious, judicious parents — receive the particular care of the pastor and the church. Such an one requires far more care and attention than an adult. There is more danger that his seriousness may be the result of sympathy, or excitement, or a desire to be like others.

After a suitable season for instruction, and proper evidence of piety, children, of whatever age, should be admitted to the church, to enjoy all the privileges of the disciples of the Lord Jesus Christ. No child, however young, that gives evidence of repentance for sin and love to the Saviour, should be denied the privilege of obeying the command of the Saviour, "Do this in remembrance of me." Such may indeed be, as one has said, "like the early, small stars of evening, very small;" but if they have been faithfully instructed, they will also be, like them, "pure, and bright, and beautiful. And they will hold on their way gloriously."

Some pastors have classes of converts to which they admit persons of any age as soon as converted. These classes they meet, at regular periods, for instruction and prayer, and in communion seasons have them sit by themselves, near the communicants. The influence of this course is found to be, in all respects, salutary.

The late Rev. Dr. Bardwell, of Holden, in August, 1830, thus wrote: —

"Since the 1st of February, of the present year, one hundred and sixty-one persons have been admitted to this church, most of whom have generally attended my Bible class instruction for the last six years, and nearly sixty of them have been members of the Sabbath school. I have a class of twenty children, all of whom are members of the Sabbath school, who are cherishing the hope that they have passed from death unto life. These children are from eight to fourteen years of age. The object of bringing them into a class has reference to their making a profession of religion. I meet them once in two months for the purpose of making personal inquiries concerning their religious feelings, and imparting to them such instruction concerning the doctrines and duties of religion as may enable them to act understandingly in uniting with the church. Of most of these children we think there is evidence of piety. Four or five of them have already been admitted to the church; others will probably be admitted, from time to time, as may be thought expedient. Some of these children have shown a maturity of mind on religious subjects which is peculiarly pleasing, and affords great encouragement to parental and Sabbath school instruction."

In the revival with which the church in W—— was blessed, the last part of 1835 and the early part of 1836, great interest was manifested among the young. There was organized a class, called 'the class of probationers,' of thirty children under fourteen years of age, who had sought the Lord early, and who hoped they had found him, according to his gracious promise. They were enjoying the special watch and care of the pastor and the church, and were receiving instruction, preparatory to a public profession of their faith in Christ.

In a Sabbath school in Massachusetts, in 1845, it was reported that ninety-five scholars had been hopefully converted, and, in addition, that there were thirty children, between the ages of five and eleven, who had expressed some hope that they had become Christ's lambs.

In a class of twelve boys, of from eleven to fourteen, nine were hopefully converted.

In a school in which large numbers were converted, it was said that some of the children gave striking evidence of conversion, and discover much knowledge of divine things. Among the large number to be admitted to the church, were some children of twelve or fourteen.

A little girl of seven wished to unite with the church, but some thought she was too young. One day she came to her mother, the tears running down her cheeks, and said, "Mother, some one said I was too young — too little — to join the church. I didn't know it was the blood, and the flesh, and the bones that made a Christian; I thought it was the heart." With this answer, which seemed to indicate that she understood herself, she was admitted to the church.

Two years after, the pastor said that there was no member of his church who walked more correctly, or who had made more progress in the divine life, than that little girl of seven years.

A few years ago, a little girl five years of age was led to love the Saviour. She was greatly distressed to think she had lived so many years without loving him. When she was about six years old, she went to her minister, — then one of the most judicious and excellent pastors in New Hampshire, — and expressed her wish to confess Christ by uniting with the church.

The venerable man received her with great tenderness, and listened with deep interest to her request, but then kindly suggested that she was very young yet to think of uniting with the church. She at once replied that Jesus says, " Suffer the little children to come unto me, and *forbid them not.*"

The good shepherd felt the force of her reply, and immediately answered, " I have nothing more to say." And in due time this lamb of the flock was admitted to the fold. For several years she honored her profession by a lovely, Christian walk, when the Great Shepherd took her to the fold on high.

And why should not the lamb — the younger and the feebler all the more so — be in the fold? If we have the evidence of true love to God, why should the age have anything to do with the question of church-membership? Why should converted children be told that they had better wait four or five years and see if they continue to be interested? What becomes of those adults who wait four or five years after their hopeful conversion, to see if — by disobedience to the command of Christ to confess him before men, and " do this in remembrance of me,"— they can get clearer evidence that they are truly his disciples? Do they ever confess him?

A mother, in a letter to the writer, says: —

"Twenty years ago, I was at a public meeting with my little daughter, who was hoping she was a Christian, and was very anxious to unite with the church, but her extreme youth was urged as an objection. The subject of admitting young children to the church was the topic of discussion at this meeting. You advocated their admission where there was decided evidence of piety, and after suitable instruction. On our return, my little girl said to me, with a glowing countenance, and an earnest tone of voice, 'Now, mother, may I not unite with the church?' I answered that we would see what our minister said about it. On presenting the subject to him, he at once decided that she was too young for such an important step, and that she must wait some years, and see if her interest in the subject of religion continued.

"She was greatly disappointed and grieved at this decision. Ever since — now twenty years — she has cherished a hope that she is a Christian, but she has never so far recovered from the shock of that early disappointment as to feel that she could make a public profession of her faith, and she probably never will. All these early aspirations to be united with the people of God seem to have been crushed, and she became discouraged, and lost her confidence that she was worthy to be a member of the church of Christ."

How sad is this history! And it is only a specimen of many, many similar cases.

After a most careful observation and extensive inquiry, for the forty-five years of our public Sabbath school labors, we hesitate not to affirm that a much smaller proportion of children who unite with the church dishonor their profession than of adults.

Rev. Mr. Spurgeon gives a most remarkable testimony in regard to this subject, and confirmatory of the above statement. He says that out of more than two thousand children that he had admitted to his church, he had not been obliged to exclude a single one! Would not the Saviour say, in regard to the admission of the smallest children in whom there is evidence of real love to him, to his church, "Suffer *little* children, and forbid them not to come unto me"? And will he not be much displeased when his ministers and churches forbid them thus to come? How solemn his words to those who should offend one of these little ones that believe in him!

X.

THE LIBRARY.

VERY early in the history of Sabbath schools, when there were comparatively few books published for the young, a library was regarded as almost indispensable to the existence of a school. And even now, when Sabbath school and tract societies, and many private publishing houses, have flooded the country with juvenile literature, a library is generally regarded as essential to a prosperous school.

In 1827, the annual Report of the Maine Sabbath School Union speaks of it as a subject of congratulation that Sabbath school libraries were becoming so generally popular. "We consider them," says this Report, "among the most interesting and useful means of religious instruction now employed; and probably, as a stimulus to induce the poor classes of children to come to the schools and to continue in them, they will be more powerful than anything else.

"And, further, as the children become interested in this kind of reading, it will, in many instances, extend its happy influence to the parents. Parents not given to religious reading are not unfrequently induced to read the books which the children carry home.

"Special care should be taken that no books professing to be religious should have a place in a library for children which contain any sentiments adverse to pure Christianity."

A superintendent, more than thirty years ago, wrote : —

"We have a well-selected library of eleven hundred volumes; and we consider a good library as essential, under God, to the prosperity of the Sabbath school as any other means which can be employed. Our scholars are great readers; and, by having books of the best kind to read during the week, their minds are imbued with the sublime truths of the Bible, their understandings are enlightened, their reasoning powers are invigorated, their perceptibilities are quickened, and their hearts become susceptible. Nor is this all; the parents of the scholars, many of whom are not pious, read the books their children bring home, and are thereby brought under the influence of truth, and are often led to serious reflection in reference to death, judgment, and eternity. Very much might be said respecting the advantages of a well-selected library in a Sabbath school. It would be very difficult to estimate the amount of good, real and prospective, which we owe, under God, to the library connected with our Sabbath school. A Sabbath school without a library must present a very dreary aspect."

Another superintendent says : —

"We have found our library, which contains about one hundred and eighty volumes, a main-spring in our school. While it stimulated to exertion, it became a teacher of religion by examples. Next to the Sabbath school institution as a blessing to our land, a library is the happiest thought. This noiseless teacher among us has found its way to many abodes of the honest yet uninformed, and has been efficacious in dispelling a cloud of errors and prejudices that has been collecting for years. It has taught, in some degree, that ignorance is not a necessary concomitant of religion."

Says another superintendent: —

"We have a library of six hundred volumes. The books are well selected, and contain much information and instruction on all matters of religious interest. We cannot help comparing the condition of members of Sabbath schools now, with the Christians and young people of former days, in the matter of information. Some, now in our Sabbath schools, can remember the time when there were no books of religious instruction fitted for the youthful mind. The only reading for children was fairy tales. And even older Christians had but few of those written helps which at the present time are so abundant. Children's books, making plain the doctrines of the gospel and clear and practical the duties of life, memoirs of pious men, histories of missions, &c., are, or may be, in every house. If knowledge is power, then we see an engine of great power in the Sabbath school library. We feel confident that it has already been of incalculable advantage, both to the teachers and scholars, and I may also add, with emphasis, in many cases to parents. The books from our library are sent out weekly to the number of more than two hundred to preach the gospel in many places where it would be difficult for the minister or lay Christian to find access. We would not silence the tongue of one of these little, yet eloquent, pleaders for 'whatsoever things are true, whatsoever things are honest, whatsoever things are just, whatsoever things are pure, whatsoever things are lovely, whatsoever things are of good report,' and for all that is virtuous and praiseworthy. No; we would rather increase their number yearly an hundred-fold. We would thus unloose and put in requisition, weekly, one or more of these unpretending yet powerful helpers in the formation of the character of the young; yea, these messengers of God, that have already been a blessing to many an impenitent parent's conscience and heart."

Says another superintendent: —

"We have experienced signal advantages from our Sabbath school library. It has furnished a powerful inducement to faithful attendance on the school. And, what we esteem of special importance, it has excited among the youth generally a taste for reading, especially of religious books. More books of this class are now read among them than of any other."

The first library of the Sabbath school in Framingham, which was established in 1816, was bought in 1821. A small sum of money was raised by personal solicitation from the leading church-members and others, and a selection made from the comparatively limited number of children's books then published. The library was composed of small books, mostly in paper covers, some of which might properly be called tracts. The following list is a sample: "Shepherd of Salisbury Plain;" "Gooseberry Bush;" "Worlds Displayed;" "Pleasures of Piety in Youth;" "Little Henry and his Bearer;" "New Testament Stories;" "The Robber's Daughter;" "The Two Lambs;" "Alfred and Galba;" "Hymns for Infant Minds."

This small library of small books was yet a matter of great consequence to the school. It was a good collection for those days. The books were mostly new to children, and they were of an interesting character.

In 1819, the pastor of the First Church in Cambridge, stated the object of the Sabbath school, which was organized four years before, to the congregation, and a collection was afterwards taken to purchase small books to be distributed among the children, as an encouragement for punctual attendance, correct lessons, and good behavior. In 1827, books and tracts were collected by subscription for a juvenile library. A board of trustees was chosen, with the pastor at the head. He was also chosen librarian. In July, 1831, the trustees were authorized to make selections from the library to form a Sabbath school library for the Shepard Congregational Society; and in 1835 both of the libraries were brought together under the name of "Juvenile and Shepard Sabbath School Library." *

After the reorganization of the school in 1831, the library comprised two hundred and five volumes, and it became an important means of keeping up an interest in the school, and drawing in pupils.†

The library of the First Parish Sabbath school, in Charlestown, which was organized in 1816, was established in 1826, and comprised three hundred and thirty volumes, and was increased the next year to five hundred and fifty.‡

A writer in the "Sabbath School Visitant," in 1829, said:—

"I began to make some calculations about the amount of reading which is produced in our country by means of Sabbath school libraries. I thought probably there were three thousand copies of each library book in circulation; each copy is read annually by two hundred persons. Then

---

* History of the First Church in Cambridge, pp. 180, 181.

† History of First Sabbath School in Framingham, pp. 35, 69.

‡ Semi-centennial Celebration of the First Parish Sabbath School, Charlestown, p. 62.

multiply three thousand by two hundred, gives, in America, six hundred thousand persons who read a book annually. These six hundred thousand persons read not only one book, but probably fifty-two each, and some more. What a channel is this, thought I, for the dissemination of useful knowledge. O, who would be such a monster as to oppose an institution that promises such benefits to our country!

"While these thoughts were passing, I fell asleep, and dreamed that there was a Sabbath school union in every state and in every county of our country, and an association in every township; and that every township had a Sabbath school in every religious society; and that every school had a library of useful books; that instead of three thousand there were twenty thousand libraries, and each book read by four hundred individuals, which would make each kind read by eight millions annually. When I thought of this, my country seemed to rise in peace, waving in perennial greenness, and presenting to the world a scene of prophetic millennial glory."

Although it has, for half a century, been almost universally considered indispensable, in a well organized Sabbath school, to have a library of carefully selected books, yet there has been no department of this institution where there has been so much difficulty in finding out the best way of managing it.

The great desideratum has been, how to distribute the books with the least interference with the exercises of the classes. The plans adopted have been very numerous. In some cases the scholars have all gone to the library before the school is opened, or at the close, each to exchange his book; in others, different classes, one or more at a time, through the whole session of the school, have gone up for this purpose; in others, the librarians have gone round, with armfuls of books, to the classes, interrupting the recitations of each class, while the scholars selected their books; in some cases the library books have been exchanged on a week-day, but this has been inconvenient to those who live at a distance. Many inconveniences have been found in connection with all these and many other plans that have been adopted.

The Sabbath School and Bible Class Association in the Theological Seminary at Andover, in 1830, took up this subject of the management of the library, with much earnestness. The students generally were requested, during their vacation, to visit all the Sabbath schools they could, and ascertain the manner in which the libraries were conducted, and be prepared, on their return, to give a careful report.

The next term, the association appointed a committee to examine these reports and make out from them what they might consider the best mode of conducting a Sabbath school library. At another meeting of the association the committee reported, in substance, the following plan: —

All the classes in a given school must have the same number of scholars, say six, and be arranged according to their numbers, one, two, three, &c.

Each class was to be supplied with its six books, which they were to exchange among themselves for six weeks. At the end of six weeks each class was to pass its six books to the next class; that is, number one was to pass its books to number two, number two to number three, and so on through the school.

This was reported by the committee as being the nearest perfect of any plan they could contrive. In this plan there would be very little for the librarian to do. There would be no change of books except in the different classes, and that only once in six weeks; and then it would take but a minute or two, at the opening or at the close of the school, for the classes to pass on their books. This would avoid all noise and all interference with the recitations of the various classes.

The committee also suggested that it might be well for the library to contain six copies of each book, so that all the members of a given class would read the same book the same week, and then change them every Sabbath.

In the discussion that took place in considering this report, it was interesting to see how soon this perfect plan of the committee went to pieces. To begin with, all the members of some of the classes might not be present on the Sabbath this plan was adopted, so that some classes might not have more than three or four books to pass to the next class; or such a thing might happen that some members of some of the classes might, now and then, be absent, or might forget to bring their books, and then the same difficulty would arise.

To this it was replied that the librarian must be prepared to meet this difficulty by having a certain number of extra books to take the place of those that were absent.

But it was concluded that it would not be long before, by the absence of scholars or of their books, the whole beautiful plan would be broken up.

Then, again, it was suggested that, by this plan, the larger and the smaller scholars would have the same class of books, without regard to which ones would be appropriate to their age and capacity. And so the plan reported by the committee was not recommended to the schools.

For many years past, most of our schools have adopted the plan, as, on the whole, the best that has yet been devised, of "library cards and numbers." Catalogues are furnished to all the families in which there are scholars in the school; each scholar has a card on which he writes the titles of several books, either of which is desired. These cards, with the names of the scholars, are placed in the books of a given class, and all returned to the librarian, who replaces these books with those desired, and leaves them with the teacher of that class, to distribute at the close of the school. The books and the scholars are all numbered; and the librarian keeps his record of the books by means of numbers corresponding to the numbers of the scholars, on small tin or pasteboard labels, which are placed on hooks by the numbers corresponding with the numbers or names of the scholars. When a book is taken out, the number of the scholar is placed over the number of the book. That is the charge of the book to that scholar; and he cannot have another book till his number is restored to the number of his name, or placed over the number of another book. In this way, there is no conversation between scholars and librarian. All the exchanges are made in silence.

This plan seems to obviate most or all of the objections that have been felt in regard to all former plans.

A printed label, like that on the next page, is pasted inside of each book.

A subject of much complaint, in connection with the library, has always been the great loss of books.

In 1844, we learned the following fact, which is a striking illustration of the evil here complained of.

A library, four years before, contained four hundred and fifty-four volumes. At the end of that time it contained only two hundred and three volumes! Showing that two hundred and fifty-one books had been lost or not returned, in four years! It is to be feared that the

LIBRARY

OF THE

SABBATH SCHOOL,

No member of the School is to be allowed to have out more than one Book at once, nor to retain any Book more than two weeks in succession.

Readers are requested to be careful in using this Book, and punctual in returning it. To injure a Library Book, or to retain it longer than is right, is to do an injury to others which cannot be easily repaired.

history of many of our libraries would reveal a fa. nearly if not quite as melancholy. While thousands of children and youths, in our land, are destitute of Sabbath school books, it is surely wrong — it is sinful, that so many of these volumes are lost or thrown aside to gather dust upon the shelves. Christ's lesson to his disciples should be studied by the members of our Sabbath schools: "Gather up the fragments, . . . that nothing be lost."

The following facts, in regard to several libraries in Massachusetts, show that much depends upon the management of the librarian. Says a superintendent:—

"Our library is exerting a most happy influence. Since our present librarian has had charge of it, — nearly five years, — not a single book has been lost. Under its present excellent regulations, it has increased from two hundred and ten to four hundred and fifty-two volumes, many of which are valuable books calculated for the adult portion of the school. Although the strictness of the present librarian at first caused some to be offended, who had taken out books under previous librarians, yet to that strictness is to be attributed the present prosperity of the library. There is double the amount of reading from it that there was formerly, one hundred and fifty volumes being frequently out at a time, scattered through every part of the town. In going through our manufacturing establishments, the books of the library are scattered among the operatives, exerting, as it is believed, a most happy effect. Although its privileges are extended to all the members of the congregation, yet many, it is believed, join the school in order to get a more ready access to the library. A lad ten or twelve years of age, formerly connected with our school, told me, a few days since, that he did not like the school he was connected with, and wished to come back to ours; and gave as a reason, our having such a good library. We consider our library an indispensable auxiliary to the school, while the school retains the same relation to the more public ministrations of the word."

The library of the Sabbath school in East Medway,

in 1844, embraced about eight hundred volumes. It is adapted to persons of every age and capacity, and is open to the whole congregation. It is a *society*, as well as Sabbath school, library. There is one fact in relation to it, worthy the special attention of all the members of our Sabbath schools, viz.: although the library is so large, and is accessible to the whole congregation, young and old, yet not one book, at the time the last examination was made, in 1844, had been lost for three years! Mr. D. Walker, who generously gave one hundred dollars towards its establishment, on condition that the society would give as much more, was the librarian; and it was owing very much to his care and skill in its management, that it had been so well preserved. He kept an accurate record of every book that was taken or returned, and seemed to have led all to form the habit of using their books with care and returning them with punctuality. He thought it was better for his own family, than it would have been had he given his donation of books directly to them; inasmuch as they had access to a larger number of volumes, and had also been led to make greater exertions to form this important habit of care and attention in the use of books.

In 1844, the following fact was communicated: —

"The library connected with the First Congregational Sabbath school in Methuen, was reorganized in June, 1836, and then contained about three hundred volumes. Additions have since been made to it from time to time, so that it now numbers six hundred and seventy-seven volumes. Since its reorganization — a period of more than seven years and a half — not a single volume has been lost! During the year ending the 1st of last July, 1843, two thousand seven hundred and fifty-five volumes were delivered from the library, and this is supposed to have been about an average delivery for the last five or six years. Aside from our pastor, no one thing has exerted a more healthy influence amongst our people, than the library. As it is open to the whole congregation, a good portion of the books have been selected to meet the wants of adults. At the time of its reorganization, nearly a hundred volumes on the catalogue were not to be found; and when the attempt was first made to enforce the rules of the library, some thought the librarian too particular; but all are now satisfied that its present prosperity is owing to the rigid observance of those rules. Since the reorganization of the library, the amount of reading from it has nearly doubled. During the time referred to, three different individuals have had charge of the library, which goes to prove that there need be no difficulty in selecting a librarian in any of our religious societies, who can keep a library together if he tries."

SELECTING BOOKS.

Much care should be taken in selecting books for the library. Those published by Sabbath school societies — as they profess to be issued under the careful examination and supervision of committees appointed for the purpose — are supposed to be, and ought to be, safe without further examination. But the miscellaneous works, by private publishing houses, it may be the wisest course to examine before they are placed in the library.

The Unitarian Sabbath School Society of Boston has a committee to examine all books published for the young, and only those approved by this committee are admitted into any of their Sabbath school libraries.

Some of our churches have such a committee, and no books, by whomsoever published, excepting those recommended by that committee, can find a place in the Sabbath school library. This caution, though requiring much time and labor, is certainly a safe one. And no Sabbath school society even has any just grounds for complaint of such an inspection of its issues.

No book should have a place in the Sabbath school library, however excellent for week-day reading, that is not suitable to be read on the Sabbath.

Some schools have a secular department of books in their libraries, intended especially for week-day reading. But such a department should be entirely distinct from the other, and the books should be given out on a week-day. Any book from either department, taken from a Sabbath school library, will be likely to be read on the Sabbath day.

An excellent system of replenishing the library, adopted by some schools, is to have a committee examine all books for the young as soon as they are published, and those approved are at once added to the library. This secures fresh additions continually, thus keeping up an interest all the while. Where additions are made only once a year, the new books soon become old, and in a measure lose their freshness and interest.

HOW TO MAKE OLD LIBRARIES AS GOOD AS NEW.

Many children, it is feared, have formed the habit of reading very hastily. Some do but little more than get a general run of the story, and then hasten to exchange it for another, to be treated in the same way. And some only look over their books, examine the illustrations, &c., and learn but little else about their contents. In a short time they will take up a book and just look at it and say, "I've had this;" and very soon, in this way, they have had all the books of the library, and have also lost all their interest in them, though they cannot tell a word about what any volume contains. Whereas, if they could be made acquainted with a single incident in any one of them, by the librarian or a teacher, they would eagerly devour its contents.

To remedy this evil, in some schools, every book has been called in, and, perhaps, covered anew, and then the teachers are requested to spend a few moments in asking each scholar to give a little account of the book he has had the previous week. In some cases the whole class is supplied with a copy of the same book, and it is divided into three or four parts, one part for a week, and the whole class examined on that part. Where this plan has been adopted, the books are read with all the interest of new ones, and read, too, with great profit. A good book needs to be read more than once. One teacher says his little girl, not four years old, will read a book over and over till she has it all by heart.

This plan of requiring the children to give an account of what they have read, will soon compel them to read with care. This will greatly assist them in remembering what they have read, and aid them in acquiring the habit of communicating their ideas, in familiar conversations and extempore speaking, with fluency and ease.

A teacher in 1830 says: —

"I required every scholar to take home his book, and told them I expected to hear a particular account of the contents from each one, the next Sabbath. The next Sabbath, the account they gave was very loose and disjointed, but as all except one gave evidence of having tried to remember what they had read, and to relate it in the best manner they were able, I allowed them to take out new books. I found every week that there were decided marks of improvement; and after continuing this course a few weeks, it was quite animating to see them enter the class with bright, smiling faces, beaming with intelligence, each anxious to relate the contents of her book. After a few weekly efforts, one little girl, under nine years old, gave me a correct account of fourteen different characters introduced into her book, after only one week's reading! And one week ago, a number of the class gave a handsome relation of a story consisting of a variety of characters, and containing over a hundred pages. The advantages of this method I have found to exceed every other I have ever tried, to rouse the intellectual and, I think I may with truth add, the moral energies of my class; for never have I found such easy and natural openings for pressing home upon the heart and conscience the momentous truths of the gospel, as since I adopted this plan. I am surprised at the improvement already made in a ready utterance. They catch not only the thoughts of the writer, but his very expressions; and the remarks of these children, and their turn for conversation, have recently been noticed with surprise and pleasure by many persons besides their fondly attached teacher." *

"I MUST TAKE THAT OR NONE."

A librarian, in giving out books, found great difficulty in satisfying the wishes of the scholars. One took a book, opened it, turned over a leaf or two, and returned it, saying, with a sour look and dissatisfied tone, "I don't want this book; it isn't a pretty one."

* Sabbath School Treasury, p. 221.

Another took the book that was handed to him, and cast his eyes over the pictures a moment, and said, "I've had this." A second book was given him, and he did the same. Another scholar just looked at a volume which the librarian held out for him, and as the appearance of the cover did not quite suit his taste, turned away his head, saying, "I don't want that book; I've had it before."

What could the poor librarian do? Some objection seemed to be made against receiving almost every book he presented. He was quite discouraged, and was on the point of giving up all attempts to please such difficult, unreasonable, and complaining children. But just then he was cheered by the appearance of a modest, smiling little girl, who, seeing the perplexity and trouble he was in, stepped up close to him, and said, —

"My mother says, when the librarian gives me a book, I must take that or none; and I have got a beautiful book;" holding up the little volume she had taken without a word of complaint. It was a real comfort to the poor man, in his perplexity, to find one child that could be suited.

WRONG THINGS TO BE CORRECTED.

There are several things connected with the use of the library in many schools, that are wrong, and ought to be corrected.

One is the practice of carrying the books into the house of God, to be read and looked at in time of worship. This is wrong and sinful. Such conduct is enough to make all the instructions of the Sabbath school and of the sanctuary a "savor of death unto death" to those who are guilty of it.

Another thing that is wrong, is the careless manner of treating the books at home. How many of the beautiful volumes of the library are brought back — if, indeed, they are returned at all — with soiled, rumpled, and torn leaves, and broken covers! Some complain that books are so poorly bound, they soon come to pieces. But were they iron-bound, they would scarcely stand such usage as too many of them receive.

And then the careless, hasty manner in which many read their books, is another thing that is wrong. No book ought to be returned to the library till it has been so thoroughly read that a full account can be given of what it contains. And such an account ought to be given to the parents or teachers.

The young are in great danger, now that there are so many juvenile books, of forming the habit of reading without reflection — reading merely to get the story. These are the scholars most difficult to please when taking books. Half an hour is sufficient time for them to dispatch any book; and by looking over their own in this way, and those taken by their brothers, sisters, and associates, they will be able, in a few months, to say of every book in the library, they have had it, or seen it before.

Let every scholar begin to read the library anew. Take the first book that is given. No matter if it has been seen, and even read before; whether there be few or many pictures in it; whether the cover be handsome or otherwise, — let it be taken. Now let it be read so slowly and carefully that an account of it can be given, and the scholar will feel a new interest in the library, and will derive a benefit from it such as he has never before. If all will adopt this course, the librarian's troubles will soon have an end. If a scholar says he has had that book before, the librarian will know that it has been read, as well as looked at, and that the wish for another is reasonable, and he will cheerfully exchange it for a new one.

METHODS OF REPLENISHING THE LIBRARY.

The Sabbath School and Bible Class Association of the Theological Seminary at Andover published the following method in the "Sabbath School Treasury" for August, 1830: —

"When a Sabbath school book enters a family, it seldom comes out again without having passed through the hands of every individual in the family. They are consequently soon worn out, and the libraries need to be frequently replenished. Money should be raised for this purpose as often as once or twice a year; for small additions, frequently made, are found to be more advantageous than larger additions less frequently. The fact that there are new books in the library awakens fresh interest among the scholars.

"Various expedients have been resorted to in order to keep the library in repair. Sometimes the parents, and sometimes the children have been solicited to give. At one time, money has been raised by subscription; at another, by contribution; and it not unfrequently happens that a very scanty collection is the result of any one or all of these expedients together. Now it seems desirable to adopt some systematic arrangement, if possible, by which this object shall be permanently secured. The following plan has been adopted in several places with unexpected success.

"A catalogue was prepared, by the author of the plan, containing the names of all the persons in the parish whom he thought suitable to call upon for money. He then handed twelve or fifteen of these names on paper to a couple of little girls, and said to them, 'Do you go and call on the persons whose names are on this paper, and ask them each to give you twelve and a half cents for the Sabbath school library.' He put another slip of paper, with other names, into the hands of two other little girls, and bade them do the same. Thus he divided the business among a suitable number, who undertook it with much pleasure. They were strictly charged to ask for no more than twelve and a half cents of any individual. It was not long before the little beggars returned with countenances of delight, which indicated their success before they had time to relate it. The result was, a collection of about as many ninepences as there were names on the papers. No one could find it in his heart to turn away a little smiling girl, who solicited only twelve and a half cents, and that, too, for the Sabbath school library. This has been repeated twice a year in that parish, and the avails of such a collection are sufficient to keep the library in good repair."

A pastor, in 1853, said, "We want fifty dollars for our library, and I do not know how to raise it." We suggested a plan, which, on the Sabbath, he proposed to the school. He told all the scholars that he wanted them to see how much money they could raise for the library during the week. As many of them as chose could engage in the work, and they might go to anybody they pleased, and just as many as pleased might go to the same persons, and see how much money they could collect. Early Monday morning, the village was all astir with these young collectors. Some of them were at the minister's house before he was up, and before ten o'clock, fourteen of them had called on the pastor for contributions. One boy went to the richest man in the parish, and he gave him only one cent. The little fellow, as he went away, said to himself, "That isn't fair." Then he went to as many of the scholars as he could find, and sent all of them to the rich man, and, among them all, they drained him pretty thoroughly of his change. The result of this effort of the children, in which the whole people seemed not less interested than the young collectors themselves, was over sixty dollars, to enlarge their library.

This plan has been adopted in many places, with about the same results.

The members of one class in a Sabbath school presented a request to their teacher for some new books; they said they found it difficult to obtain any from the library which they had not read.

The teacher told them they must contribute for the object, and she would see that some new books were procured. They all readily contributed twenty-five or thirty cents each. The teacher took the money and gave it to the superintendent, with an account of the manner in which it was procured, and of the wishes of her scholars. The superintendent immediately appropriated the money, and procured as many new books as there were scholars in that class.

These books, after he had numbered them, he gave to the teacher, with the request that she would retain them in her class, exchanging them once in two weeks, according to the practice of the school, till each scholar had read them all, and then return them to the library.

This plan excited so much interest in that class, that the superintendent mentioned it to the school, and invited other classes to try the same experiment. The result was, so many of the classes contributed, that the superintendent found no small difficulty in procuring new books enough to meet the demand. The library soon comprised a very full assortment of books; and these books were much more highly prized by the members of the school from the fact that they had aided in their purchase.

XI.

ADULT CLASSES IN THE SABBATH SCHOOL.

ALTHOUGH the institution of Sabbath schools was originally intended merely for children, and particularly the children of poverty and neglect, yet quite early in its history in New England, persons of all ages began to connect themselves with it as pupils. Bible classes, or, as they were then called, "adult" classes, were formed for the mutual study of the Scriptures.

In 1828, an aged man, connected with the South Congregational Church, Andover, used to remain at the session of the school, Sabbath noon, and always manifested much interest in watching the school. The superintendent asked him, one day, if he could hear the children recite. "No," said he; "but I love to see them; and then I can hear you, when you make remarks at the close."

"Well," said the superintendent, "should you not like, while waiting, to have a teacher come and sit down with you and talk about the Bible?"

"Yes," he replied, earnestly; "and I guess I can get some others to join with me."

This soon grew into a class of elderly men, numbering over thirty. There was also formed a class of about the same number of aged women, while most of the young people of both sexes were in the school; and no one ever intimated that he was either too old or too wise to be in the Sabbath school studying the Bible.

From this time the attendance of older persons increased very rapidly all through New England. For many years the schools generally embraced a larger portion of the congregations than most of them do at the present day. An imaginary visit to a few of the schools at that early period will be interesting and instructive.

Here, in a school in Maine, in 1832, we see parents and children — the child of four years with the hoary head of fourscore — attending to the same lesson from the Bible. In another school, in the same state and year, we find an adult class composed of persons past middle age, and who have as little need of Sabbath school instruction as any in the parish; and yet they regard it as a boon and a privilege which they would not willingly relinquish. In it they find both profit and enjoyment. In another school, in 1833, we have the grateful sight of four generations engaged in the social study of the sacred Scriptures, and of which the superintendent says: "If holy angels and the spirits of the just made perfect look down with satisfaction upon earthly scenes, is it not upon a scene like this?"

An old gentleman of eighty years, says, "Well, I'm in the Sabbath school yet." "You have been studying the Bible now so long, don't you find it becomes rather dry?" "No, no," says the aged disciple; "the older I grow, the newer and better it seems."

A few years later, let us enter a school in Franklin County, Mass. It belongs to the parish where the president of one of our colleges then ministered. He informs us that the Sabbath before he counted only eleven of all his congregation who, at the close of the morning service, turned away from the Sabbath school. In another school, in the same county, we find enrolled as members five hundred and twelve, when the entire membership of the parish is only five hundred and thirty-six. How beautiful the scene, — nineteen twentieths of all the people, embracing all ages from three to eighty-two, feeding upon the bread of life!

A superintendent, as we enter his school, informs us that all the members of the church who can conveniently attend are in the school. Another, that there are only three members of the church out of the school without a reason.

Thus we might go from school to school by the scores, if not the hundreds, and hear the statements: "Our school includes most of the society, old and young." "All the resident members of the church but six or eight, who are prevented by sickness or the care of families, are members of our school." "Our school consists of almost all the stated members of the congregation." "In our school are mingled together those who are tottering on the brink of the grave and those who can but imperfectly lisp the commandments of God." "Nearly all the stated congregation are connected with our school; and if there is any portion of the school that prizes more highly than another its advantages, it is the adults." "About two hundred adults have associated themselves for mutual instruction in connection with the school. They seem to take as much pleasure in the exercises as any of the children; and their example has had a happy influence upon the school." "Almost every one in the society, from four years old to eighty, are engaged in our school, either as teachers or scholars. It is accounted almost a disgrace for any one not to attend; and but very few of those who would attend to any good thing, fail in attending the Sabbath school. One mind seems to influence all, old and young. And all are making good progress in the knowledge of the word of God."

In many schools these classes of adults were called "classes for mutual instruction."

These classes, every Sabbath, choose one of their number to act as teacher, or "monitor," as they were sometimes called, for the next Sabbath. All were to study the lesson assigned for that Sabbath, and be prepared to answer or ask questions. While one was to act as leader, all were to feel an individual responsibility to help make the exercise interesting and profitable.

One mode of conducting such a class is given as follows: —

"On the Sabbath, the teacher introduced the lesson to the class by proposing questions, when they immediately enter upon a free discussion, and interchange of views and opinions relative to the various parts of the passage before them; and each member communicates any explanatory remarks with which he may have met, or which his own mind may have suggested. The teacher also brings forward whatever illustrations his more careful investigation of the subject has furnished him; and, so far as he is able, solves the difficulties, and answers the questions which the class may propound.

"The following method is more generally adopted where such classes exist. It differs from the one just described only in this respect. Instead of having one permanent teacher, the members of the class officiate in rotation; each for a Sabbath or a particular number of Sabbaths.

"Another method is like the other two, except that it recognizes no one as a teacher. All feel themselves under equal obligation to examine the lesson and contribute to the interest of the exercise.

"A number of ladies, from forty to seventy years of age, joined the Sabbath school, and associated themselves together for mutual assistance in the study of the Bible. The interest created in this class was very great. Rarely is there seen more interest manifested in a class of girls than was exhibited by these mothers. One member of the class, about fourscore, whose memory had been considerably impaired by age, said, 'I have never seen the time, for a great many years, that I could wish to be young again, till since I commenced going to the Sabbath school, but I now feel the great need of the memory of my youth.'

"In a Sabbath school consisting of four hundred scholars, two hundred were adults, some of whom were over sixty. These two hundred adults were associated together in studying the Bible on this plan of mutual conference and instruction.

"All who reflect upon the plan here suggested, in connection with the examples given, must feel that no insurmountable obstacle lies against the general adoption of the system of mutual instruction."

The late Rev. Dr. Bardwell, when settled in Holden, said, in January, 1830, when his people were favored with an extensive revival: —

"Within the past two months our Sabbath school has increased from two to nearly four hundred, about one half of whom are adults up to sixty years of age. The adults have the same lesson with the rest of the school. They appoint their own teachers; indeed, their plan is that of mutual conference and instruction. In our Bible class, consisting of young persons from fourteen to thirty years of age, the course of instruction is intentionally varied from time to time. Sometimes questions are proposed by the teacher and sometimes by the scholars; and sometimes topics are given out to be written upon. Nearly all of the members of this class have been brought into the kingdom."

What sight can be more interesting than that of a Sabbath school thus engaged? What can be better adapted to increase the interest of the children in the school and in the study of the Bible, than to see parents and grand-parents, and the people generally, uniting with them in this delightful work. Then the influence of these adult classes that come into school, helps to revive the school and give it new life.

A school in 1836 had become very languishing. It was suspended during the winter. At the end of three years, during which time it had continued to decline more and more, the question was asked, —

" What can be done to save the school from extinction and make it efficient?"

In answer to this question, one man said, "I will go in, become a member of the school as a scholar, unless I am needed as a teacher, if the church, as a body, will do the same."

The church immediately acceded to the proposal, and united with the school. The school was at once revived, and went on prosperously.

There is scarcely anything, save the visitations of the Holy Spirit, that will exert such a reviving, encouraging influence on a school, as a large accession of classes.

It will almost reinfuse vitality where the spark of life has expired; and it always imparts new animation and encouragement to a school, however flourishing it may have been before.

This subject was urged in an address to a congregation in the neighborhood of a city. At the close of the address, the pastor invited all the members of the congregation who were willing to unite with the school, to meet with it the next Sabbath. And the next Sabbath that school of three hundred members received an accession of about forty. Every one can see that such an accession, even to a comparatively large school, must have been most inspiring. Every teacher and pupil felt animated and encouraged.

The presence of the older people in the Sabbath school magnifies and gives character to the institution. It takes away the excuse from any among the children and the young people, "that they are getting too old to belong to the Sabbath school." And where this excuse is offered, and the young people leave the Sabbath school, the cause may usually be found in the fact that adults are not connected with it.

There is no way in which the church can more strongly commend the Sabbath school to the young than by their personal attendance as learners.

This social study of the Scriptures by the older members of the church is one of the best ways to cultivate their own Christian graces. The familiar and social study of those pure and sublime thoughts of God, and the free interchange of thought and feeling in regard to them, will ennoble, and elevate, and purify the whole inner man. Under the combined research of a whole circle of Christians, longing, and laboring too, for new and clearer views of truth, the Scriptures will be opened; gems of unsurpassed beauty and richness will be discovered; yea, it will be seen that, —

> "A glory gilds the sacred page,
> Majestic, like the sun."

Mutual sympathy and interest will be excited. All that cold and cruel distance too often existing among the members of Christ's own family will be annihilated. Heart will warm heart, till, by their mutual warmth, they melt, and flow out, and mingle into one. What does the church need so much as this familiar intercourse, this mutual bond of sympathy and love, this mingling of heart with heart? What a moral power over others this state of things would give the church. How would such a united, sympathizing brotherhood of Christians, all actively engaged in searching the Scriptures, silence the gainsayer, and bring all to "gaze and admire," though they might "hate the change."

Then the adults, as well as those in early life, find the study of the Scriptures a source of mental improvement. The memory, the judgment, the taste, and all the intellectual faculties, are cultivated and strengthened. It prevents that entire neglect of the mind which the cares and business of the world too often produce. The exercises of the Sabbath school, if engaged in with zeal, will prove a better discipline to the mind than the exercises of the best conducted lyceum. This advantage alone, were there no higher, should induce all, young men and maidens, old men and children, to engage in this work.

While the adult members of the church and congregation are largely represented in many of our Sabbath schools at the present day, this is by no means so general as in these former times. And in this respect, as well as in many others,—notwithstanding all our improvements in the conduct of this institution,—we can learn wisdom from the past.

Several years ago there was a large and flourishing Sabbath school in the town of N——. This institution had taken a deep hold on the affections of the church, most of whose members manifested their interest in it in the best possible manner, viz., by their personal attendance. The school was often a scene of much religious awakening, when one and another, of different ages, were converted.

Mr. A——, a member of the church, was a conscientious Christian. His advantages for intellectual improvement had been quite limited, and, what is not the case with every one in similar circumstances, he was sensible of his deficiency in this respect, and consequently was very diffident. For a long time he was unable so to overcome this diffidence as to connect himself with a class in the Sabbath school. He longed to be united with his brethren in the study of the Scriptures; he felt that it was the very thing for him; he needed just such assistance in understanding the Bible as he should there be likely to obtain. But he could not overcome his timidity; it was too great a trial to think of exposing his ignorance. Perhaps he had never heard of the adage, " Not to know is bad; not to ask is worse."

But Mr. A—— had also another trial; he knew that he was not only depriving himself of a rich privilege by standing aloof from the Sabbath school, but he was also exerting a bad influence by his example on his unconverted neighbors. He was a professing Christian, and if he neglected the Sabbath school, many others might be encouraged to do the same. The thought of this was a severe trial to his feelings; and, after much study on the subject, he finally fixed on a plan by which he hoped to avoid exerting any unfavorable influence on others, however much he might suffer himself by yielding to his diffidence. The plan was this: every Sabbath, as soon as the morning services were closed, and the Sabbath school began to assemble, he betook himself to the neighboring woods, and there, alone, passed his intermission. He hoped in this manner at least to prevent the injurious influence which his example would be likely to have on others, were he seen passing the Sabbath school hours around the house of God.

This plan certainly deserves the attention of those professors of religion — if there be such — who are accustomed to spend their intermissions in groups around the sanctuary, under the horse-sheds, or, still worse, in the bar-room of the tavern, in company with their impenitent neighbors, conversing about their farms and stock, "the times," the weather, &c.

Mr. A—— was at length enabled, after many struggles and prayers, so far to overcome his diffidence as to join a class in the Sabbath school; and ere long he could hardly find terms sufficiently strong to describe the pleasure and the profit he was receiving in the social study of the word of God. And we doubt not that every diffident Christian who will engage in the study of the Scriptures in the same way will find a similar pleasure and profit.

AN AGED CHRISTIAN'S TESTIMONY.

Mr. H—— had almost numbered the days of the years allotted to man on earth. He had long been a constant reader of the Bible and a professed disciple of Jesus, and from a child had sat under the preaching of the gospel. Under these circumstances, it is natural to suppose that his mind would have become thoroughly imbued with the truths of the Scriptures. And no doubt this was the case, and that his knowledge of the Scriptures compared well with that of most who have enjoyed similar privileges.

Some time since, this aged disciple united with a class of men in the Sabbath school for the mutual study of the Bible. In this exercise he became deeply interested, and was always present. At a Sabbath school meeting, having referred to his past habit of studying the Scriptures, he said he used to think he understood them as well as others who had enjoyed the same advantages; but he could now see that he knew comparatively nothing about the Bible until since he connected himself with the Sabbath school. He now had a complete chain of the truths of the Bible, from Genesis to Revelation. He felt that the school had been a great blessing to him, in leading him to a more careful and connected study of the word of God, and that nothing would induce him to leave it.

It was the opinion of Mr. H—— that comparatively few Christians, not engaged in this manner of studying the Bible, though they may read it, ever do really study it. And it is very certain that, without study, the chain of the truths of Scripture spoken of by this aged Christian can never be obtained.

It is a very important fact, that almost every one who engages heartily in this mode of studying the word of God bears a similar testimony to its beneficial influence upon his mind and heart. It is also an important fact, that those who once become interested in the social study of the Bible are not often inclined to give it up.

This testimony and these facts should encourage the adult members of our Sabbath schools to unabated diligence in studying the Scriptures, and should also lead them to use their influence in persuading all the adult members of our congregations, and especially all members of our churches, to avail themselves, so far as is practicable, of the same precious privileges which are proffered to all without money and without price.

YOUNG MEN.

There is no class in the community whose attendance on the Sabbath school it is so difficult in many places to secure as that of young men. And, when we consider the influence they are exerting, and are destined hereafter to exert on the world, there is scarcely any class whose attendance seems so desirable. All the sacred and momentous interests of the church and of the various benevolent institutions which are the glory of our age and of our land, and all the interests of our literary and civil institutions, will soon be bequeathed to them. No Christian, philanthropist, or even patriot, can look on those to whose possession an inheritance so rich, and to whose guardianship interests so precious, are to be committed, without the deepest emotions.

Woe to the world if these guardians of the church and of the nation are not wise and faithful! And where is our security that they will be either wise or faithful, if they neglect the only fountain of wisdom and the man of their counsel, and never offer the prayer of the young man Solomon, "Give me now wisdom and knowledge; a wise and understanding heart"? In no way can young men better cleanse their way, and prepare themselves to meet and sustain the responsibilities that are coming upon them, than by taking heed thereto, according to the word of infinite wisdom. And in no way can they give their dying parents better security that they are committing the interests of the church and of the nation to faithful hands.

The beloved disciple well understood the power and influence of young men when he said, "I have written unto you, young men, because ye are strong." Ye are in your prime of fitness for active service. What an illustration of this was that same disciple, who received from his divine Lord the appellation "son of thunder."

With what safety might the interests of the church and of the world be intrusted to the supervision of the young men of the present age, did they possess the sterling character of John, the youngest of the twelve? O, that the remaining words of that disciple were as applicable to them as those already repeated, "And the word of God abideth in you, and ye have overcome the wicked one." There are some young men of whom it may be said, "The word of God abideth in them," and according to that word they are taking heed unto their ways. The Lord increase their number an hundred and a thousand fold!

The influence of those young men who are connected with Sabbath schools is strongly felt on others around them; and all that is wanting, in a multitude of cases, to engage many of their associates in the same delightful employment, is a friendly invitation. Young men who are already interested should give that invitation, give it kindly, give it courteously. None can do it so well and with so much promise of success.

Soon after a revival in the First Church in Charlestown, in 1841-42, a large class of young men was formed. The teacher reported twenty-eight members of the class, six of whom soon after united with the church, and five more were indulging hope. The attendance was usually good, and the class uniformly attentive, and apparently interested in receiving instruction. Much good was anticipated from the formation of this class. The erroneous impression, so common among young men, that they are "too old to attend the Sabbath school," seemed to have given place to the better one that "none are too old;" and the influence of this class upon the remainder of the school was highly salutary.

LARGE BOYS.

There is a class of pupils who are just between the periods of childhood and manhood,—large boys,—that should receive the special attention of the guardians of Sabbath schools. High-spirited, inclined to throw off restraints, often reckless, generally overestimating themselves, perfectly confident of their own wisdom, and somewhat ashamed to be numbered among children, these large boys are not only often inclined to leave the school, but are among the prominent candidates for temptation and ruin. They should have the teachers of their choice, if it can be done consistently. Certainly they should have one of the ablest, most discreet, as well as most godly men of the church, a person, if possible, who understands this class of pupils, who can appreciate their feelings, and knows how to acquire an influence over them.

There are good men whom the large boys respect; and there are other good men who, for some reason or other, cannot gain their confidence. A teacher of the former description should be chosen for such a class of pupils. If he sees them often, shows himself their friend, encourages in them habits of industry and true manliness, holds up before them great and good examples, suggests principles on which success in life depends, while he inculcates the great truth that "the fear of the Lord is the beginning of wisdom," he will gain their confidence and esteem. It is important that this class of large boys be retained in the school, not only for their own benefit, but also on account of their influence over the younger class of boys and the whole school.

XII.

INFANT DEPARTMENT.

INFANT classes in the Sabbath school, or infant departments separate from the main schools, began to be formed as early as 1827–28. A correspondent in the "Sabbath School Treasury," for 1829, inquires if "it would not be a useful plan to introduce that part of the infant school system into Sabbath schools, which consists of Scripture questions and singing hymns? As far as I know the management of the Sabbath schools in this vicinity, the children three or four years old have but little to interest them, and do not appear to receive much benefit."

To this, the editor in a foot-note replies: "In many places in this vicinity, most of the children from two to five, are connected with the Sabbath schools, and manifest a deep interest in their exercises. In one school there are twenty under five years of age, who form one of the most attractive and diligent classes in the whole school. The teacher furnishes her little pupils with an historical verse of Scripture, accompanied with a picture, and requests them to study it till next Sabbath, when she will explain it to them. With this historical picture and text she never fails to interest them during the whole exercise of the school."

The above correspondent, a few months later, writes:

"I have heard of a Sabbath school in Boston, in which an infant class has been commenced that bids fair to succeed well."

The plan of this class is thus described: "The children are placed in such a manner as that all may see every movement of the teacher, and hear without difficulty. The exercises are commenced by reading a few verses from the Bible with explanations, followed by a short prayer. Then they sing or repeat a hymn, which the children can easily learn by repeating it, line by line, after the teacher. Passages of Scripture, from 'Series of Scripture Prints,' are then read and learned in the same way. After a hymn, ten minutes are occupied by reading, reciting, and explaining by the picture the lesson on one of the cards; then they change to some other subject, and continue to change sufficiently often, to keep up the attention of the children, closing with a doxology. In all the recitations, &c., the children speak in concert, and thus help each other along.

The following is an account of the infant Sabbath school connected with the First Baptist church in Boston:—

"In December last, 1829, the names of twenty of the smallest boys were taken from the main school, and formed into an infant class. At first they met in the gallery of the meeting-house, and the average attendance was about ten. With an apparatus consisting of seven of the pictures commonly called schoolpieces,— for which we were under the necessity of preparing questions,— the Infant School and Nursery Hymn Book, and a library which cost fifty cents, we commenced our attempts at instruction. We were not then aware of the existence of any infant Sabbath school in this vicinity, and consequently were obliged to form a plan of action as well as we could, from visiting an infant day school, which plan has not been essentially varied to the present time.

"At the ringing of the bell, both in the forenoon and afternoon, the children assemble in the vestry with the older scholars, where they remain till the school has been opened by reading a portion of Scripture, and prayer. They then retire to a small room adjoining, for instruction, and commence by singing or reciting a hymn in concert. Then they answer the questions of some one of the 'Lessons for Infant Sabbath Schools,' which book we have used since it was published. They continue alternately singing and reciting till the time of closing the school, when they sing a doxology or dismission hymn. The pictures are occasionally used to assist their memory or attract their attention. The average attendance, at present, is about thirty. Thirty-five is the greatest number that has been present at one time, though we have a much larger number of names on the roll. About one third part of the scholars now are girls.

"The success that has attended our efforts thus far is greater than was anticipated at the commencement, and we have more than once heard it remarked that it was the most interesting part of the school. The children appear to be very much pleased, and would be as unwilling as the teachers could be, to have it discontinued." *

The infant class, or infant department, very soon became a most interesting feature in the Sabbath schools throughout the country, often numbering over one hundred of these little ones. Question books, and catechisms, and library books, and little papers in great numbers, have been provided for them.

* Sabbath School Treasury, Vol. III. p. 214.

Some seem to think that almost any person will do to teach these little ones. So far from this, the very best teacher the church can furnish is not too good for this important station — right here at the foundation — at the beginning of influence.

The requirements for success in this department are many and comparatively rare. The teacher, to be successful, must be a person of special aptness to teach, of a kind and loving disposition, with a large degree of patience and perseverance, and one who feels a special love for children; and it is very desirable that there should be some knowledge of music, so as to lead the children in their frequent singing. Nothing does more to keep up an interest among these little children than singing.

The infant class connected with the Sabbath school in Pawlet, Vt., in 1830, had eighteen members, the oldest not over eight years of age. The "Sabbath School Guide" was used, and the children recited the lessons in the first part of the work. Interesting Bible stories were told them, and the scholars were questioned in regard to their meaning and application.

"Our infant department," said the superintendent in 1846, "is the hope of the church. It numbers, during most of the year, about one hundred and forty, including the principal and fifteen teachers."

"No department of the school," says another superintendent, "is more interesting than the infant department." This, at that period, was a very general report from most of our schools.

METHOD OF TEACHING CHILDREN FROM FOUR TO SIX YEARS OF AGE.

A teacher says: —

"My class consists of little girls from four to six years old. Only two or three of them can read in the Bible, and consequently I use no question book. My usual method is, to tell them a story from the Bible in the most familiar manner, just as I would tell little children any other story, in language which they can understand. For example, in giving them an account of the flood, I begin by saying, 'Once there was a man whose name was Noah. He lived a great many years ago, and a great way off. He was a good man, and he was the only good man in the world at that time. All the rest of the men were wicked, and so were the women and children. And because they were so wicked, God said he would destroy them all but Noah and his family.'

"Having proceeded thus far, perhaps one of the children becomes inattentive; and, as it is useless to go on with such a class without their attention, I resort to some such method as this:

"'Eliza,' addressing the inattentive one, 'now what way should you think God would take to destroy all those wicked men, and save Noah and his family alive? For there are a great many ways, you know, in which he can destroy men.'

"Such an inquiry as this generally brings Eliza's thoughts back to the subject, and awakens her curiosity to hear how God did actually destroy the world. After I have gained her attention in some such way, and heard two or three of the class give their opinion on the question, I then proceed through the story, and draw such practical inferences from it as a child can make. I request them all to remember the story, and tell it to me on the following Sabbath. In addition to this, I commonly give them a verse from the Bible, which, by the help of their parents, I expect they will learn, and repeat to me the next time they come to school. On the next Sabbath I ask them about the story which I last told them, and, if I succeeded in keeping their attention while relating it, they can sometimes state particulars with astonishing accuracy. I then recite their verse, and after such remarks upon it as seem important for them to hear, I proceed to tell them another story, and to give another verse."

A LITTLE TALK WITH AN INFANT CLASS.

We visited a school in which there was an infant class of about thirty little boys. On approaching this class, we noticed one intelligent, bright-eyed boy, standing up by his teacher, and listening with the greatest interest to every word of instruction as it dropped from her lips. As we began to address these children, the little boy's attention was instantly transferred to us, and his bright eye beamed intelligence. The children were asked, —

"Supposing there were a stain on your faces, in what way could you find it out?" The bright-eyed boy answered in a moment, —

"By looking in the looking-glass."

They were then told that there were a great many stains on their hearts, and they were shown how they could see them by looking into the mirror of God's law — the ten commandments. Every sin made, as it were, a stain on their hearts. Some of the ways in which they sin were mentioned; and after " Thou shalt not kill," and some of the other commandments, were repeated, they were asked if they had not broken every one of them. The little boy answered,—

"No, sir."

"Haven't you?"

"No, sir; I never killed," said he; and his lip quivered, and his eyes filled with tears, as though he was grieved that any one should think such a thing of him.

"But what have you done, which the Bible says makes you a murderer?"

His countenance fell, and his features all relaxed, while, with a frankness and a tone of penitence which cannot be forgotten, he answered, "I *strike*." "He that hateth his brother is a murderer."

After some further conversation, the children were asked, "Why is it best to become Christians while young?" The countenance of the little boy again kindled with intelligence, and with the greatest earnestness in his looks and the gestures of his little hands to give impressiveness to what he said, he answered, "Because it is just like bending a little tree,— it will grow just as you bend it. But if we do not become Christians till we are old, it is like trying to bend a great tree,— it won't bend."

Very little children understand much more about the important truths of the Bible than we sometimes suppose.

XIII.

WOMAN'S MISSION IN THE SABBATH SCHOOL.

Whatever may be said on the questions of "woman's rights" and "woman's sphere," she has ever had a most important and interesting mission in connection with the institution of Sabbath schools. This institution has opened before her a broad and most inviting field for Christian labor and influence. Here she finds the most ample scope for all her warmest love and most ardent zeal in the cause of the Master. No object of benevolent labor can be more appropriate and congenial than this mission of love and mercy among the young.

The whole history of the institution, from the days of Raikes till now, shows that this class of disciples have been among the most zealous and successful workers in the cause. Young women, bright and earnest, have special advantages oftentimes for this work. They have time, and spirit, and tact. They have no ruts, but are ingenious in methods. Many a mission school in some dark alley or filthy corner has been planted by such a disciple; and under her unwearied toil and prayer, light, and purity have broken in, and made all radiant with love, and peace, and holy joy. Many a wilderness has been made to bud and blossom like the rose. In the place of revelry, and profaneness, and broils, have come up the voice of prayer and the songs of praise and worship.

It would be interesting to know how large a proportion of the earlier Sabbath schools in this country and in Europe were organized and conducted by Christian women. Though Robert Raikes is called the founder of Sabbath schools, yet nearly all, if not all, the teachers he employed to conduct them were females. The first three schools established in Massachusetts — one in Beverly and one in Concord in 1810, and one in Boston in 1812 — were established and taught by young ladies. It is said that a Sabbath school was started in Paterson, N. J., in 1794, by a little girl eleven years of age. She collected the children of the factories together, and taught them from Sabbath to Sabbath, until she had as many as sixty under her care. She was a teacher for forty years.

In most of the semi-centennial celebrations of Sabbath schools that have been held the past several years, the historical reports have shown that they were organized by women.

Then in most of our Sabbath schools, from the first, the number of female teachers has ever been larger than that of male teachers. With very few exceptions, the infant department has always been under the care of such. All seem to concede that this is woman's mission — woman's appropriate sphere of labor. We should almost as soon choose a man as a nurse for our infant children as to be the teacher of an infant Sabbath school.

This class of teachers have also been among the most successful in leading their scholars to Jesus. Many of the most wonderful cases of religious interest in the

Sabbath school — of whole classes converted, as many a superintendent can testify — have been in connection with the labors of female teachers. A pious young lady, who had been successful in leading a large class of Sabbath school girls to Jesus, was asked, " What is the secret of your success in teaching?" She answered, without a moment's hesitation, " Prayer."

She was in the habit of having her class every week at her own house, and there prayed with them and talked about their salvation. The result was that nearly every scholar under her tuition became a Christian.

Some years ago there were three female teachers in Maine who were rejoicing over the hopeful conversion of eighteen scholars each. A female teacher in Massachusetts says : —

"Nineteen persons have enrolled themselves as members of my class. Of this number, two were previously professors of religion, and sixteen have, I trust, passed from death unto life, and are now members of the church of Christ. The remaining member, who indulged a trembling hope, has taken her flight from time, and, it is hoped, now walks with the Redeemer in glory."

A teacher had for a long time been unusually anxious for her class of six little girls. On the Sabbath previous to a protracted meeting, which was held in a neighboring parish, she urged them all to attend. On the second or third day of the meetings she saw her superintendent, and, taking him by the hand, while tears of Christian joy were gushing from her eyes, she exclaimed, " Can you believe it? all my class are rejoicing in hope!"

A teacher, who had witnessed five conversions in her class, says of one of them : —

"She is much engaged in the Master's cause. She has been an instrument in the hands of God of two or three other conversions."

This teacher was in the habit of meeting her class once a week for religious conversation and prayer. She was also in the practice of giving a religious tract frequently to each of her scholars, with the request that they would read and give it away where they thought it would do the most good. One of these tracts was given to an intemperate sailor. He took it with him, read it, and on his return he appeared to be a reformed man.

These are only specimens of facts that might be given to almost any number.

Many a missionary among the heathen looks back to the instruction of a warm-hearted female teacher in the Sabbath school as the means of awakening the first desire to carry the gospel to the benighted. Some such teachers have kindled a missionary spirit in a whole class who are now scattered to the ends of the earth, and through them these teachers have thus rolled an influence round the world. It has touched every continent, every island, every shore, and it will not cease to roll on till it shall reach every hamlet, every dwelling, every soul, and incense and a pure offering shall ascend from every heart on earth, as from one great altar unto God. What work can be made more noble, more glorious than this?

Who can contemplate the influence of such a noble Christian woman as Miss Mary Lyon without the greatest admiration? What multitudes of youths, under her instruction, have been inspired with her own ardent spirit, her own love of everything good and holy. Where is the spot on earth that has not felt her influence?

And such, in her measure, every female teacher in the Sabbath school may become. Next to the parent and the pastor, no one has a more blessed ministry in leading young souls to Jesus. Let, then, every Christian female, whose circumstances will allow, and who longs for some sphere of usefulness, enter this field of labor. There is no spot in the whole vineyard of God more inviting; none where the soil is more mellow and ready for the good seed of the word; none where the rains and the dews of divine grace are more richly bestowed, and none where the seed more readily springs up, or where it yields a more golden and abundant harvest. Let every Christian female remember the declaration of the psalmist: "He that goeth forth and weepeth, bearing precious seed, shall doubtless come again rejoicing, bringing his sheaves with him."

XIV.

MISSION SABBATH SCHOOLS.

Mission Sabbath schools in cities are very different from those in most of our country towns. And hence much that is said, in the discussions on this subject at conventions, from the standpoint of the city, is wholly inappropriate to that of the country. These schools in the cities are, to a great extent, among foreigners, or the poorer and more neglected class of children. In country towns they are in remote neighborhoods and outskirts, not necessarily among the poor and ignorant only. In the country these schools are more frequently called "neighborhood," or "branch schools." They purposely avoid the word "mission" or "missionary."

The fewer of these outside schools the better, if the children and youth can be induced to attend the schools at the churches.

Some twenty-five or thirty years ago, the question came before the late Bowdoin Street Congregational Church, in Boston, in the days of its prosperity, "What shall we do for the neglected children and youth of our city? Shall we form mission schools, as some of the churches are doing, or shall we try to gather these neglected ones into our own school?"

The decision was to gather them into their own school, and seat them with their own children. And the result was, that that Sabbath school, in one year and a half, was increased from one hundred and fifty scholars to three hundred and fifty. Of the infant class of about one hundred children, all but fifteen or twenty were gathered out of the streets, whose parents were not accustomed to attend public worship on the Sabbath.

A class of eighteen Swedes was gathered, thirteen of whom, in a year and a half, were hopefully converted and united with that church. And the pastor said of them, "They learned the 'language of Israel' before they had learned our own language."

Outside neighborhood schools in the country, where the young might have been gathered into existing schools, lead to unnecessary expense and labor; and they encourage many to be satisfied with the exercises of the Sabbath school, who would otherwise attend worship.

Then such schools sometimes lead to an unnecessary multiplication of feeble churches. Every little neighborhood of a few families, to save themselves the trouble of going two or three or four miles to church, may, by the establishment of a Sabbath school, be led to attempt the formation of a new society, thus rendering all the societies in town too weak for healthy and vigorous existence.

A few years ago, a Sabbath school missionary came to a pastor in Massachusetts, and wanted to organize schools in the various school districts of the town. The pastor told him that he did not wish such schools organized. It would injure the schools already existing. There might be one or two out-districts where schools might possibly be established, if any person could be found to enlist in the work.

The missionary, nevertheless, went to work and organized six Sabbath schools in different districts. The result was that a large portion of the members of the school at the church, who resided in those districts, left the church school and united with the local school. And most of them very soon made these schools a substitute for public worship, and gave up going to church; and it almost broke up the school at the church.

In about two years, only two of those six schools existed, and one of these was under the care of errorists. The influence of the whole movement was most disastrous to the spiritual interests of the young in every part of the town. It was the result of "zeal without knowledge."

A Sabbath school missionary, some years ago, visited a minister in Central New York. That minister understood that his special object was to organize Sabbath schools in the outskirts of the town. He received him cordially, and, as the missionary seemed labor-worn, persuaded him to be his guest for a few days for relaxation and rest. He then told him he understood his work, but that he did not wish any of it done in his town. He said:—

"For three years I preached every Sabbath evening in a neighborhood three miles distant, where the people did not attend my preaching at the church or any other. Some time since I told them I could not go there any more. For three years I had visited them every Sabbath and conducted worship with them. It was no further for them to go to my church than it was for me to visit them; and I invited and urged them now to attend worship at the church. The result was that nearly all are now my constant hearers at church and attend my Sabbath school. Should you go there and establish a Sabbath school, it would soon satisfy many of them, and they would no longer take the trouble to come here to attend public worship."

The missionary at once saw the force of the minister's statement, and felt that there was danger of establishing too many outside schools.

Special efforts should first be made, both in the country and in the city, as in the case referred to above, to secure the attendance of all at the church schools. Then, if for any reason — distance, social position, or poverty — there are places where they cannot be brought to the Sabbath school and the sanctuary, the Sabbath school must be carried to them. These districts are often literally missionary fields. They are the rough and stony places; but they are not to be left uncultivated. It is regarded as bad husbandry for a farmer to leave any such unimproved and unsightly corners on his premises. How much more so for the church to do it. If every church would extend its watch and care over all within a circuit of six or eight, or even five miles around its centre, most of the neglecters of this institution — if persuasive argument and any reasonable amount of effort can avail — might be gathered into the Sabbath school.

Many of the churches are now each maintaining a branch or mission school. It is a centre of attraction around which the sympathy, the prayers, and the charities of the church cluster. It is a portion of the vineyard they are specially cultivating. We are always interested where we have invested our money or given our labor. We find it in this work more blessed to give than to receive.

Reports are made in regard to it at the Sabbath school concert and the church meeting. And this interest and labor all react in promoting a quickened zeal and a true missionary spirit upon the whole church. Thus is the church doing its legitimate work, — going out into the highways and hedges, inviting and compelling them to come in to the gospel feast.

Some years ago there was a very interesting branch or mission school connected with the former High Street Sabbath school, Providence, R. I., taught by a poor, infirm woman. She was a regular and an interested attendant at the Sabbath school and the church so long as she was able to leave her home. When deprived of this privilege, she induced several poor children in her neighborhood, who were accustomed to spend the Sabbath in play on the streets, to come to her room and receive instruction from her.

This school, in the extreme outskirts of the city, was a branch of the High Street school. As such it was regarded by the church and all the members of the main school. It was always reported at the Sabbath school concert, and was often made the subject of special prayer.

Many among our efficient and active churches have grown out of these mission or branch Sabbath schools. The Prospect Street Congregational church in Cambridgeport has formed two such churches — the Pilgrim, and the Chapel church — in this way. The Rockville church in Peabody, Tower Hill, Lynn, Chambers Street chapel, Boston, West Congregational church, Portland, Me., &c., were started as neighborhood Sabbath schools; and also the famous Lee Avenue church, in Brooklyn, N. Y., which was called the model

Sabbath school of the world. They were, in most cases, started with this ultimate result in view.

This kind of labor for the outskirts was begun very early. Indeed, almost all the earlier Sabbath schools were of this character. When church schools were established, those who became interested in the work began to look out the distant and destitute portions of the neighborhood or town. As early as 1833, the Congregational church in Fall River, in addition to the school at the church, sustained eight other schools in the town and vicinity from one to seven miles distant, embracing in all three hundred scholars. Some years ago the Congregational church in Augusta, Me., had seven Sabbath schools under its care. In March, 1815, a society was organized in Winthrop, Me., the expressed objects being "to discourage profaneness, idleness, gross breaches of the Sabbath, and intemperance." This society continued in operation till 1832, having, in the meantime, established Sabbath schools in seven school districts.*

The work of mission Sabbath schools, therefore, is not a new enterprise that has sprung up within a few years. It has long proved a very important work in its reflex influence upon the church. There is scarcely any labor like this that so effectually enlists the services of the churches. It is a broad field for the exercise of the talent of private Christians. Here the longings of every one to be useful will find ample scope.

In 1859, a minister said:—

"In one part of my parish I held a meeting, and urged upon the people the importance of having a Sabbath school

---

* Centennial Celebration at Winthrop, Me., 1871, p. 40.

for their children. I then invited those who were disposed to favor it to remain and consult about it. Not one remained.

"But a poor widow of seventy, the only member of my church in the district, felt that she could not have it so. She lived all alone in a retired spot, and she went from house to house through the neighborhood, talked with the parents, and invited them and their children to come to her house Sabbath afternoons. As the result, she soon had a delightful school of about thirty members. The next time I saw her, she was rejoicing in her school, and said, —

"'We have great need of some books to interest the children. Do you know of any way we can get some?'

"I happened to have a couple of packages of children's books in the buggy, and when I brought them to her, she exclaimed, —

"'O, that is just what we need. If you had given me as many pieces of gold, you would not have made me so happy.'

"And I believe it. That school is her meat and drink, and company in her loneliness."

In 1817, the Chillicothe Association of Sabbath School Teachers, Ohio, says: —

"The town has been divided into eight school districts, in each of which there is a school, under the direction of competent teachers. To secure the regular attendance of the scholars, parents, guardians, and masters are requested to enter them by subscriptions for the term of one year, engaging to provide for them the necessary books. The society has under its care four hundred scholars. They are taught to read the Scriptures, and memorize select passages. They are also taught to sing the praises of God. The schools are brought together monthly, to sing in concert, and have an address from a minister of the gospel." *

A Sabbath school association was formed, in the spring of 1841, in Marietta College, Ohio, for the purpose of establishing Sabbath schools in all the destitute neighborhoods within a reasonable distance, and to furnish teachers for schools already established, where they were needed. That summer this association conducted twenty-three schools, in which about one thousand scholars were taught.

The Mason Street Sabbath school in Boston was established in 1817, by the Society for the Moral and Religious Instruction of the Poor in Boston. In the early days of this school, more than one hundred of the children between five and fifteen years of age could not tell their letters; and one, about twelve years old, on being asked about Jesus Christ, replied, that she had never heard of such a person! Some of them had never attended a place of worship till taken thither by the teachers of the Sabbath school.

In 1839, at the twenty-second anniversary, it was stated that nearly three thousand children and youth had come under religious instruction in that school, and more than one hundred and forty teachers had been connected with the school.

* Boston Recorder, Vol. II. p. 142.

XV.

GATHERING IN NEW SCHOLARS.

A GREAT variety of plans have been adopted during the fifty years of our connection with Sabbath schools for gathering in the neglected and those that neglect this institution. There are probably but few places where this work is not still needed.

In a large parish in the suburbs of Boston, some years ago, the common plan of offering rewards for new scholars was adopted. Almost every Sabbath new scholars were brought in and rewards given. One day a bright little girl came to the superintendent, and, with a discouraged look and tone of voice, said, "Mr. ——, the other children get rewards, but I can't get any, although I keep trying to get new scholars."

"What is the reason you cannot get any new scholars?" said the superintendent kindly to her.

"Well, the fact is, I do not live in a pick-up neighborhood."

There may be some such neighborhoods; but the number, it is believed, is very small, and various expedients to bring in new scholars must still be devised.

On addressing a school in one of our New England manufacturing cities, a few years ago, we suggested the following plan to increase their number. Let the superintendent appoint a class of boys and a class of girls to visit as many as they can during the week, and urge them to attend. Next Sabbath let them report how many visits they have made, how many persons have promised to attend, and how many of them are then present. Then let two more classes be appointed in the same way, and keep up this measure through the season.

In one case where this plan was adopted, the first two classes appointed made, during the week, sixty-six visits, and twenty-seven of those visited promised to attend, of whom twelve were present the first Sabbath after they were invited.

This plan was adopted in the above school; only a class of young men and a class of young women were appointed, as the school embraced a large number of operatives belonging to the mills. The next Sabbath the young men reported that fourteen persons had promised to attend, and half of them were present. The young ladies reported that thirty-five had promised to attend, and fifteen of them were present. The next spring the superintendent wrote: "At the time of your visit our Sabbath school numbered one hundred and sixty scholars. We adopted the plan you proposed and have followed it ever since, and I now have the pleasure of reporting to you a school of five hundred and fifty-seven members."

In some cases the parish has been divided into districts, and a committee of the teachers appointed, sometimes of teachers and scholars, and sometimes of one scholar from each class, to visit, within a given time — a month, or week, or day, frequently the 4th of July — every family, and invite every member to attend. In this way many a school has been increased fifty and even one hundred per cent.

Some schools have appointed what they have called a "vigilance committee," whose business it is to watch about the sanctuary and visit any places where the neglecters of the Sabbath school may resort, and kindly urge them to attend. This plan has prevented noise about the church, and has also been the means of increasing the schools.

In one school in 1838, after the pastor had preached on the subject, a committee was appointed to circulate a paper through the parish to obtain the names of all who would join the school. This plan was attended with great success. In three months the school was increased from about one hundred, all under fifteen years of age, to three hundred and twenty-nine, and about one half of them were over sixteen years of age.

A female teacher some years ago resolved, at the beginning of the year, not to go to the Sabbath school a single Sabbath that year, without taking with her, if possible, at least one new scholar. She attended fifty-one Sabbaths, and she brought into the school fifty-one new scholars who had never attended a Sabbath school before! And they were also led to attend public worship regularly, and eleven of them were hopefully converted during the year. How eventful in good would be such a resolution by every Sabbath school teacher.

A very successful device in securing new scholars has been the giving of an illustrated certificate to both the new scholars and to those who bring them in.

In some cases the members of the infant classes are all invited to get new scholars, and are promised a little book or pretty card for every new scholar they bring into the school. These little ones will go directly home to their parents, — if they are not already connected with the school, — and with earnest looks and words, say, " Mother, or father, the superintendent says he will give me a beautiful book if I will get a new scholar into the school. Now, mother, or now, father, won't *you* go?" Of course they will go. How can they help it? Many and many a parent has thus been brought in, whom no one else could persuade to attend.

We visited a school in 1836 where there were several classes of adults for mutual instruction — one a class of young men. In passing round among these classes, we suggested the following plan for increasing the number of similar classes.

Let these classes all disband, and each member, or each two, form the nucleus of a new class, to be collected by the personal efforts of this member, or couple. In this way a class of six members might multiply itself into three or six classes, each with equal number with the original class. This simple plan has three important feature.

1. These personal efforts to obtain new members will greatly increase the interest of those by whom they are made.

2. A personal invitation to become a member of such a class will persuade many who would remain unaffected by a general invitation from the superintendent or pastor.

3. Each class will have one or two experienced persons, who will be of great service in preventing discouragement and failure at the outset.

This plan was received with much apparent interest by the members of the above classes; and it was expected that it would be adopted and result in a large increase to the adult department of that school.

Each class in one school selected one of its number to constitute a committee for the school. It was the duty of this committee to invite all into the school who did not attend, and to secure, so far as possible, a constant and regular attendance, and report at the end of the month. The results were happy. The school was increased; and some were brought in who had never before attended.

A lad about twelve years of age found his way to a school from an adjoining town, where they had no school. The next Sabbath he brought others with him, and then others, till, through his influence, seven or eight attended from that place regularly.

"There is a large number in this school," says a correspondent, "who have been gathered in from the 'highways and hedges' of our city; and among them are some of the most promising children in the school. Many, whose parents are never seen in the sanctuary, are regular in their attendance there, with their teachers, and they have become so deeply interested, that we hope they will never forsake the assembling of themselves together in the house of God. One little girl, of this class of children, has, within the last year, brought in fifteen others to share with her the privileges she so highly prizes.

"About forty of this class of children have been provided with seats made for this special purpose, suited to their age, near the pulpit; and no seats in our house are more crowded than these."

A superintendent, some thirty years ago, told his school one day, that he wanted some new scholars for Thanksgiving. Within three weeks from that time, forty new ones were brought into the school! And twenty-five of them were obtained by one female teacher, who devoted the whole of Thanksgiving-day week to the work of finding them! Thanksgiving must have been a joyful day to that teacher, stormy though it was. Some of these new scholars were so eager to attend the school and be there punctually at the commencement, quarter before nine, in the morning, that they came to the teacher's residence as early as seven o'clock. One of them, stimulated by the example of her teacher, herself brought in five others. So soon we see the second and third generations — the children and the children's children.

The next year she obtained twenty new scholars. The next Thanksgiving-day week was very stormy. But this faithful teacher could not forego the happiness she had experienced before; and she addressed herself again to her benevolent labors. The week after, she met her superintendent, and, with a sad countenance, said, "I have not succeeded in getting new scholars this year as I had hoped to. I made last week three hundred visits for this purpose, but was able to obtain only eighteen!"

Who can estimate the good that may result from these labors? Many of these children and youth — gathered, as some of them may have been, from the lanes and by-ways of the city, and from among those but little favored with moral and religious training — may, through the influence of these labors, be saved from a life of sin and from becoming a curse to society, and trained up to become blessings to the community, and ornaments to the church of Christ.

In 1851 there were fifteen Sabbath schools in the city of Indianapolis. In the month of September there were in the city seventeen hundred children and youth of suitable age to attend Sabbath school, and all of these but one hundred and ten were connected with these schools. This was probably a larger per cent. of attendance than could be found in any other city in the world. Every family was visited once a month by members of an association comprising of the different schools. The Bible classes were composed of the first young ladies and gentlemen in the city.*

At a large evening meeting in a manufacturing village, in a front pew there were three small girls and a young man at the head of the pew, who was supposed to be the teacher, as the teachers were generally seated with their classes. In the course of the exercises the pastor said : —

"We have a Bible to give to the one who has brought into our Sabbath school the largest number of scholars who belonged to no other school, according to our promise a month ago. Indeed, we propose to give four Bibles."

He took a beautiful copy of the Scriptures and gave it to the first little girl, who had brought in twenty-five new scholars. He then gave another copy to the next little girl, who had brought in fifteen new scholars. He then took a small, beautiful Bible, and gave it to the next wee thing, who, with a great deal of effort and perseverance, had persuaded two or three to join the Sabbath school, and the good minister wished to reward her effort. The pastor then took up a substantial and finely-bound copy of the word of God, and, to our surprise, gave it to that young man, who, it seemed, had brought eleven young men into a new Bible class for young men. He was not a Christian; and yet he had, in the face of the remonstrances of his whole class,

---

* Family Visitor.

come up before a whole congregation and taken his seat with these little children, and publicly received a copy of the Scriptures. Was not that a specimen of true moral courage? And did not Jesus, as he saw that act, as in the case of the young man in the gospel, love this young man? And did he not say to him, "Thou art not far from the kingdom of heaven?" He had outwardly, in taking his seat with those little children, become as a little child.

Every school in the land should, once or twice a year at least, adopt some of these plans here suggested, or some better ones, to gather in those who are deprived of, or are neglecting the instructions of the Sabbath school. There are everywhere neglected children, a "sort of spiritual orphans," they have been called, through parental impenitence and unbelief, "aliens from the commonwealth of Israel, and strangers to the covenant of promise;" through parental neglect starving for the bread of life. Shall not teachers and Christian disciples seek them out and become foster-parents to them, and in the Sabbath school and in the house of God seek for them the bread and water of life? How many, thus reclaimed from ignorance and sin, have become bright and shining lights in the church, ministers of the gospel, and even missionaries of the cross among the heathen! Then "gather them in, gather them in."

XVI.

THE SABBATH SCHOOL CONCERT.

One of the most noticeable and attractive features of the Sabbath school has ever been the monthly concert. Thirty or forty years ago the concert was generally spoken of as one of the fullest and most interesting meetings held, enlisting alike the interested attendance of parents, teachers, and children.

A little boy, in 1830, came to his minister and asked if the concert could not be held once in two weeks, for he said that he did not know how to wait so long as four weeks.

In a report from a school, in 1839, it was said: "I doubt if we have a stated meeting that is looked forward to with greater desire, or attended with greater interest, than the Sabbath school concert."

A pastor, in 1834, said: "The children live somewhat scattered; yet they are so much interested that they go to the concert the coldest winter evenings." The same year there were sixteen schools under the care of the Congregational churches in Boston. All but three observed this meeting, and nearly all used to speak of it as their fullest and most interesting meeting.

At the concert of one school, in January, 1835, there were two hundred present. Some of the children, who had never attended before, expressed much wonder that they had not heard what an interesting meeting the concert was, and said that "nothing would tempt them to stay away in future."

A pastor, in 1837, says: "The concert is one of our most thrilling meetings; and, further, it is one of our most overflowing meetings, and most highly favored of heaven."

A single fact will show the remarkable interest taken in the concert as long ago as this meeting was held on Monday evenings. "On the evening of the concert in October," says a report, "there was a display of fireworks, firing of guns, &c., in the vicinity of the vestry. To our great surprise and joy, most of the older pupils of the school, boys and girls, came in and were quietly seated through the whole exercise of the evening, apparently unmoved by the roar of the cannon and blaze of rockets without."

We doubt whether the present day, with all our improvements, can show an example of greater interest in this important meeting.

The concert was often spoken of as an efficient aid in increasing the interest of parents, guardians, and the adult portions of the church and congregation in the Sabbath school cause, and of promoting the general prosperity of the school. It has also been the means of bringing out parents and others who seldom or never attended worship on the Sabbath. They become interested in the concert, and finally are seen in the sanctuary.

A pastor said: "We regard the concert as having a most important bearing on the interests and prosperity of the school, and as standing at the head of many sacred influences, which, like leaven, are diffusing a healthful energy through the community."

The concert was also often spoken of as the means of special religious interest in the school. In 1825 the Holy Spirit was sent down upon a school. The report says: —

"Yet it was most manifest that this inestimable blessing was obtained only through the operation of efficient means. These were various; but none more happily successful than the efforts made to interest the teachers, scholars, and people generally in the concert."

In 1832, in a school of two hundred and four scholars, more than one hundred were hopefully converted. The pastor, in speaking of the influence of the concert and other meetings for prayer, in promoting that glorious refreshing, says: —

"The Sabbath school concert of prayer was attended with special interest. A stated prayer meeting in behalf of the school was held Sabbath morning, between the ringings of the bell. Members of the church, teachers, and pupils came together for this purpose. If I had looked into the streets, and not at the hour, I might have mistaken the first for the second bell. It seemed as if the congregation were assembling."

With such a spirit of prayer, the results are not so wonderful.

In one town in Maine there were eight schools, and during one season seven of these schools enjoyed special religious interest. All these seven schools observed the concert, and also had a meeting of prayer for the schools Sabbath morning. The other school did not observe the concert, or have any season of prayer. This singular fact was noticed with interest by the people.

There was in the earlier days of this institution less

of machinery, less that was theatric and operatic in the exercises of the concert than exists in some schools at the present day. A few years ago we were invited to attend and address a concert. We found a programme all made out of nine songs, solos, duets, and choruses, and fifteen dialogues and single pieces to be spoken by scholars. The speakers were all young Misses. They came forward upon the platform, made their bows, and accompanied their rehearsals with all the gestures and other accompaniments of an academic exhibition. At the close, eight minutes were allowed the invited speaker for an address.

Variety is always essential to an interesting concert; and that existed in the earlier concerts, as it does now. There was perhaps less singing, but more prayer. The prayers were short, interspersed with the recital of interesting information or incidents respecting Sabbath schools in this and other lands; their origin, progress, present condition, manner of conducting, plans to awaken an interest; the condition of children in other countries, particularly heathen; the reading of short anonymous pieces, written by teachers and scholars, on subjects previously given out; in giving an account of the writer's own religious feelings, &c. In some instances these accounts were the first intimations that there were inquirers after the way of life among the scholars. In one school there were nine pieces written on the subject "Jesus Christ." In another school, in two years and a half, about one hundred pieces were written on various subjects, which it was said added much interest to the exercises, and helped to secure a good attendance. Sometimes, as is now very generally the case, all the scholars repeated verses, on which the pastor or superintendent would make appropriate remarks. These verses were sometimes selected by the scholars themselves, and sometimes they were connected with a subject previously assigned by the superintendent. It was an object formerly, as it is now, to make the concert as attractive as possible to the children, — a meeting which they would anticipate with pleasure, and from which they would absent themselves only from necessity.

A successful plan of exciting and maintaining an interest in the concert, extensively adopted in former years, was full monthly reports by the teachers of their classes.

The superintendent of the Sabbath school in West Boylston — which was organized in 1818, — in 1821 circulated among the teachers class-books, in which they were to keep weekly accounts of each scholar and recitation. From these class-books the superintendent made a monthly report to the school, and also a general report at the close of the season, which the pastor made the foundation of a Sabbath school sermon on the Sabbath.*

This was regarded by some superintendents of vital importance to Sabbath school operations. By this plan the condition of each class was represented every month; every fact or incident worthy of notice was brought to view, accompanied with such suggestions and remarks as the teacher felt the circumstances required, and often with warm exhortations and entreaties to their pupils. These reports were put into the hands of the superintendent, and by him arranged and read

* Semi-centennial Anniversary of the Sabbath School of West Boylston, &c.

at the concert. "By this means," another report says, "we get more knowledge of the school, and have a fuller attendance at the concert."

Another plan, adopted by many schools, that awakened great interest at this meeting, was for the pastor to give a short and familiar sermon or lecture at the close of the other exercises. In one instance, this plan excited so much interest among the people generally, that sometimes the children found fault because so many of the older people attended that all the children could not be accommodated.

The time of holding the concert has varied with different schools at different periods. The more general time has been Sabbath evening. Some hold it Sabbath noon, in place of the usual exercises of the school; and some, of late, hold it in place of the afternoon service in the church. Whatever may be the opinion or feelings of any in regard to giving up the afternoon sermon, generally, to the Sabbath school, a public meeting like the concert once a month certainly has not the same objections that some urge so strongly in the other case. All the people will attend such a meeting, and the pastor is usually present to aid in its exercises, and to close with an address.

A practice in former years, that had some advantages over that in many schools at the present time, was, that the short addresses or remarks that were interspersed among the prayers, singing, and recitations, were usually made by those connected with the school,— the pastor, superintendent, and teachers,— instead of depending on some one from abroad. In this way, the talents of the teachers were developed and cultivated, and by this exercise many a teacher became a more active helper in the church-meeting, and many a teacher was also led to see that he possessed talents that called him to fit for the ministry.

While variety is necessary to give a proper spirit and interest to this important meeting, we need not make an exhibition of the children, either in repeating verses or hymns, or in singing. And we should ever be watchful lest we overlook the great object of the concert and the school; and any forms or machinery that may tend to this will endanger the best interests and usefulness of this precious institution.

We should not forget the original design of the Sabbath school concert. Like that of the missionary concert, it was a meeting especially for prayer for God's blessing on our Sabbath schools, and on all the labors of the teachers and others in connection with them. The object of remarks, or reports from schools, or letters from missionaries and others, should be to impart such information as may awaken an interest in the object, and direct that interest so as to inspire all with the spirit of devotion.

As the concert has become so especially a meeting for the children, there must be, in the remarks or addresses that are made, more or less of incidents and stories to keep their attention. But they should always be used, not merely for the sake of repeating them to amuse or interest the children, but to illustrate or enforce some important truth or duty.

A superintendent in 1829, finding that the interest in the concert was decreasing, resolved to try an experiment. During the month he collected all the facts he could find in the religious papers and Sabbath school periodicals, which showed the utility and importance of

Sabbath schools. These facts were then arranged in proper order, interspersed with remarks and inferences, and read at the next concert. The same was done the two following months.

The effect was what might have been expected. At the next concert, when the evening was so extremely unpleasant and stormy that he could hardly expect any to attend, and almost doubted whether it were best to go himself, he found between two and three hundred present.

A pastor, in 1830, said: "The way in which the concert has been conducted, and which has excited so much interest of late, is simply this: I have read or related some anecdotes respecting Sabbath schools and Sabbath school children, which I have requested the children to remember until the next concert. At the next I first inquire of the children respecting the last meeting. I enter into all the particulars of the different anecdotes. All who have attended have been astonished at the quickness and accuracy with which the children answer the questions propounded. The children are all alive to attend the next Sabbath school concert. Nothing short of this, or some similar plan, can long sustain a suitable interest in any concert."

Many superintendents, from the commencement of the concert, have been accustomed to spend much time in preparing for this interesting meeting. The plans devised to give attraction and interest to the exercises, are almost as various as are the tastes and modes of thinking of the superintendents.

A marked feature in the exercises of the concert, at the present day, is the repetition of Scripture verses and poems by the scholars. Where small children recite, unless they will speak so as to be heard over the house, it is better that several, or a whole class, should repeat their verses together, so as to give volume to their voices.

In these recitations the design is to let every one, or most of those who are present, take a part in the exercises, and not to see how much two or three scholars can recite. At one concert, conducted, too, by the pastor, two small girls repeated each three or four chapters of Scripture, and probably not twenty persons in a large audience in the church heard scarcely as many words.

The Sabbath school in T——, in 1861, held its anniversary on the afternoon of Fast Day. Although the storms for several days interrupted some of their preparations, yet the exercises of the school, which had all been arranged by the pastor, were well performed and very interesting. These exercises consisted mostly in the repetition of Scripture by individuals, by whole classes and by the school in concert, interspersed with frequent singing by the school.

The infant class repeated "The sweetest thing," &c. in eight parts. Two little girls repeated a dialogue about the Saviour. Then the pastor repeated several verses, to each of which two or three little children responded, one at a time, by a verse. Two classes then repeated, individually, the Beatitudes, the whole school repeated together the last, "Blessed are ye when men shall revile you," &c. Then the different classes, even to the young men and women, repeated numerous and appropriate verses, sometimes separately and sometimes in concert, on the following subjects: — the Bible, Industry, Honesty and Uprightness; Peace, the duty, conditions, and future prevalence of peace; Profaneness, Intemperance, Oppression, and the Sabbath; Beneficence, the Saviour, Heaven. At the close of the verses on Peace, the whole school repeated, "Blessed are the peace-makers." At the close of the verses on Beneficence, the last of which was "How shall they hear without a preacher," &c., the whole school repeated the verse, "Go ye into all the world, and preach the gospel to every creature." At the close of the verses on Heaven, the last of which were the description of heaven, the tree of life, &c., the whole school repeated. "Blessed are they that do his commandments, that they may have right to the tree of life, and may enter in through the gates into the city."

The happy effect of these exercises was seen in the unabated attention and deep interest of the whole congregation. It was truly impressive to see those young men stand up, with so much apparent interest, with no appearance of a false shame or bashfulness, and repeat all those appropriate verses on such subjects as Profaneness, Intemperance, Oppression, the Sabbath, Industry, Honesty, &c.

On another occasion this school had for its exercises the character of God, His existence, His greatness and majesty, His omniscience and omnipotence, His providence, His holiness, His mercy and gospel invitations.

On the first, one person repeated nine proof-texts; another, the ninety-first psalm; another, the one hundred and twenty-first psalm; then singing appropriate to the subject.

On the second, one repeated seven proof-texts; another, twenty-three verses of the one hundred and fourth psalm, the whole repeating the twenty-fourth verse, "O

Lord, how manifold are thy works," &c.; another repeated from the twenty-fourth to the thirty-fifth verse, the whole school repeating the last part of the thirty-fifth verse, " Bless the Lord, O my soul. Praise ye the Lord." This was followed by spontaneous singing of an appropriate hymn. And so on through all the topics.

The more common plan has been, for many years past, to enlist all the scholars in the exercises. In some cases a promise, or invitation, or warning, or an historical fact, — as the deluge, the offering of Isaac, the captivities, the crucifixion, the conversion of Paul, or the jailer, — or some topic, — as the Sabbath, baptism, the Christian graces, or fruits of the Spirit, &c.. — is given out, and each scholar is to recite a verse relating to the subject. More frequently a single word, as holy or holiness, pride, humility, &c., and verses in which such words occur, are recited by the whole school.

Books of exercises for the concert, within a few years, have been published, and many schemes have been devised, such as large representations of the cross, the crown, the star of Bethlehem, the anchor of hope; monuments composed of various blocks, on which are written the different truths and doctrines of the Bible; temples, &c., upon which different scholars will come forward and hang cards with letters that will spell out particular words, each scholar repeating a verse beginning with his letter. If not too complicated, and if not attended with too much machinery and display, these representations may serve to fix the great truths represented in the minds especially of the younger scholars; and, if accompanied with suitable remarks by the superintendent or pastor, may be made impressive.

A plain Christian woman said she could understand "Pilgrim's Progress," but she could not understand the explanatory notes. And some of these attempts to make truth simple have been harder for the children to comprehend than the truths themselves, as plainly taught in the Bible. A little girl returned home from the concert, where there had been erected a monument of blocks, each block representing some important Scripture truth, and a dove on the top to represent the Holy Spirit. She was full of enthusiasm as she described the monument, and how they made it by placing one block upon another. "O, mother," said she, "it was beautiful! And when they got through, they put a hen on the top. O, mother, it was beautiful!"

She evidently had misapprehended the whole design of the representation. She saw only the material object, without a single idea of the great truths intended to be taught. A description, in simple language, of the various truths of which that monument was constructed, and of the Holy Spirit — the heavenly dove — who teaches us, she very likely would have understood; but this display of visible objects filled her vision and occupied all her thoughts.

This singular case is mentioned to show the need of great wisdom and care lest we complicate and obscure truth by our attempts to explain it, instead of making it plain to the understanding of childhood. The old, old story, and every truth of the gospel, should be told simply, as to a little child.

XVII.

BENEVOLENCE AMONG THE YOUNG.

Much has been said, for some years past, on the subject of Christian, systematic benevolence, and on the Christian use of money.

Premium tracts have been published, numerous sermons preached, and the religious press has often spoken with emphasis on the subject. And it is believed the spirit of benevolence, from year to year, has in consequence been rising in the churches.

But still many feel that we need a much higher standard in regard to Christian giving. There is too little principle about it. Many give only under the influence of an appeal; they have no system to regulate their charities.

Every one knows that a spirit of benevolent giving can be cultivated — can be increased by a proper course of training. There must be education on this subject. And one reason why so many church-members manifest no deep, fixed principle in regard to Christian giving, is that their education on the subject has been neglected. They have never been trained and educated to give.

It is said that the muscles with which we close the hand are much stronger than those with which we open it. Now it is the weaker, opening muscles we use in giving money, and the stronger ones we use in holding on to our money. Every one can see the importance of a frequent use of these weaker muscles, to keep them supple; else they will become so stiff and rigid that no call of charity can relax them.

Now, education on this subject, as on all others, should begin in childhood. Then the duty and the blessedness of giving for the benefit of those less favored than ourselves should be taught. Then the habit of giving should be formed — of giving what is our own, what we have earned or saved.

There is no one thing in regard to the early religious training of the young, next to their conversion, that we have considered in our fifty years with the Sabbath schools as so important as right instruction on this subject of benevolence. It is too late in manhood to expect that all the habits that have been strengthening from early life can be broken up, and new ones formed. Our hope is with the young. And it is delightful to witness the eagerness with which children will enter into any plan for the alleviation of human woe. Nothing so easily excites their sympathies as the story of pagan ignorance and wretchedness. Their hearts have not yet felt the deadening influence of that practical infidelity in reference to the condition of the heathen, and that spirit of selfishness, which prevails so extensively among the more mature in years. They believe what the Bible says of the lost and perishing state of the heathen, and their charities flow out almost spontaneously for their relief.

It has long been a part of the Sabbath school system to train its members to form the habit of giving. At first their little offerings — no matter how small, if they were earned or saved — were brought once a quarter, then once a month at the concert, and now most schools take a collection every Sabbath. And there are few, if any, exercises in which the children manifest more interest than in making their contributions.

More than forty years ago, in a large school, where a collection was taken monthly, we used to pass round among the little ones, just before the collection was to be taken, and loan a cent to any who had forgotten to bring one. One of those pupils, many years after, said she used sometimes to leave her cent at home on purpose, that the superintendent, if he loaned her one, might see that she would certainly remember to pay it the next Sabbath. She spoke with great enthusiasm of her interest in these contributions.

It has ever been a source of interest to see the various and often curious plans children adopt to obtain their money for the contribution. Going on errands, picking berries and nuts, holding a gentleman's horse, cultivating a little plot of land, raising poultry, helping mother, rising early in the morning, breaking some bad habit, &c. One little boy earned twenty-five cents by "sitting up straight." Two little boys in Maine got into a rivalry in seeing which would give the most. One Sabbath, Roswell brought twenty-five cents. Frank said he should beat him the next Sabbath. But the next Sabbath Roswell brought thirty-three cents! When Frank, with a discouraged tone of voice, said, —

"Well, my father doesn't let me pull gray hairs out of his head for half a cent a dozen, as Roswell's does; and I have no baby sister to rock for so much an hour, as Roswell has."

If Roswell earned all of his thirty-three cents in pulling gray hairs out of his father's head, there must have been a harvest of sixty-six dozen in one week; and at that rate one would suppose it would not be long before all of the poor man's hairs could be easily numbered.

These contributions in our Sabbath schools have awakened among the members a lasting interest in the various objects of benevolence. Many have been led, through this interest, to devote their lives to the cause of missions among the heathen. A missionary said she owed it to the fact that she gave, when a little child, by the suggestion of her mother, a cherished article of clothing to the Sandwich Islands Mission that she herself became a missionary to the heathen. Her dust, with that of her husband, now mingles with that distant heathen soil; but no doubt the soul of many a Nestorian will hereafter gem her crown of rejoicing on account of that little offering she made in her childhood.

The hundreds of thousands of dollars which our New England Sabbath schools, by their small weekly collections, have sent in donations of books all over the great West, have been silken cords — unnoticed by statesmen and politicians, it may be — that have greatly helped to bind together these different sections of our great country. Few are the men and women now, in any part of the West, who cannot remember — and they can never forget — their deep interest, perhaps their tears of gratitude, when told in the Sabbath school that these pleasant and attractive books and papers were the gift of New England children, and that many of those children earned the money to make the gift by acts of self-denial and severe toil.

A vigorous prosecution of this work of training the young to habits of benevolence will do more in bringing forward a generation of large-hearted, liberal Christians than all the various plans that can be adopted to awaken the spirit of benevolence among adults. Parents and teachers have a great responsibility, and also great encouragement, in regard to this work. The man who quarries the stone in a distant mountain is no less really engaged in erecting the temple, than he who lays the stone upon the rising walls; and the humble Sabbath school teacher, who instils lessons of piety and benevolence into the impressible mind of childhood, is no less really bearing a part in the magnificent enterprise of converting this world to Christ, than the man who forsakes all the hallowed endearments of life, and goes forth to erect the standard of the cross amid polar snows or tropic suns. Indeed, many a teacher thus faithful has been the honored means of training those who have gone on this errand of mercy to the heathen. And the number and the character of those who shall hereafter go forth on this same errand will depend, under God, in no small degree, on the instruction given to the young in regard to the claims which the heathen world, and the claims which Christ has on them.

The district secretary of the American Board for the Valley of the Mississippi, many years ago, said, that more good was accomplished for the American Board in awakening a missionary spirit, by the Sabbath school libraries sent West, than as if all the money those libraries cost were put directly into the treasury of the Board. And he gave this illustration: —

"Louisa Ralston, or What can I do for the Heathen," found its way, in connection with other books, through the benevolence of some Sabbath school in

Massachusetts, to L——, Kentucky. This little book was read by the children. Such was the interest awakened among a company of fourteen or fifteen young girls, that they organized a missionary society on the plan proposed in the book. In one year and a half this society of fourteen or fifteen young girls paid into the treasury of the Foreign Missionary Society two hundred and forty dollars! The price of that book was about twenty cents.

Very early in the history of Sabbath schools, juvenile benevolent societies began to be formed, and they have existed, more or less generally, ever since. They have taken all sorts of names, according to the taste and fancy of the members. Among these names are the following: "Robert Raikes' Juvenile Association;" "The Twig Society;" "The Gleaners;" "The Fragment Society;" "Sabbath School Missionary," or "Temperance Association;" "Golden Sheaf," &c. Some schools select, at the beginning of the year, the special object they will aid. This serves to increase the interest and the amount collected.

XVIII.

JUVENILE MUSIC.

SINGING by the children has become a marked feature in our Sabbath schools, both in connection with the weekly exercises and with those of the concert. Some suppose this is one of the more recent improvements that have been introduced to give interest to the institution.

Much more attention has been given to the subject, it is true, within comparatively a few years, than was given in the earlier history of Sabbath schools. Numerous volumes of juvenile hymns and tunes have been prepared and published; and more has been done to instruct the young in music, and to prepare them to take part in the exercise of song in the school and the concert.

And yet it is interesting to see how early singing by the children was practised in many of the Sabbath schools. The hymns and tunes were the same that were used in church, and the children did not seem less interested in singing them than do the children of the present day in those prepared especially for them.

In what has been said about the various modes of conducting Sabbath schools, it will be remembered that singing was common in most of the earlier schools mentioned, as a part of the opening and closing exercises.

An excellent judge of music in the Theological Seminary at Andover, in a review of the "Sabbath School Psalmody," by Mr. Ezra Barrett, published in the "Sabbath School Treasury," dated March 27, 1829, says:—

"I have long felt anxious that something might be done to promote singing in our Sabbath schools. To me it is one of the most delightful and inspiring acts of sacred devotion; and I have no doubt it would have a most happy tendency could it be more generally introduced into our Sabbath schools, and executed with propriety, as it might be, by the scholars."

A single sheet was published, in 1829, containing seven tunes, and three verses for each tune, for use in Sabbath schools.*

It was common, as early as 1832-33, to hear superintendents say that successful efforts had been made to instruct the children in sacred music; that the singing in the school on the Sabbath and at the concerts was performed by them, and that it had contributed much to the interest; and that they thought it desirable that juvenile singing should be introduced into all the Sabbath schools. A superintendent, in 1832, said:—

"There was no exercise in which the children took so much delight as in singing hymns. A hymn suited to their capacities was chalked on a blackboard, and committed to memory by the whole school. This was sung, when all had learned it, in some simple tune adapted to the words; and if the Sabbath school room may ever be said to resemble 'a little heaven below,' it was while the hundred youthful voices united in a song of praise."

* Boston Recorder for 1829, p. 36.

In 1836, the Massachusetts Sabbath School Society began to publish hymn and tune books adapted to the circumstances and wants of the schools. Among these were "Sabbath School Songs," and "Sabbath School Harp," prepared by the late Dr. Lowell Mason; "Juvenile Music;" the "Sabbath School Melodist;" the "Massachusetts Sabbath School Hymn Book;" "Vestry Songs," &c.

For the first eight or ten years after the establishment of this society, in 1832, there was hardly any subject connected with the management of Sabbath schools that received more attention, or that awakened more interest, than this singing by the children. A new impulse, it was everywhere reported, was given to the school by this exercise, and the interest increased from year to year. It was spoken of as a delightful employment for the young. A superintendent, in 1837, says: —

"An employment which, if engaged in with correct motives and feelings, seems more than any other exercise on earth to place us by the very side of those who have tuned their harps on high, and are now singing the song of Moses and the Lamb. Why may not infant voices, here in the Sabbath school, be made to catch the strain, and praise — as the redeemed will praise in heaven — the Lamb their Redeemer!"

Another says: —

"After the concert is over, you will hear aged fathers and mothers exclaim, 'Did you ever hear anything like it? How the little creatures did sing!'"

In order to make this interesting exercise effective for good, the children should be reminded that the singing in the Sabbath school is not a mere musical concert or singing school, but that it is a religious exercise no less than praying; and that it is as improper to be thoughtless and irreverent in our songs as in our prayers. It is the words we are to think of, and not merely the tune.

A little mission Sabbath school boy, as he took a seat in the car, began to hum to himself, "We'll anchor by and by." When asked what that meant, he answered reverently, "I suppose, sir, it means that we shall rest in heaven." He was humming that Sabbath school song not merely for the music, but also for the words.

Two or three hundred little children at a Sabbath school convention, all arrayed as for the opera, sang, —

> "The angels are coming,
> Don't you hear them?"

Almost the whole audience was affected, not a few to tears, but many of those thoughtless little fairies were nudging each other, looking about and laughing, without the least evidence that they thought of what they were singing; and in this, it is to be feared, they have the example of many older singers.

Then, in many of our schools, comparatively few of the boys engage in this delightful service. A proper attention to these two things on the part of superintendents and teachers — more thoughtfulness and reverence in this exercise, and the enlisting of the boys and all the members of the school to take part in it — would make this exercise a great power for good in our Sabbath schools.

In some of our schools, at the present time, it is the practice to sing, at least once, from the book used in the church. This practice will serve to prepare the scholars, as they come forward in life, to take part in the singing, in public worship, either in choir or in congregational singing, as the case may be.

Most of the young are now taught to sing in the public schools. Then, in many of our Sabbath schools, there are those who are accustomed to meet the members, before or after the regular sessions, for practice. All this attention to this beautiful science ought to furnish the church with all needed help in the service of song.

XIX.

TEACHING THE CHILDREN TEMPERANCE.

> "The drunkards will never be dead,
> And I'll tell you the reason why:
> The young ones they'll grow up
> Before the old ones die."

THE jolly soldier who added this chorus to all his bacchanalian songs understood what he sung. There is philosophy in his words. He well knew, if all the children and youth of the land could be enlisted in the cause of temperance, the drunkards would all die out with this generation, and intemperance, with all its woes, would disappear. Many believe this can be done, — at least, that by this method a vast amount of good can be effected.

In 1829, a correspondent of the "Sabbath School Visitant and Magazine" said: —

"I perceive, by the New York papers, that something considerable is doing by the Sunday schools in that city in aid of the cause of temperance. And surely, if any cause of public concernment demands the entire co-operation of this humble yet powerful institution, it is the cause of temperance. Our efforts heretofore have had in view only those above the age of childhood. It was well to begin there; but if we stop there, we leave the work more than half undone. Our children may exhibit, when they arrive at maturity, the sad reverse of all our reformation. If we would lay the axe at the root of this devastating evil, we must plant an abhorrence of it in the minds of the young. We must make upon their minds such an impression of the evil of intemperance, as that ardent spirits shall forever be associated in their thoughts with all that is detestable in conduct or horrible in crime."

The Massachusetts Sabbath School Society, from its organization in 1832, by its various publications, and visits to the churches and Sabbath schools, has been laboring for this object. Some of the most interesting and effective temperance publications of the times have been found among its books.

At first, the plan was to enlist the members of the Sabbath schools, so far as possible, in the parish or town temperance society; then "juvenile temperance" or "total abstinence" societies were formed; then "cold water armies;" and now these temperance organizations for the young are often called "Bands of Hope."

In 1832, a juvenile temperance society was formed in one of our Sabbath schools, which embraced almost all the youth. They held frequent meetings during the intermission on the Sabbath, and they purchased and distributed publications of different kinds on temperance; and it is confidently hoped that all the youth trained up in this way will be secured against this great evil of intemperance.

The Essex Street Sabbath school in Boston reported in 1836 that they had formed a "juvenile temperance society," and enrolled in it one hundred and fifty of the scholars, with the consent of the parents. In 1837, many schools in different parts of Massachusetts reported that nearly all the members were connected with temperance societies. The school in Pepperell, in 1838, reported one hundred and fifty under fifteen years of age, members of the "juvenile temperance society."

In 1839, special efforts in promotion of the temperance cause were made in the Tabernacle Sabbath school, Salem; and more than seven thousand signatures to the temperance pledge were obtained by the pupils of that school. Thirty members of the infant classes obtained from three to one hundred and fifty names each. In Granby, in 1842, the "Cold Water Army" connected with the Congregational Sabbath school numbered about three hundred. Thus early in the temperance movement were efforts made to enlist the young.

The following incidents show that young children can thoroughly understand the total abstinence principles: One little boy's definition of temperance was, "Not to drink any rum, and but very little cider." Another one's definition of total abstinence was, "Not to taste the first drop." A little boy, hardly able to speak plain, when asked if he did not intend to drink any cider, should his father ask him to, quickly replied, "No, because I am a totaler."

A little boy of six years, whose older brothers had joined the temperance society, came to his father one evening, when there was to be a temperance address, and made this original but significant request.

"Pa, I want to be temperanced." His father understood his wishes, but told him he felt unable to go out with him to the meeting that evening. But the little fellow's entreaties to be temperanced were so importunate that they prevailed, and his father accompanied him to the meeting. After the address, the lad's name was set to the pledge of total abstinence, and he was thus temperanced to his entire satisfaction. And he understood, too, what it meant to be temperanced.

"Mother," said little Charley, "there is going to be a temperance meeting this evening, and father has had an invitation to go; and I want to go too. May I, mother?"

"Yes, my child, you may go if your father does."

"Mother, you look very sick, but I guess you will be well when father comes home, for he has been talking with a gentleman about drinking rum, and father almost cried; and I think they are going to do something. I mean to make father go; mayn't I, mother?"

"If you think it will make him any better, you may."

"You need not be afraid about that, mother, for the gentleman said it would make him a great deal better."

So little Charley went to the meeting. About nine o'clock, the door opened, and in ran the little boy, almost out of breath, exclaiming, "Mother, mother, father is going to be a good man,—he is, mother. They have made him write his name on a piece of paper which they call the temperance pledge. Now, mother, I guess he won't be so cross nights, and break all the cups and saucers, and behave so like a madman. Ain't you better, mother?"

"Yes, my child; if this be true, I am well."

"If he acts like my little brother,—be good a little while, and then be bad,—I mean to go and find that gentleman, and ask him to come and see him, and talk to him, and make him a good man."

"Well, my child, I hope with all my heart that you will succeed."

And he did succeed. And may the Lord bless him, and all others who try to reform.

Here is a child's pledge: —

"Good people, old and young, in all parts of the world, are joining the temperance cause. And why should not I? Have I not a right to? I hope I have. I will join. Here, then, with heart and hand, I put my name, and declare myself a friend of temperance, — an enemy of all intoxicating drinks. I will say No to every drop. Those who will may laugh, but I hope never to be ashamed of my resolution. May the great Being above aid me!"

The ministry of children has often been of great service in the temperance cause in enlisting other children, and also older persons, and even their parents, and in reclaiming the intemperate.

This is strikingly illustrated in the following incident, which occurred some twenty-five or thirty years ago: —

A female teacher, feeling a desire to do something for the cause of Christ, resolved to collect some poor children into a Sabbath school, where they might receive religious instruction, of which they and their parents were then entirely ignorant. The first family she visited was that of a poor, miserable drunkard. His wife and children, and everything around them, bore the marks of poverty, degradation, and wretchedness. They had four small children, only two of whom, Martha, of six years, and her little brother Francis, of four, were old enough to attend school. After learning that clothes would be furnished for them, the father consented to let his children attend. They soon became deeply interested in learning about the Saviour. Although they lived a mile from church, they were usually first at school. Martha was taken sick, and for some time deprived of the privileges of her school. One morning, as she began to recover, she appeared unusually pleased on receiving a visit from her teacher. "The children," said the mother, "have been almost impatient for you to come; they have a new plan in view. For a few days past their thoughts and conversations have been about the temperance society. Martha has come to the conclusion that she can live all her days without tasting another drop, and wants to sign the pledge. I have tried to put them off by telling them I did not know that children so young were permitted to join. But they would not give it up."

Said Martha, "O, I think if mother and Francis and myself join, we can persuade father to."

"Francis," said their teacher, "do you think you can always refuse the sweet bottom of the glass when your father offers it?" "Yes; I will stick and hang as long as I live." Their names were taken, and they were requested to get their associates to join with them. Martha at once exclaimed, "I will see H. C——; I guess I can get her to join, for her mother drinks as much as pa does, and the little children surely suffer for victuals and clothes. O, mother, I wish we could get them to join the temperance society."

As soon as she was well enough to walk out, she went to the house of Mrs. C——. She first enlisted little H. in the cause; then they told the mother about it, and entreated her to join. She was awakened by the earnest solicitations of these children; and they did not leave her until she had promised to think of the subject. At the end of three days she put her name to the pledge, and ever since has been a temperate woman.

Encouraged by past success, they commenced the work at home. They not only begged of their father to put away the poisonous stuff, but daily, in secret and at his side, they prayed that God would give him a new heart, that he might love and serve Him on earth, and be prepared to dwell in heaven; Francis, in particular, would kneel by him and earnestly beg God to give them all new hearts, and save his poor father from the drunkard's grave.

Whenever the father came home at night under the influence of intoxicating liquor, cross and angry, his mouth was shut when he saw his little son kneeling with his Bible before him, begging that he would repent, for no drunkard could enter the kingdom of heaven. By the decision and zeal of his children he was silenced and confounded. Neither by flattery nor persuasion could they be made to taste one drop of ardent spirit, or even to take water from a glass where it had been used. One night little Francis was taken suddenly ill. His father arose and brought him some water. He no sooner took it than he exclaimed, "It is in your rum-tumbler; I can't take it!" When he was so sick that he was not expected to live, he refused to have rum applied externally, because he had signed the pledge.

The prayers of these children have been heard and answered, for many months have elapsed since this once miserable drunkard has tasted the poison; and it is hoped the prayer they now offer will also be heard, and that he will yet be seen "clothed and in his right mind, sitting at the feet of Jesus."

A LITTLE TEMPERANCE TALK TO THE YOUNG.

When I was a boy, it used to be a great wonder to me why the rivers did not all run out. Have you never felt a similar wonder? You stand on the banks of the Connecticut, for example, and see that immense body of water rolling past you; and thus it has been rolling for generations, for centuries. Now why does not the water all run out, and the river become dry?

In the town of Glover, Vt., there was a pond, some years ago, from which a small stream ran that carried a mill. Some men, one day, cut a small place to increase the stream. The bank through which they cut proved to be quicksand; and suddenly it gave way, and the whole pond ran out, and left nothing but a very small brook. The road now passes right through where the pond was. They call it the " Runaway Pond."

Now why do not the rivers run away in the same manner? Most of you probably know that, although the source of rivers may be of a small spring, or a small pond or lake, yet all along, on either side, there are smaller rivers, streams, brooks, and tiny rills, constantly running into them. Now if we could cut off all these smaller streams, and thus stop the supplies, the rivers would run out and become dry.

Young friends, do you know that there is a mighty river rolling its dark and bitter waters through our land, and is carrying destruction and woe wherever it flows? It is the river of intemperance. And many good people feel alarmed, because they think this river is becoming more and more swollen, and that it is threatening a more fearful desolation than ever before.

They are now asking in what way this river can be dried up. Like other rivers, there are numerous smaller streamlets constantly running into it. The only way, then, is to cut off these supplies, and let it run out and dry up.

Some one says, "Drunkards are drinking young men grown up." There, then, is where drunkards come from. To stop the increase of drunkards, then, we must cut off the supply; we must have no more "drinking young men." But how can we prevent this? Where do the "drinking young men" come from. Why, they are large boys grown up; and large boys are made out of little boys. Large boys and little boys, and large girls and little girls, are the springs, the little rills, the sources, from whence drinking young men and drinking young women come who grow up into drunkards.

Now, young friends, is it not quite plain what we are to do if we wish to cut off all supplies to this river of Intemperance, and let it dry up? In other words, if we would let the old drunkards die off, and have no more to take their place, there must be no more sipping little boys and girls to become tippling large boys and girls, to grow into drinking young men and women; then there will be nobody to grow up into drunkards. Is not that just as plain as that the stopping of all little streams will dry up the rivers, or preventing all little fires will prevent all large ones?

Now, boys and girls, good people who have become so alarmed at the increase of intemperance the past few years, are making an effort to stop it, just in the way I have been describing, — by cutting off all the supplies, — preventing, if possible, every boy and girl in the land from beginning to sip and drink, so that there shall be no more "drinking young men" and women to grow up into drunkards.

What do you say to this, young friends? Are you willing to unite with us in this work? Are you willing to aid in preventing all that sorrow and woe that darken the homes and settle down upon the hearts of the wives and children of poor drunkards?

If you would take for your next Sabbath's lesson what the Bible says about drunkards, strong drink, &c., you would be alarmed at the greatness of this sin of intemperance. And no one who tastes or touches or handles the intoxicating cup is safe. All drunkards were once moderate drinkers; no one ever meant to become a drunkard.

The only safety, then, is to resolve, with the little boy, "not to taste the first drop." Will not all in this Sabbath school make that resolve, as a New Year's gift to the cause of temperance? Such a resolve may not only save you from personal danger, but it will influence others in the work of cutting off the supply of drunkards, so that our land may no longer be called a "land of drunkards."

As I have been "reasoning of temperance," have any of my young friends trembled, in view of the danger from this evil? Then do not, like Felix, say, "Go thy way for this time," but resolve now never to taste, touch, or handle any thing that will intoxicate.

PRIZE COMPOSITIONS.

A few years ago, a total abstinence society in this state, with which we were connected, offered prizes to the scholars in our high and grammar schools for the best compositions on the "Evils of Intemperance, and the Remedy." In two years, seven thousand scholars, in one hundred and fifty towns, accepted the offer, and wrote on this subject; and one hundred and eighty prizes, of from two dollars to ten dollars, were awarded.

This plan is, in some respects, one of the most important ones ever adopted in connection with the interests of temperance. It is beginning at the right place, with the young. All these five thousand children and youth who have written on the subject, have committed themselves to the cause. The very effort they have made to describe and illustrate the evils of intemperance, and to point out the remedy, has impressed them as no temperance lecture could have done.

The amount of reading on the subject has been truly wonderful. All the books on the subject, in the Sabbath school and public libraries, have been sought for; and messages have been sent to the city for works on temperance and intemperance. There has been much conversation in the family, and all the knowledge of parents, and older brothers and sisters, and friends, has been laid under contribution to aid in this work. This has awakened new interest in the subject in these families, and especially in those in which prizes have been obtained. A prize of ten dollars was obtained by the daughter of an intemperate father, who in consequence has been reformed. All the members of these schools have also had their attention turned especially to the subject.

Then, in nearly every town where these prizes have been given, there have been held public meetings, at which the prize compositions have been read and the prizes publicly presented to the successful competitors, followed by addresses. These meetings in some instances have been very largely attended. The people seemed to have felt honored in the honor conferred upon their sons and daughters.

Then the society is selecting some of the more interesting of these prize articles for publication in pamphlets, and also in permanent volumes. The committee of award were greatly surprised at the merit of many of these compositions, especially from the high schools. They would do credit to much older and wiser persons. While the subject of all was the same, there was great variety in the manner of treating it. Most spoke of the evils of intemperance upon the community, the family, and the individual. Some of the papers were replete with sound, logical argument; some contained touching illustrations, and some an array of statistical facts. Most referred, in presenting the remedy, to the "woman's movement," some with hearty approval, others with doubts and hesitation; some were for the most stringent prohibition, and others would rely wholly on moral means; some would abolish the manufacture of spirits entirely, and others felt that the remedy of this great evil must be principally in the right training of the young.

Many of the papers were long enough for a sermon, and showed a great amount of research and earnest thought.

The result of all this cannot be otherwise than most salutary in its influence upon the writers, the families, the schools, and the communities where this plan has been adopted.

Some there may be — and even many — who, in after life, when appetite or companions have tempted them, have broken away from their early pledges. They may have quieted their consciences by saying that they took the pledge when they were so young they did not understand what they were doing, and hence they ought not to be held by it. Be this as it may, there can be no doubt that vast numbers have been protected by their early pledges, and by what they then learned about the evil of intemperance, from the snares of this destroyer.

It is true that great care and judgment should be used on this subject. No child should be encouraged to sign any pledge till he has been thoroughly instructed as to its meaning and solemnity. It should be remembered that children are creatures of imitation; that they are sympathetic and impulsive. But, with due care, they can be confirmed very early in the right way.

The late Rev. Dr. Alexander said, "It is the children — the children — that we want; for are they not the stuff that states are made of?" No wonder some communities, cities, and states, with their rulers, judges, and citizens, are so bad, considering the bad stuff, the poor material, they have been made of. But a whole generation of children and youth, pledged to temperance and virtue, would be splendid stuff out of which to make splendid states. Then —

"The drunkards *will* be dead,
And I'll tell you the reason why:
Young 'totalers' they'll grow up
As fast as the drunkards die."

XX.

SABBATH SCHOOL CONVENTIONS, CELEBRATIONS, AND PICNICS.

In September, 1855, one thousand Sabbath school teachers of Massachusetts, in answer to an invitation from the teachers in New York and Brooklyn, visited those cities. They were received in the Crystal Palace, where were gathered many thousand children connected with the various charitable institutions — the Orphan and Half Orphan Asylums, Home for the Friendless, Mission Schools, &c., who were addressed by some of the visitors.

Meetings were held in each city for social interviews among the friends of Sabbath schools, and for the discussion of various practical subjects connected with the Sabbath school work. This gathering greatly stimulated all who participated in it in their labors in this cause. The teachers from Massachusetts returned with fresh zeal and interest in promoting the efficiency of their respective schools.

Soon after this, Sabbath school conventions began to be held in different states, and now they have become quite common. When they first commenced, many supposed they were a new thing, the outgrowth and evidence of special interest and progress in the Sabbath school work. But, so far from being new, it was but the revival of a plan that had had its day, and a day of great success, and been discontinued.

The Worcester North Conference Sabbath School Society held a Sabbath school convention in 1833. The next year it held a similar convention at Templeton. All the schools but one belonging to that county society were represented by delegates. The forenoon was occupied in hearing reports from the various schools, most of which had enjoyed revivals. About forty connected with the school in Athol had been hopefully converted; thirty-three in Gardner, eight of whom were between the ages of seven and ten; a whole class of twelve or fourteen young men, and all but ten of the Misses from twelve to twenty years of age, were among the number; forty in Phillipston, six between the ages of seven and ten; thirty in Templeton; and one hundred in Ashburnham.

A convention of the friends of Sabbath schools within the limits of Middlesex South Conference was held on the 18th and 19th of August, 1835, at Hopkinton. There was a very general representation of the ministers, superintendents, and delegates from the various schools and churches. The exercises of the convention were almost precisely like those of the conventions of the present day: dissertations, essays, and discussions on various subjects, as "Obligations of the church to sustain the Sabbath school;" "Duties of teachers and superintendents;" "How shall the library be rendered in the highest degree useful?" "Importance of a department for the instruction of teachers;" (and that in 1835! Is there any thing new under the sun?) "The cultivation of a spirit of systematic benevolence in children, with special reference to the efforts of the day;" "Plan for infant children's meetings;" "The importance of systematizing truth in Sabbath school instruction;" "How shall unconverted parents be made to feel an interest in the Sabbath school?" "How shall a Sabbath school be induced to read the Bible?" &c.

At two o'clock P. M., on Wednesday, the children, to the number of about three hundred, were collected into the body of the house and addressed.

Practical resolutions were also discussed and adopted. And in the discussions on some of these topics fifteen or twenty persons took part.

Essex County Congregational Sabbath School Society held a convention in 1835, and in the account of it published in the periodical of the Massachusetts Sabbath School Society at the time, there is an earnest appeal for all the county societies of the state to hold such conventions.

A convention of the Sabbath schools in Kennebec County, Maine, was held at Hallowell in 1836, which was a meeting of great interest. Delegates were present from eleven towns. Several dissertations were read on specific questions, and sixteen resolutions were presented, accompanied with interesting and appropriate remarks. There were thirty-seven schools reported from seventeen towns.

The same year, on the 24th of August, Worcester Harmony Conference Sabbath School Society held a convention at Grafton, at which most of the schools belonging to the society were represented by delegates, and there was a large attendance of pastors, superintendents, teachers, and friends of the cause.

Among the subjects which elicited animated and

useful discussions were the following: "What are the objects to be arrived at in Sabbath school instruction?" "What are the obstacles to success?" "How can the church be made to take a deeper interest in Sabbath schools?" "How can the coöperation of parents, and the attendance of adults generally, be secured?" "What are the peculiar and appropriate qualifications of teachers, and what are their most prominent deficiencies?" &c. The next annual convention of this same society discussed, with great interest and effect, several other equally practical subjects.

In all the exercises of these early conventions there was the greatest harmony. It is pleasant, at the present time, when such meetings have become so common through the country, to look back and see how perfectly those of more than thirty years ago correspond, in most particulars, with those of to-day.

There is one respect in which they differed from many of the present conventions, and in which, we think, they had the advantage. They were generally confined to the schools of a single county or conference, and were consequently less unwieldy; and they were also confined to a single denomination, and were consequently more unrestrained and harmonious. We have attended two state union conventions, where the best part of two sessions was occupied in an excited and somewhat bitter discussion of a remonstrance sent in by one denomination that they were not properly represented on the offices of the convention! At another state union convention, an Episcopal minister, well known as intensely denominational, delivered an earnest essay in vindication of the rite of infant baptism. At the same time the Baptists of that association were holding, in the same city, a Sabbath school convention of their own. Then there are always some strongly sectarian persons at such union meetings, who seem inclined to gain *eclat* by a special show of liberality, and they are ever referring, in their prayers or addresses, to " this delightful scene of union, where we can meet on this broad Christian platform our brethren of different denominations," &c. All this " unpleasantness " is avoided, and the meetings are less expensive, and much more effective for good, when confined to a smaller number of schools and those of a single denomination.

For several years past the Baptist churches of Massachusetts, and the Congregational churches of Hanover, Marshfield, Scituate, and Woburn conference, have adopted this plan of denominational conventions, and with the greatest success. These meetings are a sort of reunion of those especially interested in the work; and there is the utmost freedom and earnestness in the discussion of all practical subjects relating to the interests of their own denomination. A long experience and careful observation have led us to the belief that denominational conventions are always the most interesting and effective.

More than forty years ago many of those interested in the right training of the young became alarmed at the noisy, riotous, and irrational manner in which many were celebrating our national independence. The influences of such celebrations were seen to be injurious to the moral training of the young.

This state of feeling led to the more appropriate and delightful mode of commemorating the anniversary of our nation's freedom by Sabbath school celebrations, where the young were instructed in the great principles of civil and moral freedom. In the year 1836 there were eight or ten such celebrations among the schools connected with the Massachusetts Sabbath School Society, some of them embracing most of the children and youth from thirty or forty schools. In some cases they were Sabbath school and juvenile temperance celebrations.

Everything was done, by singing, addresses, and various entertainments, that could be, to make these occasions interesting and profitable to all present.

For many years a large number of schools observed the Fourth of July in this manner, and, in many cases, at the time of the celebration, or on some Sabbath near, took up an "independence offering," to aid in establishing and sustaining Sabbath schools in the destitute sections of the country.

In 1844, these celebrations were very numerous, and they passed off with much interest; and the improvements in the manner of commemorating the birthday of our national independence, within five or ten years, was truly wonderful.

In some cases Independence Day was made the occasion of a general canvass of the parish or town to get in new scholars.

In 1834, several schools were greatly enlarged by a general visitation of all the families within the limits of the parish on the Fourth of July. Large committees were chosen, who employed the day in presenting the claims of Sabbath schools in every dwelling, and in inviting every man, woman, and child to become members. Wherever this experiment was tried, the results were most happy. Classes of adults were formed, and children and youth from the highways and hedges were "compelled to come in." The committee themselves, by their very efforts, were made more active and faithful teachers. In one family visited there were the parents and fourteen children. None of them attended the Sabbath school, though efforts had often been made to secure their attendance. This Fourth-of-July visit, however, proved successful in gaining the permission of the parents for some of the children to go. Soon they became much interested in the school. A new child was fitted out every Sabbath, till most of them were enrolled as members. Ere long those parents and several of their children were hoping in the mercy of God.

In the same year, the Sabbath school society in one town, embracing the different evangelical schools, chose forty-one persons to visit, on the Fourth of July, every family in town. Each visitor had his particular field allotted to him, containing from six to ten families, and in such connection as to make the work of visiting light. Every individual, adults and children, was to be invited to attend the Sabbath school, leaving it for each one to decide where.

The result was most gratifying. In some families, where, at least, much indifference was supposed to exist, some of the visitors were rebuked for having so long neglected this department of duty, and urged to come again.

This undertaking made all the families acquainted with the fact that they might avail themselves of the advantages of a Sabbath school. It served to make the teachers — and most of the visitors were such — acquainted with the field of their labors. It showed that God is with them that devise and execute liberal things, and that he will not fail to water them that labor to water others.

These Fourth-of-July celebrations and visitations, so common years ago, it is believed might be revived, with very great benefit to the young and to the cause of Sabbath schools, at the present day.

Within the past fifteen or twenty years, Sabbath school picnics and excursions have become a prominent feature of most of our Sabbath schools. Many of the members of the schools in our cities and large towns find this the only opportunity through the whole year to visit the country and breathe its pure and invigorating air, and gaze upon the fresh grass and beautiful flowers with which our Heavenly Father has clothed and decorated the hills and the valleys, and upon the trees of the wood as they clap their hands.

If these excursions and annual gatherings in the woods are properly directed, they may be made very useful. They may be the means, not only of keeping up an interest in the school, but of bringing in new scholars. They will show the children, too, that, at a proper time, and in a proper manner, the church, their pastor and teachers, as well as their parents, are glad to please and entertain them to make them happy. When they see this, they may be more ready to make returns by their constant and interested attendance on the instructions of the school.

This feature of our Sabbath school is, to a great extent, comparatively a modern one. Though there are not wanting individual cases of something like this.

One measure in A——, more than forty-five years ago, which produced a great amount of good feeling, both among parents and scholars, and did much for the interests of the school, was the following : An invitation was given to all the girls under sixteen years of age, who belonged to the school, and those who would unite with it within two weeks, to make the wife of their pastor some social, religious visits. These visits were made on different days, and by three divisions. First, all under eight years of age; second, those between eight and twelve ; and third, those between twelve and sixteen. At the three meetings, eighty were present. They were entertained by infant and Sabbath school anecdotes, familiar religious instruction, &c. Some of the first division were asked if they belonged to the school ? They answered, " No, ma'am." They were then told that none were expected at the meeting but Sabbath school scholars.

" But," said the little girls, " we are going to the Sabbath school." The next Sabbath, a new class had to be formed. A similar invitation was given to the boys under sixteen years of age, to make their pastor a visit. When the hour arrived, sixty were present. It was a season of peculiar interest, and profit to the children, and was long remembered.

XXI.

EVILS RESULTING FROM SABBATH SCHOOLS.

The institution of Sabbath schools, though it has proved to be a great blessing to the young and to the world, like most good things, can be perverted, and there are some who do pervert it. One evil resulting from this institution, apprehended and even complained of as already existing, is, that parents are making it a substitute for parental instruction — that they are throwing off responsibility upon the teachers.

So far as this is the case, a note of alarm and of warning ought to be given, and it should be sounded loud enough to startle the slumbering conscience of every parent who is guilty in this matter.

But no one surely can regard the evil here spoken of as necessarily incident to this institution. The evil exists only where the institution is perverted. Sabbath schools are designed only as an auxiliary — a help to parents in the religious instruction of their children. It is not intended to lessen one iota of the parent's responsibleness in this work, but only to aid him, — to supplement, so far as may be, his efforts.

In reference to far the larger portion of the young, it is true — however lamentable the fact — that the Sabbath school is the only source of personal religious instruction they have, except so far as they receive it from their pastors. They either have no parents — they are orphans — or they have such as concern not themselves with the religious education of their children. Sabbath school or not, it is all the same to them. To these multitudes of the young, surely no one will object that this institution comes forward with the kind offices of the faithful, pious parent.

The only ground of apprehension is, that pious parents are transferring their responsibilities to the teachers of the Sabbath school. And so far as this is the case, it is a serious evil, and it is a most unnatural evil.

Sabbath schools a substitute for parental instruction! Why, a parent may as well transfer to this institution his obligation to maintain prayer and communion with God in secret, or good works before men. If he is to throw off his obligation to teach his children the fear of the Lord, and to bring them up in his nurture and admonition, and to watch for their souls as those that must give account, he may as well hire a family priest, and commit to him the whole care of his own, and the salvation of his household, and give himself no more concern or solicitude for anything but the present life. And indeed this would be a far better course than to give up the religious instruction of his children to a Sabbath school teacher, who could meet those children only one hour in a week; for the priest could more fully meet the requirement, "Thou shalt teach them diligently unto thy children, and shalt talk of them when thou sittest in thine house, and when thou walkest by the way, and when thou liest down, and when thou risest up."

It is not merely for the good of the children that God has placed this work in the hands of parents, but it is for the personal good of parents themselves. Nothing will more rapidly promote the parent's own growth in grace than the prayers and instructions which deep parental solicitude will call forth. All this inestimable good to the parent is lost entirely when he gives up his individual responsibility in the religious instruction of his children to the Sabbath school teacher. The institutions of the gospel are in harmony with each other. Jerusalem is builded as a city that is compact together. The buildings, closely joined together, strengthen each other; and the citizens, pursuing their various avocations, all help one another. Thus the ministry of the word encourages the Sabbath school, and the Sabbath school helps to gather the young to the house of God and prepare them to understand and receive the word of life. Religion in the family also helps the teachers and scholars of the Sabbath schools in their duties, and the teachers add their prayers and faithful teachings to aid parents in the training of their children.

In the days of our Puritan fathers, the afternoon public exercise on the Sabbath was, in some cases, a catechetical one; but this was never understood to supersede faithful catechising in the family, but rather presupposed it. And so, now, we would have every family to be as much as possible a Sabbath school. If our Sabbath schools flourish, such family religion will flourish; and if such family religion flourishes, Sabbath schools will flourish also. The influence will be reciprocal.

An extensive observation for many years shows that those parents who are most faithful in family instruction are the most faithful and successful teachers in the

Sabbath school. And the most numerous, the largest, and the most flourishing Sabbath schools are in localities where there is the most constant preaching of the gospel, where there are the largest churches, and where families may be supposed to maintain the best Christian order. The church should be a city compact together; the family, the ministry, the Sabbath school, and all our institutions of benevolence, morality, and religion, should stand close, compact together.

But the Sabbath school, as an auxiliary, no parent will be in any great danger of overestimating. Properly viewed, it will be found to increase, rather than lessen, the obligations and responsibilities of parents. It will furnish favorable opportunities for personal conversation with children, and greatly aid the faithful parent in this important duty, which is so much neglected by many.

Another evil in connection with our Sabbath schools, of which many complain, and, it is feared, have reason to complain, is that many scholars are acquiring the habit of studying the Bible superficially, or of neglecting a suitable preparation of their lessons. The nature of this evil may be exhibited by a single fact.

The Sabbath school bell had rung, and James had found his Bible and question book, and was just ready to start for school.

"James," said one to him, "you had better leave your Bible at home; you will not need that at school."

"O, yes, I shall; I shall want it to find the references."

"But you ought to have looked those all out and committed them to memory in getting your lesson, so that you could recite them without the Bible."

"But our teacher lets us read them. We never look them out till we get to school, and the teacher asks the questions."

This boy, it was found, seldom looked at his lesson at all till he came to recite. And the teacher did not require his scholars to commit any of the lessons to memory. All they did was merely to look out the references, and read them as the teacher asked the questions.

Here is, indeed, a very serious evil. Should it become general, it would render the whole system of Sabbath school instruction comparatively worthless. What would be the value of our public schools if conducted in this manner? The Sabbath school certainly promises but very little good to any where there is not, on the part of superintendent, teachers, and pupils, thorough and earnest study of the lesson. It is a school, and that implies study.

Another growing evil of our times, resulting from Sabbath schools, is the non-attendance of children upon the public services of the sanctuary.

There has been no one thing that has caused so much anxiety among great numbers of good people, as this evil, which has been so rapidly developed the past few years. In various ways the note of alarm has been given, but the evil goes on with increasing strength. In many of our large congregations scarcely a score of children will be seen at public worship. They attend the Sabbath school, and then turn their backs on the sanctuary and go to their homes; thus we are training up a generation of church neglecters.

Till within comparatively a few years, one of our favorite, and, as we thought, most persuasive arguments, in commending this institution as an auxiliary to the church, has been that the Sabbath school is increasing the number of those who attend on her ministry. Whole families and whole neighborhoods, we have been wont to say, through the influence of this institution, are allured to the sanctuary. But now the Sabbath school is taking away from the house of God most of the children and youth even of Christian families, and leaving only a worshipping assembly of adults. We no longer see, as in former times, households, whole families of parents and children, going in company to worship God, as the Israelites went up in tribes to the temple.

Our children are thus losing all the interesting associations of childhood connected with the sanctuary. Who can estimate the happy influence of the habit formed in early life, of frequenting the sanctuary every Sabbath day? There can be no substitute for a constant and regular attendance by young and old, on the preaching of the gospel. Nothing can compensate for the loss of it.

It should be remembered that the pastor is ordained just as much the pastor of the children and youth, as of their parents. He is the shepherd of the lambs not less than of the sheep; and nothing except the parents should come between him and the lambs of his flock. We have often said to the young, and shall continue to say in the most emphatic manner, " If you cannot go to but one, — the church or the Sabbath school, — go to church, whatever becomes of the Sabbath school."

What if the children do not comprehend all, or even but a small part of the sermon? Will any one say they are not to be encouraged to learn anything they do not fully understand? How many of them, then, must give up the study of grammar, and geography, and arithmetic, and philosophy, till they are capable of fully understanding them? The importance of these studies, and the full meaning of everything connected with them, they cannot, of course, understand yet, as they will by and by; and much of the instruction from the pulpit they may not now comprehend as they will when their minds become more enlightened and their understandings more enlarged. And yet who has not often recalled, in after life, what he heard in the house of God in his childhood, but did not then understand, and found it of inestimable value? The wicked sea-captain, in his last sickness while at sea, some will remember, recalled the answer to the question, "What is justification?" which he learned in childhood without understanding a word of it, and by those wondrous truths, now all made plain by the Spirit of God, he was cheered in the dying hour with the hope that through faith in the righteousness of Jesus Christ he had obtained justification.

But little children do hear and understand more than we sometimes think.

A little girl five years old, in the neighborhood of Boston, attended church with her parents, a few weeks since. The text was in Rev. ii. 4: "Nevertheless I have somewhat against thee, because thou hast left thy first love."

"Well, what would a child of five years be likely to understand on such a subject?"

On Monday her parents had some little conflict of opinion on some subject, and when the father had gone, the child said, "Mother, you mustn't forget what the minister said yesterday, about leaving your first love!"

A minister, as he took his leave of a family in his parish, which he was visiting, placed his hand on the head of a little child about two years old, and said a word respecting the Saviour.

"That child," interrupted the mother, "does not understand anything about that subject."

How little did that mother suspect that this single remark of her minister, was fixing an important truth in the mind of her child, never to be effaced!

Some months after this interview, the minister was in another family, and was told that this little child had just been there on a visit, and one day said to them, —

"The minister has been to our house, and he told me that Jesus Christ came into the world to die for little children!"

This incident shows that children, at a very early age, often notice and treasure up whatever they hear on religious subjects; and it should encourage parents to commence the religious instruction of their children early.

Children who can attend the public school six days in the week and six hours a day, and then be all fresh for their sports, surely can attend the Sabbath school, and at least one service at church, one day in a week, without any alarming weariness.

Another subject that should be referred to in this connection, is the want of proper reverence in the house of God, that is sometimes manifested by those children and youth who do attend public worship.

We do not wish the young to have any superstitious regard for the sanctuary; but there is a reverence and a decorum of manners that they always should manifest in the house of God. All play and levity should be avoided. Such conduct is profaning a sacred place.

No boy would think of entering a gentleman's parlor without removing his hat, and maintaining propriety of conduct. Certainly as much regard to proper behavior should be shown when he enters the holy place that has been dedicated to the worship of the great God.

The Psalmist says, "Holiness becometh thine house, O Lord, forever."

The wise man says, "Keep thy foot when thou goest to the house of God."

And the apostle says, "Attend upon the Lord without distraction." "Let all things be done decently and in order."

Complaints have been made that some children and youth, even members of the Sabbath school, when entering the house of God, or warming themselves around the register, and also during divine service, are not sufficiently careful to maintain that stillness, sobriety, and general reverence and decorum of conduct that becometh the sanctuary of the Most High.

A lesson on this subject can be learned from the heathen.

Plutarch tells us of a Spartan youth who held the censer to Alexander whilst he was sacrificing. A coal fell upon the arm of the youth; and he suffered it to burn there, rather than, by crying, disturb the rites of their heathenish superstition. And yet how many thoughtless youth do many things, even when suffering no pain, that greatly disturb the worship of the holy God!

Many are often grieved to see children and young

persons, in the midst of the services of the sanctuary, engaged in reading their library book, or "Well-Spring," or in some even more improper behavior, in the house of God.

Such conduct is disrespectful to the preacher, often annoying to worshippers around them, and very irreverent towards God. All are pleased to see the young interested in their books and papers at proper times, but never during the services of the sanctuary.

Perhaps this subject should receive the thoughtful attention of the people generally. A traveller in England, some years ago, said, "There is one thing that I see in England everywhere in places of worship, that I long to see in our New England. I allude to the deep, solemn composure all over the congregation at the close of the service, when the benediction is uttered. It lasts for half a minute. Not a head is raised, not a foot stirs, and there is a reverence apparent."

XXII.

THE FAMILY.

Under this general head we have grouped various scenes and incidents connected with the family, that have fallen under our observation, or have been suggested to our thoughts, which, though somewhat miscellaneous and disconnected, are deemed worthy of preservation for the use of others.

RELIGION AND THE FAMILY.

Sin has spread a withering blight over all the relations of life. Nowhere has its influence been more destructive than in the various relations of the family. And still, the united, affectionate family — even where the rains and dews of divine grace have never fallen — is one of the most verdant spots in our world. Here one common bond of sympathy and love binds all hearts together. The dear names of father and mother, brother and sister, are music to each other's ears. Each helps bear the other's burdens. Envy and selfishness seem to have so far yielded to the power of even natural, unsanctified affection, that the happiness of each is to see the others happy. This is, indeed, a comparatively green spot in the midst of a surrounding desert.

But let the rains of heaven be shed down upon this spot, and what a change! A more abundant luxuriance now springs forth on every side, and it is clothed with a far deeper verdure and a far richer beauty. Religion purifies and sweetens all the tender and endearing relations of such a family. It adds a silken cord to the bonds of sympathy and love. It diffuses a softening, hallowed influence among all its members; and makes the good parent, the obedient child, the affectionate brother and sister, the amiable companion, a better parent, a more obedient, loving child, a more affectionate brother or sister, and a more amiable companion. Religion produces such a union of feeling and sentiment that a discordant note seldom mars the harmony of their lives. If one suffer, all suffer alike with him; and if one rejoice, all are made happy.

Religion erects, too, in the pious household, an altar, around which all the members daily assemble with united and joyful hearts. The priest of the household now opens the sacred volume. The world for a little season is dismissed; every passion is hushed, every bosom quieted, every mind awake, and every thought is fixed. The words of eternal life fall upon the ear as if from the lips of the Almighty. The song of praise now unites every voice in sweet melody; then all bow in solemn prayer, and offer incense and a pure offering to their Maker. Here, around this altar, their union and love are most perfect and endearing.

> "Their souls, by love together knit,
> Cemented, mixed in one,
> One hope, one heart, one mind, one voice,
> 'Tis heaven on earth begun."

If there is here below an emblem of the household of the blessed, it surely is the united, affectionate, Christian family. What power there is in that religion which can make such a scene in such a sin-blighted world as this!

And there is efficacy in this religion, could it pervade every heart, to convert every family into such a scene; to sweeten all the relations of kindred and friendship, and to change earth into heaven. God speed the day when all our homes shall be Christian homes.

THE DARK CLOSET.

Mrs. W—— was the mother of ten children. She ever sought by precept, example, and prayer, to bring them up for Him. The salvation of a particular child was sometimes a special burden upon her soul; and more than once, as she believed, a special answer to her importunities in that child's behalf was granted. For many years she has had the great happiness of seeing all her children members of the church of Christ.

The quiet, Christian spirit of that mother, and her fervent prayers in the closet, were her chief sources of religious power over her children. She did not talk with them on the subject of religion directly as much, perhaps, as some mothers do; but there was a religious atmosphere around her at all times. Every child breathed that atmosphere, and felt her influence. They all believed their mother to be a sincere Christian.

One of the sons, when but a lad, became interested in religion. In seeking a place of retirement for his secret devotions, where he would be undisturbed, he thought of a large closet out of the spare chamber. That closet was the repository of blankets, comfortables, and various kinds of bedclothes. It was large, and without any window. When the door was shut, it was total darkness,— no eye but that of "Him who seeth in secret," could behold any one who there sought retirement from the world.

In that dark closet that lad erected his altar for secret prayer; it was his Bethel. And none but God can ever know the Bethel-seasons he there enjoyed, in communing with his Saviour, before he left his home to prepare for the work of the gospel ministry.

Some years since, in one of his visits to his dear old home, as he arose in the morning, he had a desire to visit the dark closet, and see how it would seem to "shut the door and pray to his Father which is in secret," as he was wont to do in his young days. He opened the door, and what a scene greeted his eyes! There in the centre of the closet stood a chair, and before that chair there was a cushion in which were deep prints, where some one evidently was accustomed to kneel in secret prayer. And who could it be? Who but that blessed mother who had prayed all her ten children into the kingdom?

What a hallowed spot did it seem to that son! A thrill of sacred awe came over him, and a voice almost seemed to say, as it did to Moses of old, "Put off thy shoes from off thy feet, for the place whereon thou standest is holy ground."

We gaze with interest upon the desk at which a distinguished author composed his works of world-wide fame; at the studio of a great artist; at the chair where sat a renowned statesman or hero. But what are all these to the prints in that cushion, where knelt that "mother in Israel," in her communings with the Saviour, and where she "had power with God"?

MINISTERS' AND DEACONS' CHILDREN.

Some years ago we were led to make some careful investigations in regard to the children of ministers and deacons, and also of pious parents generally.

The special object of these investigations was to refute — as they did most satisfactorily — the oft-repeated proverb, that "the children of ministers and deacons are worse than other children."

Our inquiries extended to all the families of Orthodox Congregational clergymen and deacons in every town in Massachusetts which we visited in the course of our labors as secretary of the Massachusetts Sabbath School Society, and in the neighboring towns so far as information could be obtained. The results were as follows: —

In two hundred and forty families of ministers and deacons there were eleven hundred and sixty-four children over fifteen years of age. Our faith in regard to the conversion of children under that age, we are sorry to say, was not as strong then as it is now. Of these eleven hundred and sixty-four children, eight hundred and fourteen — about three fourths — were hopefully pious; seven hundred and thirty-two had united with the church; fifty-seven had entered the ministry, or were engaged in their preparatory studies; and only fourteen were dissipated, about one half of whom only became so while residing with their parents. In eleven of these families — four of them ministers' and seven deacons' — there were one hundred and twenty-three children, of whom all but seven were hopefully pious; seven of them were deacons and fifteen ministers. In fifty-six of these eleven hundred and sixty-four families there were two hundred and forty-nine children over fifteen years of age, and all of them were hopefully pious.

Investigations similar to the above, and about the same time, which were made by a gentleman laboring in the Sabbath school cause in the state of Connecticut, include two hundred and seven families of ministers and deacons. In these families there were nine hundred and thirty-seven children over fifteen years of age, of whom six hundred — almost two thirds — gave evidence of piety, and thirty-six of them were in the ministry, or in a course of preparation for it. Twenty were intemperate, but one of the parents of several of them were accustomed to the use of strong drink, or were opposed to the temperance cause. The results of both of these investigations united are as follows: —

In four hundred and forty-eight families there were two thousand one hundred and one children over fifteen years of age, of whom one thousand four hundred and fourteen were hopefully pious; ninety-three were in the ministry or fitting for it; and only thirty-four dissipated! And all the remaining children, with very few exceptions, were respectable and useful citizens.

Can results like these be obtained from the same number of families — taken impartially, as these were — of any class or profession of parents, especially of those who are not professing Christians? How false and unjust, then, the proverb, that "Ministers' and deacons' children are worse than other children."

Leigh Richmond, in his directions to his children, said, "Never lose sight of this, that the more public my name, character, and ministry is become, the more eyes and ears are turned to my children's conduct."

They are expected, in knowledge and circumspection, in religion and morals, in opinions and habits, to show where they have been educated, and to adorn, not only their profession, but their parents' principles.

It is no doubt true that any impropriety of conduct in the child of a minister, or other officer or prominent member of the church, appears worse and becomes more notorious, and indeed may actually be worse, more aggravated, than similar conduct in the child of any other parent. The former child, too, if he become wayward, will probably be more reckless in his waywardness, and plunge deeper into the gulf of sin and ruin, than the latter, because he will have to break over greater barriers in forsaking the path of virtue. But that a larger proportion of the former class of children than of the latter, or anything like as large a proportion, do become wayward, our statistics most clearly show is not in accordance with facts. Indeed, they show that there never was a proverb more unjust and false than the one in regard to this class of children.

The character of the facts presented in these statistics is interesting, probably, beyond the expectations of almost every one; and their interest will be greatly increased if we consider some of the peculiar obstacles with which this class of parents have to contend in the education of their children.

The Sabbath — that day when everything conspires to aid other parents in the religious instruction of their children — is with the minister a day of labor, fatigue, and anxiety; a day in which he can command but little time and but little strength, either of body or mind, to devote to his family.

Again, the employment of the minister is very unlike

that of most other parents, — the farmer, the mechanic, and even the merchant, — which will enable a father often to take his sons with him, and exert an almost constant influence in forming their characters. A large part of his time the minister must be shut out from the world, engaged in severe mental labor that demands his entire and undisturbed attention.

But one of the greatest obstacles with which ministers and deacons both have to contend, in the religious education of their children, is the influence of the irreligious. This obstacle is, indeed, felt to a great extent by all Christian parents.

A clergyman, whose parents were not professedly pious, with whom we once conversed on this subject, said it used to be his daily study and effort, when a school-boy, to persuade or provoke the children of religious parents to do things that he knew were wrong, — to quarrel, and swear, and lie, — thinking that their improper conduct would afford a sort of license to do wrong himself. This kind of influence is exerted peculiarly on the children of ministers and deacons. Deep plans and combinations are often formed to lead them into sin. Who has not witnessed the cruel and fiend-like efforts of these vile wretches who congregate and lounge about the drunkard's resort, to tempt this class of children to taste their cup of shame, or indulge in their other wicked practices, for the purpose of dishonoring the holy religion and the profession of their fathers? So strong is the power of ridicule and shame on an unsanctified heart, that many a youth has been tempted to plunge into open sin, just that he might prove to his wicked associates that his father's title, "parson" or "deacon," which they in ridicule had applied to him, was inappropriate.

These are some of the peculiar obstacles with which this class of parents have to contend; and yet it appears, from the facts contained in our statistics, that a large proportion of their children, through the blessing of God on parental instruction, are hopefully converted; and they are among the most virtuous, respectable, useful members of society. That there have been instances, ever since the days of Eli, the priest of Israel, where some of this class of parents have come short in duty, and where their children have, in consequence, become wayward and profligate, no one will pretend to question; but these instances do not compare, in number, with those that have always been occurring in connection with any other and every other class of parents.

THE CHILDREN OF PIOUS PARENTS.

Several years ago we gathered some facts in regard to the influence of Christian homes very encouraging to pious parents, and not less suggestive and admonitory to irreligious parents. These facts were as follows: —

In one neighborhood there were in all ninety-eight families. Of these families, both parents in twenty-seven were hopefully pious; and of their one hundred and twenty-five children over fifteen years of age, eighty-four, or about two thirds, were hopefully pious. Four of these children were ministers, five deacons, and but one of the forty-one unconverted children was dissipated. But his father, though a professor of religion, was in the daily habit of using intoxicating drink.

In nineteen of these families only one parent in each was professedly pious, and in every case but one that parent was the mother. Of the ninety-five children over fifteen years of age, in these families, thirty-one, or about one third, were hopefully pious, four of whom were ministers of the gospel. Of the sixty-four unconverted children, seven were dissipated; but five of them had the example of dissipated fathers.

In the remaining fifty-two of the ninety-eight families included in the investigation, neither parent gave evidence of piety; and of their one hundred and thirty-nine children over fifteen years of age, only thirteen, or about one tenth, were pious; and not one of these became so while living at home. Twenty-five of the unconverted children were dissipated.

There were two families in that neighborhood in which there were ten children each. The outward circumstances of the families were much the same. They both attended the same meeting on the Sabbath. The parents in one family, while they were moral, kind to the poor, and good neighbors, were not professedly Christians; and not one of their children has ever become personally interested in the subject of religion. The parents of the other family were members of the church. The domestic altar was established when the family was instituted, and it was ever maintained; and all the ten children became members of the church, nearly every one while under age. Three of the sons entered the ministry, and two others studied with the ministry in view, but in the providence of God did not enter that sacred profession; and two of the daughters became the wives of clergymen.

In a town in Maine, some years ago, there were three brothers who resided near each other, all with large families; in two of them there were ten children, and in one eleven. The parents of two of these families, including the one of eleven children, were members of the church of Christ, and maintained family prayers; and they had the satisfaction of seeing all their children " walking in truth," and honoring a Christian profession. The parents in the other family were not professedly pious. They were moral and upright in their dealings with men, observing conscientiously the last six of the ten commandments, but their hearts were not right towards God. They were kind and affectionate to their children, but they did not, by example and instruction, " bring them up in the nurture and admonition of the Lord;" and only one of their ten children gave evidence of having become a child of God, and three of them became wayward and intemperate.

How can we account for facts like these, without acknowledging the power of parental influence?

CONFIDENCE IN THE DIVINE PROMISES.

Mr. C—— and his wife both made a profession of religion soon after their marriage. They maintained the lives of consistent Christians, and were highly respected both as Christians and as neighbors, and were much prospered in the pursuits of life.

Mr. C—— was taken suddenly ill, when about forty years of age, and died, leaving his wife a widow, and his five children fatherless, the eldest of whom was fifteen. As the wife closed the eyes of the companion of her life and the father of her now orphan children, she sunk into her chair, and exclaimed, with unshaken confidence in the divine promises, " Leave thy fatherless children; I will preserve them alive."

Some of the neighbors, who had come in out of respect

to the departed, and to sympathize with the bereaved, said, " What will become of this family of little children ? "

A godly deacon arose, and addressing the people, said: "I believe in the promises of God to such children. See what this mother has just said. These children now have this promise to rest upon ; it did not take effect in their case till their earthly father was taken away. I almost feel willing to become responsible for their future prosperity."

This shows the strong confidence he felt in the promise of God, while others were unbelieving. And the subsequent history of these children showed that his confidence was not misplaced.

The very next year, the eldest child — a son in college — was converted ; and three years after, another son, both of whom became devoted and useful ministers of the gospel. The three younger children were daughters, and they all became hopefully pious successively, according to their ages, and at about the same age. The eldest and the youngest of the daughters died in the triumphs of faith, and the remaining daughter is now adorning her profession as an active disciple of the Lord Jesus Christ.

Just as the youngest daughter was dying, she was asked if she could think of any passage or hymn that expressed her views and feelings in relation to her past life.

" Yes," she replied, —

" 'I send the joys of earth away,' " &c.

She dwelt on each verse as descriptive of her feelings, either in reference to her present condition, or to the different periods of her past life.

How surprising that any Christian, in any circumstances of affliction, — with all the precious promises of God before him, verified as they are by the constantly occurring events of his providence, — should ever lack confidence in his heavenly Father! How full of consolation is this incident to the pious widowed mother, and to the orphan children of pious parents.

"Leave thy fatherless children: I will preserve them alive."

A MOTHER'S VOICE IN PRAYER.

D—— was, from his birth, "lent unto the Lord," to minister in his temple "all the days of his life." His early conversion, and his preparation for the sacred office, was the burden of parental desire and the subject of frequent and earnest prayers. Long and severe was the trial of their faith, but the promises of the God of Abraham kept them from despair.

At an early age D—— entered college. During the first part of his course, his attention was frequently turned to the subject of personal religion. But the serious impressions of those seasons gradually wore away, leaving him, each time, apparently farther and farther from the kingdom of heaven. His mind became restless and uneasy. Sceptical thoughts respecting the religion in which he had been educated, now and then were suggested to his mind. These he began to cherish, till at length he had built up quite a little system of infidelity — a system of fashionable religion that leaves the feelings of the natural heart undisturbed. This he found perfectly congenial to his own state of mind. He searched the Scriptures daily, that he might defend the views he was endeavoring to embrace. But every time he sat down to this work, he found many things entirely opposed to his system, which he was obliged to wrest or reject.

One day, during his last collegiate year, while engaged in his dreadful work, he found the Bible so inflexible — that its teachings were so utterly different from what he wished them to be — that, in a paroxysm of rage, he threw the sacred volume into one corner of his room, where it lay upon the floor, unhonored and unread, for six months. He then resolved to spend his life in doing all he could in destroying the religion of the Bible. Such was the desperation and such the mad resolve of this young infidel.

D——'s last vacation was spent at home. One day, as he was amusing himself with some work of imagination, his mother entered the room. Her expectations in reference to this son had so often been disappointed, and her hopes so long deferred, that her heart was well-nigh sick, and her faith almost ready to fail. His college course was now soon to close, and a profession for life to be chosen, and the son of her prayers and vows was still unconverted. Her heart yearned over him, and, with all the tenderness and affection of a mother, she began to address him on the subject of his salvation. But he suddenly arrested her remarks, and said,—

"Mother, I respect your motives, and would not do anything to injure your feelings; but, I may as well tell you now as ever, I do not believe anything about this religion. It is all an imposition!"

O, it fell upon that mother's ear like the knell of death, and she cried out, "O, my son, my son!" and sank into a chair, sobbing aloud as though her very heart were broken.

This unexpected burst of maternal grief touched, for a moment, the cold, infidel heart of D——; but he soon arose and left the house. He retired to a bookstore, where he diverted his thoughts and amused himself till he supposed "the storm had passed away at home," and then returned.

As he was ascending the stairs to the sitting-room, a faint, plaintive voice arrested his attention. He stopped and listened. It was that mother, still in the chair where she had fallen, amid broken sobs and many tears, pouring out the anguish of her soul in prayer for her son. That voice, like an arrow from the quiver of the Almighty, entered the heart of D——, and he cried out involuntarily, "My God!"

That mother's voice in prayer rang in his ear continually. It followed him back to college; it was with him in his studies, and he heard it in the visions of the night; and it gave him no rest or peace till he found them in cordially embracing that God and Saviour to whose service his parents had given him with so much prayer and faith from his infant days.

We have had the pleasure of standing in the pulpit of D——, where is preached, not that fashionable, heartless religion that lulls the conscience into the sleep of death, and robs the divine Saviour of his crown, but that religion which represents the "natural heart" as "enmity against God," and holds up "Jesus Christ and Him crucified" as the lost sinner's only hope of salvation. Shall not this incident strengthen the faith, encourage the hope, and increase the importunity in prayer of every Christian parent?

PATTERNING AFTER MOTHER.

Oliver Crosby was a youth sixteen or eighteen years of age. He was the youngest of a large family of children. From very early life he manifested unusual sensibility and tenderness on the subject of religion, and the friend whom he made his principal counsellor, and to whom he ever unbosomed his feelings on this subject with the utmost freedom, was his own dear mother.

One day he was reading some work on education, and his mother was sitting near him. At length he stopped, and, addressing himself to her, said, —

"Mother, you do not know how much you have been watched. When I was small, I used to watch you in everything you did, so as to see what it was right for me to do. If I ever wanted to do anything that I thought might be wrong, I used to devise every plan to find out what you thought of it, and if you approved, I always felt safe in doing it. I never thought of going to father. I used to think that he had to see about supporting the family, and that you had everything to do about the soul; so I used to pattern after you."

"Why, my son," said the astonished mother, "what did you think when you saw me do things that were wrong?"

"I knew," replied the son, "that you used to say that you were a sinner, like other people, but I used to think that everything was right that you did. I could not believe that mother did anything that was wrong."

The effect of these remarks on the feelings of that mother was of course almost overwhelming. She was ready to give herself up to bitter weeping when she found how great her influence over her children had been, and how little she had realized it. "Had I only known," she said, "that I was observed in this way, how differently I should have felt, especially when indulging in feelings that were wrong." And yet there are few mothers whose feelings were more uniform, and whose influence was more salutary, or who have witnessed greater blessings on their children.

It is a most solemn truth that, in most cases, children do pattern after their parents, and especially their mother. Do parents generally realize this? Do they think that they are watched in all their words and actions, in all their intercourse with each other and the world, and in all their conduct towards their children? Do they remember that even what is wrong in them will be seen by the watchful eyes of their children, and be regarded and copied as proper and right? How can a parent think of this subject and not, like this mother, be overwhelmed, and ready to exclaim, "Who is sufficient for these things?" But there are most precious promises to encourage the pious parent. "My grace," says the Saviour, "is sufficient for thee." "As thy day, so shall thy strength be." "If any of you lack wisdom, let him ask of God, that giveth to all men liberally and upbraideth not, and it shall be given him."

"HOW SHALL WE ORDER THE CHILD?"

The prayer of Manoah, "How shall we order the child, and how shall we do unto him?" is one that many Christian parents often feel like offering in regard to the proper training, and especially the proper discipline, of their children. If ever they need divine wisdom and guidance, it is in reference to this subject.

Some years ago we became acquainted with the following case of discipline, that may be useful to some parents in similar circumstances.

Among the rules of conduct which the Rev. Mr. B—— early taught his children they must strictly observe, were these two, namely, never to take anything, however small, without the permission of the owner; and always to speak the truth.

Henry, his oldest child, one day, when about four years old, saw the boys around the house where his parents boarded busily engaged in trundling their hoops. They seemed to be full of glee and happiness. The little fellow, as he watched their happy sports, longed to be a partaker with them, but he had no hoop. At length, as he went under the shed, he espied an old iron hoop. He seized it with joy, and began to mingle with the other boys in their amusement.

When he came in, his mother said to him, "Henry, where did you get that hoop?"

"One of the boys gave it to me," said he. But his countenance and faltering voice betrayed his guilt.

Mrs. B——, not being able at that time to give the subject the attention which its importance demanded, related the particulars, and gave him up to his father.

Henry at length confessed that he found the hoop under the shed, and that he had told a falsehood. Thus he had broken two of the established rules of the family. The father told him he could not settle the business then, as it was Saturday night; but he would attend to it Monday morning, and that he might think of it till then.

Monday morning, after breakfast, Mr. B—— took his little boy into his study, and, without saying a word, tied his hands together, and then tied them to a nail.

As he commenced doing this, the little fellow began to tremble and beg to be forgiven.

"But, my son," said the father, "I cannot forgive sin. God alone can do that, and I must leave you here to settle this business with God."

At this the child became greatly agitated; but the father left the room, turned the key, and went across an adjoining room to the stairs, so distinctly that the child should know that he was left alone. As the key turned, Henry gave two or three distressing cries, and all was silent.

The father waited fifteen or twenty minutes with the greatest solicitude, and returned. As he entered the room, the little boy stood with his eyes cast down, looking very pensive and sad, and so absorbed in thought that he seemed not to have noticed his father's return.

"My son," said the father, "has God forgiven you?"

"I don't know. How shall I know, father?"

"Why, my son, if you are really sorry that you have sinned, if you trust in the Saviour for pardon, and are resolved never to do so again, you may hope that God has forgiven you. But, my son, how shall I know that you have asked God to forgive you? You have once told a falsehood; how shall I ever again know when to believe you?"

The broken-hearted child immediately dropped on his knees, and, raising his little hands, he offered up to his heavenly Father his simple, child-like petitions for forgiveness. This was too much for a parent's eye to witness, or his heart to endure.

The father untied the penitent child, now tenfold dearer to him, if possible, than ever before, freely forgave him, so far as he had offended him and violated the rules of the family, and then sent him to his mother, to seek her forgiveness also.

That child was never afterwards known to indulge in the least equivocation. Years afterwards, whenever he wished anything, he would say, "Father, I should like such a thing, if you think it is best."

This single case of discipline, though it was truly affecting, and must have been peculiarly so to that parent's heart, may prove the salvation of the child. It may instrumentally save him from bringing his parents down-broken-hearted to the grave, and of plunging his own soul into the gulf of despair.

A MOTHER'S BURDEN CAST ON JESUS.

"Cast thy burden upon the Lord, and He shall sustain thee." "Casting all your care upon Him, for He careth for you."

These precepts are strikingly illustrated in the following simple narrative : —

Mrs. L—— is the mother of a large family of children. Having given herself to the Saviour, she ever sought to "bring her children up in the nurture and admonition of the Lord," and she was afterwards sustained and cheered in her advanced years, as she had long been, in seeing all her "children walking in truth."

Several years since, one of her younger sons went to a Western city to commence a course of study for the ministry. Three of her sons were already in different stages of preparation for that sacred office. This son was to proceed by land to the place of his future home, and his baggage, containing most of his clothes and books, was to be sent in a large box by water.

A part of the evening previous to his departure, he

with the other children was absent from home, and the mother was engaged in packing that box; and a mother only can tell the feelings with which she undertakes the sad yet pleasant office. Her son, still in early youth, with the morrow's light was to leave the parental roof to seek a home among strangers. As she dwelt on this important era in his history, at length parental solicitude suggested to her mind the possibility that this box, with its precious treasures, might never reach her son. This suggestion raised a tempest of anxious thoughts: " What would my poor child do should it be lost? How he would suffer, far away from a mother's care, without these articles I have toiled so many long evenings to prepare for his comfort. They must not, they *cannot* be lost!"

Thus, for a time, she bore all this burden alone, and it well-nigh crushed her aching heart. At length she said, " Why should not I cast this burden upon my Saviour? Why not tell Him of my sorrows?' She fell upon her knees, and poured her complaint into the ear of her sympathizing Saviour.

She again resumed her work, but the burden was still upon her heart. Again she prostrated herself at the Mercy-seat, but no light came to her mind, when, for the third time, she knelt beside that box, and earnestly sought submission to her Father's will. And now her Saviour, who had so often appeared for her, interposed in her behalf, saying, " Daughter, thy tears are seen; thy prayer is heard. According to thy faith be it unto thee."

That burden was now removed, and she was able to say " Thy will be done," and she felt a sweet assurance that her prayer had been heard. She cheerfully finished her work, and then commended anew that precious treasure to her Saviour. Ever after she felt a confidence that His eye would watch over it, and that He would bring it in safety to the hand of her child.

The next morning that son, having been commended at the family altar to a faithful God, took a tender leave of kindred and home, and commenced his long journey to a land of strangers. His box was also started on its still longer and more adventurous tour, but its safety was insured by a mother's prayers and a Saviour's promise.

At length a letter brought the strange news that the box had not arrived, and that the boat, on which it was probably shipped at New Orleans, had been wrecked on the great western river. This was strange news, indeed, to the mother; but still she trusted in her Saviour's faithfulness. Other letters from time to time came, detailing the inconvenience, and almost suffering, this loss had occasioned the absent son.

Several months after the boat was wrecked, and the son had given up all hope in regard to his lost treasure, one day, to his great surprise and joy, it was brought safely to his room. He learned that the boat, on which it was shipped at New Orleans, was wrecked hundreds of miles from him, and the baggage on board was mostly lost. But his box, under the guidance of a watchful providence, was borne upon the bosom of the river, and landed safely upon the shore.

"But will it be found? And if found, will it not fall into the hands of those cruel wreckers, who fatten upon the losses of others?"

Yes, it will be found, and it will be protected; for that mother's prayers have insured its safety. All the waters of that mighty river, and all the avaricious men that swarm along its shores, cannot countermand the Saviour's purposes in regard to it. As a protector was divinely guided to the Hebrew infant among the flags of the Nile, so an honest man, a protector, is directed to this lost treasure upon this western river's bank. The directions, though so long exposed to the floods and the storms, he finds uneffaced, and at once sends it on its way. After a few days its adventurous wanderings are completed, the mother's faith is sufficiently tried, and it is safe in the possession of its owner, its contents all in the same good condition as when that anxious mother wept over them, closed so carefully every chink, and in faith committed it to the care of her Saviour.

Anxious mother, burdened Sabbath school teacher, careworn disciple, " cast your burden — all your cares — upon the Lord, for He careth for you."

HOW DR. BELL TRAINED HIS BOYS.

Dr. Bell believed in boys. He had seven of his own. He believed, with Abraham, in the duty of "commanding his children and his household," and in the Solomon mode of family discipline; but, while he ever insisted on prompt and implicit obedience from his children, a look was generally sufficient to secure it. The rod was, like his lancet and some of his deadly poisons, only for extreme cases, which seldom occurred. No child ever thought of hesitating, or asking " Why ? " when a command was given.

Dr. Bell believed in treating his boys as associates, and not as slaves. He was ever ready to talk with them, and to enter into all their plans, and show an interest in whatever interested them. He was once a boy himself; and he had not forgotten, as a great many seem to, how a boy feels and what a boy wants.

When his eldest son was about three years of age, Dr. Bell purchased a large farm at Hillside, in one of the finest agricultural towns in Central Massachusetts. He was led to this both from his own love of agriculture, and because he felt that the farm was the best place for the early training of his boys.

This farm was pleasantly situated, about half a mile from a village. The panoramic view from the large farm-house, with its cluster of barns and various out-houses, was called one of the most beautiful in the state. The village, in its natural appearance, was a little gem in the centre of a small valley, surrounded with verdant fields and gentle slopes. But morally, this village was much like the " cities of the plain." The evil spirit of rum ruled in almost every family. Many of that generation have gone to the drunkard's grave, some in their youth.

On all public occasions the men and boys of the village and of the surrounding country there congregated, and gave loose to almost every wicked passion. On "Election Day"—the chief and well-known holiday of those times, and then more observed in Massachusetts than the Fourth of July—it was a scene of rioting and confusion. Shooting-matches, horse-racing, the bowling-alley, cock-fighting, profanity, and drunkenness were the employments of the day. What a neighborhood in which to train a family of boys! There was no Sabbath there, and a God was scarcely acknowledged except in oaths.

Dr. Bell showed no little wisdom and tact in managing his boys on these occasions. All other boys went to the village; and how could he safely deny his from doing what all others did? He well knew that, should he take such a course, without providing some other amusement at least equally attractive, they would be likely to become impatient of restraint, and by and by seek to break away from his control.

When Dr. Bell first began the practice of medicine, he procured a lad to attend his horse, go on errands, and help about the house. In a few days this lad was taken with that distressing illness for which the doctor had among his medicines no remedy — homesickness; and he ran off home to his grandmother. The good old lady, perhaps, never experienced that kind of illness, and did not know how to sympathize with the poor child; and, giving him a good grandmotherly scolding, she sent him back.

In a day or two he was home again, feeling worse than before. Grandmother sent him back once more, with the assurance of what he well knew how to dread, if he returned again.

This threat aroused all the wicked there was in him, and he burst out, in the midst of his sobs, and his words a little mixed: "Well, when I get to be a big boy, I guess I shall come when I go, and please when I'm a mind to, for all nobody."

Dr. Bell well knew that his boys, if restrained from the amusements which all other boys enjoyed, — if he simply forbade their going to the village, and left them to find their means of recreation as best they could, — might for the time being hush down their sense of oppression and wrong; but they would say in their hearts, if not in words, "When we are older we shall come when we go and please when we're a mind to."

But how did Dr. Bell meet the emergency? As soon as his boys became large enough to think of the attractions of the village, he at once said, " I must provide something for them more attractive." He sent invitations into town, three miles distant, where the family attended church on the Sabbath, to the sons of the minister and of four or five other families with whom they were especially familiar, to spend Election day at Hillside Farm. They all gladly accepted the invitation, and there was a company of twenty or twenty-five boys gathered to celebrate the great holiday. No labor or expense was spared in providing entertainment and every kind of amusement for this young and happy party.

And what should be their amusements? Should they be left to themselves to devise them as best they might? No. Dr. Bell entered into all their scenes of recreation with them. When one amusement began to lose its power to please, he would suggest another. When they played ball he kept tally. And how it thrilled every young heart when he occasionally lent a helping hand, and united with them in some favorite sport of his boyish days.

According to the universal custom of those days — a custom at which we are now amazed as we think of it — all the men and boys, and even many women and girls, partook, on all joyous occasions, of the social glass, and Dr. Bell brought out to his young friends the tall fluted glass of lemon punch; and the good mother, who fully entered into all the plans of her husband in the right training of their children, did her best to prepare an attractive dinner, in which the huge plum-pudding and the shiny "Election cake" were prominent.

Few companies of boys ever enjoyed election as did this one at Dr. Bell's Hillside Farm. When they separated at the close of the day, it was with the most enthusiastic declarations. "What a good time we have had!" "Splendid!" "Capital!" "No boys ever had a better!" &c. Not a boy of Dr. Bell's but was more than satisfied with their father's plan of keeping election; not one who ever again wished to be with the low rabble at the village.

The next year this party of boys all spent their election at the parsonage, and had a good time; the next at Esquire T.'s; and so on. They went round about once and a half, when they were old enough to find their amusement in some other rational way, and unite in social visits with their sisters.

And then, when the young people who had attended the dancing-schools, and spent their earlier holidays at the village and the tavern, united in a sleigh-ride and a ball, Dr. Bell was ever ready to propose a ride for his children. They always saw that it was not to avoid expense, if they were not permitted to unite in the amusements of others, but it was their father's wish to shelter them from temptation to evil.

Dr. Bell's mode of training his boys proved a happy success. Before he was called to leave his ten children fatherless, he and his praying wife had the great pleasure of seeing all of them choosing God as their "father, and the guide of their youth;" and half of them enter the sacred office as ministers, or the wives of clergymen.

EFFECTS OF PARENTAL INDULGENCE.

The sad effects of the improper indulgence of children, the neglect to exercise proper parental authority in restraining them from wrong, and in bringing them up in the nurture and admonition of the Lord, are strikingly seen in many examples given us in the Scriptures.

Look at the domestic trials of David. See him fleeing for his life from a rebel son, who seeks the paternal throne at the price of a father's blood. We learn the cause of these severe trials in what is said of Adonijah, another rebel son, who also had exalted himself to be a king, and usurped the throne in his father's old age. "His father had not displeased him at any time, in saying, Why hast thou done so?" Such indulgence never did, it never can, secure filial respect, love, and obedience. Look at the awful judgments sent upon Eli and all his family, in consequence of his neglecting the exercise of parental authority. His sons "were the sons of Belial." They made themselves vile, and the father restrained them not. "Their sins were very great before the Lord," and they called for the most rigorous and severe exercise of parental authority. Instead of this, the indulgent father, when he heard of their vile conduct, mildly says, "Why do ye such things? For I hear of your evil dealings by all this people. Nay, my sons, for it is no good report I hear."

This afflicted father, for his cruel lenity, must not only suffer by seeing his sons making themselves vile, but he must be pained to the very heart by a message from God, that his sons are to be slain by the sword, as a judgment upon himself for not restraining them from sin. And to make his affliction still more severe and intolerable, he is told that this iniquity of his house shall not be purged with sacrifice or offering forever. O, with what bitterness of soul must the father reflect that his own indulgence had not only caused "men," by the sins he had neglected to restrain, "to abhor the offering of the Lord," but had also caused the premature and violent death and everlasting ruin of his children.

How different would be the state of many families in our day, which are now scenes of unhappiness, confusion, and discord, were parental authority properly maintained; were parents, like Abraham, to command their children and their households after them.

The happiest families, the most affectionate and dutiful children, are those where the most perfect and unconditional submission to parental authority is maintained. Indulgence at the expense of authority always begets disrespect and insubordination.

Why do so many parents of the present day affect to lightly esteem, or even ridicule, the advice of the wise king of Israel,—advice given, too, under the special guidance of the Holy Spirit,—"Correct thy son, and he shall give thee rest; yea, he shall give delight unto thy soul. Thou shalt beat him with the rod, and shalt deliver his soul from hell"?

With what eloquence will these passages enable parents to describe to their children the reasons why they insist on their obedience, and do not indulge them in all their childish and unreasonable whims. They can show them that however trying to parental affection, they must restrain them from sin and disobedience, or break themselves the commands of God, and incur his awful displeasure and judgments.

There is a strong conviction in the minds of many that family government has, of late years, greatly declined among us; that indulgence has taken the place of authority. Many of our public school teachers assert that it is far more difficult to govern their schools and secure the obedience of their scholars, than it used to be in former years. And they attribute this to parental indulgence, and a want of the proper exercise of authority in the family. The influence upon the community at large of a decline in family government must be most baneful.

INCONSIDERATE THREATENING.

Henry B——, when a little boy about three years old. accompanied his father and mother on a visit to his grandparents. He was of just the age to attract notice and be petted. His grandfather called him his little man, and dandled him on his knee; his grandmother covered his cheeks with kisses, and filled his hands with sweetmeats; and many were the marks of attention and little presents by which his uncles and aunts excited his sweet smiles and won his young affections.

This was a gladsome day to little Henry. For many weeks after his return, the sweets of that visit were made almost the only theme of his chatter. Among the presents which endeared to him his uncles and aunts, was a tiny bow and arrow. For hours he would amuse himself in the yard in shooting at flies, many of which he greatly frightened. At length he began to fire in the house, with no small danger to the windows, and to the eyes of his baby brother. His mother showed him the danger, and told him he must not do it any more. This he soon forgot, and began again to fire at the marks and flies on the walls and the ceiling. His mother saw it, and, without any consideration, told him if he did it again she should burn his bow and arrow.

Henry's memory was rather short, especially in relation to anything that interfered with his play. In a few days he again resumed his favorite amusement in the house, as if no danger had been threatened to his bow and arrow. His mother reminded him of what she had threatened.

Poor Henry! He knew his mother never broke her word; yet he pleaded as for his life, and promised not to disobey again. Till now the mother was not aware how much he valued his bow and arrow. She did not know that it had become the idol of his heart. She now regretted that she had spoken so inconsiderately, with so little reflection as to the consequences. But she could not recall her word, or commute the penalty, without injuring parental authority.

As she cast the toy into the flames, poor Henry clasped his little hands, and walked to and fro before the fire in the greatest agony. He watched the idol object till it broke asunder and fell among the embers; then, with a deep-drawn sigh of despair, as though his very heart were broken, and casting an anxious look into the face of his mother, whose heart was also ready to burst, he exclaimed, —

"There, it's all gone!" And long did he mourn under this infliction, and refuse to be comforted.

No one who has never felt the same can conceive that mother's feelings. Gladly would she have fasted days, could she have recalled that rash threatening, and have restored to her distressed child the object so dear to his little heart. She did not reproach herself because she had prohibited firing in the house; that prohibition was proper. Neither because she had threatened punishment in case the offence were repeated. Henry's disobedience deserved punishment, perhaps as severe as was inflicted. But that mother did reproach herself for the inconsiderateness with which she threatened the punishment. She did not stop to think of the consequences of its infliction. She did not stop to choose the kind of punishment that would best answer the purpose for which it was intended.

For many years that event was fresh in the recollection of that mother. There was hardly an act of her whole life, as a mother, that she so much regretted. She said, —

"Parents should reflect before they threaten punishment, and ponder well the consequences of its execution."

This is a remark of wisdom. By not acting in accordance with it, many parents acquire the habit of threatening unnatural punishments, which they never dream of executing. By such false declarations they sin against God, destroy in the minds of their children all respect for their authority, and all confidence in their word, and all regard to truth themselves.

DECEIVING CHILDREN.

It is a very unwise and pernicious practice with some parents to use deception in seeking to influence and govern their children. This practice, like frequent and inconsiderate threatening, is soon understood by the children, and loses its power to influence them.

Dr. Bell was called to visit a sick boy twelve years

of age. As he entered the house the mother took him aside, and told him he could not get her boy to take any medicine except he deceived him.

"Well, then," said Dr. Bell, "I shall not give him any. He is old enough to be reasoned with."

He went to the boy, and after an examination, said to him, "My little man, you are very sick, and you must take some medicine. It will taste badly, and make you feel badly for a little while, and then I expect it will make you feel better."

The doctor prepared the medicine, and the boy took it like a man, without the least resistance; and he would take from his mother anything the physician prescribed, but he would take nothing else from her. She had so often deceived him, and told him "it was good," when she gave him medicines, that he would not trust to anything she said. But he saw at once that Dr. Bell was telling him the truth, and he trusted him. He knew, when he took the bitter draught, just what to expect.

A mother came with her boy, eight or ten years old, to a dentist. The little fellow had for days been suffering all the cruel pains of the toothache. She had used in vain every possible influence to induce him to go with her and have the offending tooth extracted. But he could not forget that she had once before persuaded him to have an aching one removed by assuring him that it would not hurt him much. But O, how it did hurt him! She deceived him then, and he would bear the pain rather than be so deceived again. Had she at first frankly told him it would hurt him, but it would be only for a minute, and he must be brave and bear it like a man, it would all have been well. But the suffering at length became so terrible, that he was induced by his mother's new methods of deceiving him, and by her promises of rewards, to go with her again to the place of torture, as he regarded it.

He had no sooner reached the dentist's office than the tooth ceased to ache, and he resisted every effort of his mother to have it extracted. He screamed, and fought, and struggled, till the dentist, wearied with the delay, and out of patience with this exhibition of bad training or want of government, said to the mother, "Madam, do you want me to extract that boy's tooth?" She replied that she did; when he quietly took the boy, before he had time to suspect what he was going to do, placed his head firmly between his knees, and removed the tooth. The ungoverned child, as soon as he was released, ran round the room, screaming, "You shan't pull it! you shan't pull it!"

These simple incidents contain instructions of deep importance, deserving the careful consideration of every parent. "Honesty," with children as well as with others, and in all things, "is the best policy."

THE SINS OF OUR YOUTH.

The penitent David, as he looked back and thought of his early days, exclaimed, "Remember not the sins of my youth." And afflicted Job cries out in his distress, "Thou makest me to possess the iniquities of my youth."

Two aged disciples, one eighty-seven years old, one day met. "Well," inquired the younger of his fellow-pilgrim, "how long have you been interested in religion?" "Fifty years," was his reply. "Well, have you ever regretted that you began so young to devote yourself to the cause of the Saviour?" "O, no," said he, and the tears trickled down his furrowed cheeks; "I weep when I think of the sins of my youth. It is this which makes me weep now."

Another man of eighty, who had been a Christian fifty or sixty years, was asked if he was grieved that he had become a disciple of Christ? "O, no," said he; "if I grieve for anything it is that I did not become a Christian before."

We visited a woman of ninety, as she lay on her last bed of sickness. She had been hoping in Christ for half a century. In the course of conversation she said, "Tell all the children that an old woman, who is just on the borders of eternity, is very much grieved that she did not begin to love the Saviour when she was a child. Tell them 'Youth is the time to serve the Lord.'"

Said an old man of seventy-six, "I did not become interested in religion till I was forty-five; and I often have to tell God I have nothing to bring him but the dregs of old age."

Said another man, between sixty and seventy years of age, "I hope I became a disciple of the Lord Jesus when I was seventeen;" and he burst into a flood of tears as he added, "and there is nothing which causes me so much distress as to think of those seventeen years — some of the very best portions of my life which I devoted to sin and the world."

This testimony is only a specimen of the testimony of all Christians on this subject. Why, then, are we not more earnest in our endeavors to convince the young that their present forgetfulness of God will be the occasion of many a bitter tear of sorrow when they are old, even should they hereafter be converted? They will then cry out with David, "Remember not the sins of my youth;" and with Job, "Thou makest me to possess the iniquities of my youth."

A FEARFUL ENTAILMENT.

Impenitent parents are entailing impenitence, with all its consequent temporal and eternal calamities, upon their children. This is, indeed, a fearful entailment. But it accords with the testimony of the Scripture. God said, amid the thunderings and lightnings of Sinai, "for I the Lord thy God am a jealous God, visiting the iniquities of the fathers upon the children unto the third and fourth generations of them that hate me." In speaking of the judgments of God against the wicked, the prophet Jeremiah says, "Thou recompensest the iniquities of the fathers into the bosom of their children after them." And this will not be unrighteousness in God, because the children will be induced, in the natural course of things, to imbibe the corrupt principles and copy the bad examples of their parents.

The history of the kings of Israel and Judah teaches the same lesson on this subject. As one king after another is introduced to us, it is almost invariably said, "And he did evil in the sight of the Lord, and walked in the way of his father." Sometimes they did worse than all that were before them. Such were Omri, and Ahab his son.

On account of the high-handed wickedness of Jeroboam, in forgetting Jehovah, the Lord denounced destruction upon his whole house. This denunciation was soon after fearfully fulfilled. Nadab, the son of

Jeroboam, succeeded him, doing evil in the sight of the Lord, and walking in the way of his father. After three years, Baasha conspired against him and slew him. He no sooner established himself in his usurped dominion, than he slew all the house of Jeroboam, and he left not to Jeroboam any that breathed, until he had destroyed them, according unto the saying of the Lord."

The same destruction was also denounced, in turn, against this wicked usurper and his posterity and the posterity of his house and all his kinsfolks and friends, because he walked in the way of Jeroboam. And this threatening was perfectly fulfilled a short time after by Omri, who usurped the throne of Elah, the son of Baasha.

Ahab, being stirred up by Jezebel his wife, sold himself to work evil in the sight of the Lord. The sins of these wicked parents were speedily visited upon themselves and their children, and their house was made like the house of Jeroboam and like the house of Baasha.

No one can read the stories of Achan, of Korah, Dathan and Abiram, of Gehazi, &c., without trembling in view of the terrible calamities which they, by their sins, brought upon themselves, their sons and their daughters, their wives and their little ones, and upon all they possessed.

And how many and affecting are the examples in our day, in which irreligious, and especially vicious and intemperate parents, are making a fearful entailment of evil for this life and the future, upon their children!

And what more natural than that their children should be preparing themselves to receive such an entailment? While young, how unsuspecting, how credulous! Whatever instruction is given, whatever example is set by a parent, is received and followed with the most unquestioning confidence. Let a parent neglect the Bible, profane the sacred name of his Maker, violate the Sabbath, indulge in the intoxicating cup, and disregard all the duties of the gospel, and his children, with the sanction of parental example, will not hesitate to do the same. And why should they? What more natural than that they should imbibe the sentiments and feelings, and walk in the footsteps of their parents? Like parents, like children.

And we are driven to the painful conclusion that impenitent parents, by their instruction and example, are entailing impenitence, with all its consequent temporal and eternal calamities, upon their children; that, because they are forgetting the law of their God, God is also forgetting their children.

INFLUENCE OF PIOUS BROTHERS AND SISTERS.

There was a family of seven brothers and three sisters, all of whom became interested in the subject of religion in early life, and all became members of the church of Christ. They will never forget their feelings when only one of their number remained unconverted. All their sympathy and interest seemed to concentrate upon that brother. With what prayers and entreaties did they labor for his conversion! And when their prayers were answered, there was joy in their hearts like that among the angels in heaven when a sinner repenteth.

The son of a clergyman, some years ago, was hopefully converted while a member of college, at a distance from his home. He was a child of many prayers. Like Samuel, he had been "lent unto the Lord;" and it was for His service in the sanctuary that these pious parents were educating him. But their hope as yet was deferred, and their faith was still tried. Under these circumstances, what emotions of joy and gratitude to God must the intelligence of that son's conversion have awakened in that father's and mother's bosom! Similar intelligence, from that same favored institution, has often gladdened the hearts of distant parents and friends.

But what was the particular way in which God saw fit to answer the prayers of these parents, and to show that he was faithful to his promises? In other words, what were the special means of that young man's conversion while at a distance from his home.

He was favored not only with praying parents, but also with a praying brother and sister; and they were the special means of leading him to the Saviour. A few weeks before the concert of prayer for our literary institutions, this pious brother and sister,— the latter then absent from home,— wrote letters almost simultaneously to their impenitent brother in college. These letters, warm from the hearts of a dear brother and sister, and breathing forth such tender and anxious expressions of fraternal and sisterly piety and love, reached his heart, and awakened the inmost feelings of his soul. This state of mind rendered the concert of prayer, when it arrived, a meeting of great interest to him, and he was soon led to rejoice in hope of pardoned sin. This brother was converted into an active Christian. The influence of religion, in its purity and power, does indeed, or it should always make those who truly embrace it active Christians.

Soon after he became interested, he, and an associate

with like ardor, went to a neighborhood several miles distant, where the people had few, if any, religious privileges, and where there was but little interest manifested in religious things. They there set up a prayer-meeting, and soon established a Sabbath school of sixty scholars, both of which were the means of awakening much interest among the people.

Such are the happy results, as already seen, that have followed the efforts of that pious brother and sister in behalf of their unconverted brother.

What an encouragement these incidents should afford pious brothers and sisters, and, indeed, all Christians, to labor for the salvation of their impenitent friends. How great must be the influence of the daily lives of truly Christian brothers and sisters in their homes!

XXIII.

SABBATH SCHOOLS AN AUXILIARY TO THE CHURCH.

It may not be inappropriate to close this account of "Fifty Years with the Sabbath Schools" with one of the author's sermons on "Sabbath Schools an Auxiliary to the Church."

"And God hath set some in the church, first apostles, secondarily prophets, thirdly teachers, after that miracles, then gifts of healings, helps, governments, diversities of tongues." — 1 COR. xii. 28.

God has furnished the church, in performing the great and responsible work intrusted to her hands, with many and efficient auxiliaries. He has permitted her to lay everything, to the utmost of her power, under contribution for assistance in this work. And in the text we are informed that he has appointed or ordained various orders or ranks in the church, for the accomplishment of this object. Among these are specified teachers and helps. The precise meaning of these terms, or the precise duties assigned to these orders, it is now perhaps difficult to determine. But that they were employed, to a greater or less extent, in communicating instruction to the ignorant, in teaching the doctrines of religion, and in rendering various assistance to the apostles, — the ministers, the servants of the church, — is more than probable. Although the apostle, probably, had not in mind, in recording these words, the modern institution of Sabbath schools, yet it is obvious that Sabbath schools may very appropriately be denominated helps. They are helps to the ministry in discharging the duties of that high and holy office; helps to Christian parents in bringing up their children in the nurture and admonition of the Lord; and helps to the church generally in training up her sons and daughters for her own service, and in all her efforts for the conversion of the world. And it will be my object, in this discourse, to consider the institution of Sabbath schools as a help — an auxiliary to the church in her labors for the salvation of men.

I. I remark, then, in the first place, that this institution aids the church *by increasing the number of those who attend on her ministry.*

The great work of the church is to proclaim, especially through her ministry, the messages of salvation to men. She is to persuade as many of them as possible to be reconciled to God. Whatever has a tendency to increase the number who listen to these messages aids the church in her labor; for the more there are to hear her proclamation, the greater will probably be the number who will accept the salvation she proclaims.

Now, to do this, is a direct tendency of Sabbath schools. Few are the churches that do not acknowledge the attendance of whole families, through the influence of this institution. And whole neighborhoods, too, — where there was no sanctuary, no Sabbath, and no voice of prayer, and where vice had long held undisputed sway, — through this instrumentality have been renovated, and most of the inhabitants now go in company to the house of the Lord, and an altar of prayer is erected in many a dwelling, and a throne for the Saviour in many a heart.

The following testimony of a pastor might be made respecting many of our churches: —

"I consider the Sabbath school as an institution, in connection with every religious society, of the highest importance, and as intimately connected with its prosperity in every respect. Nothing, under God, is effecting more for my church and society than the Sabbath school. It is a powerful auxiliary to the enlargement of both. It has done wonders here in bringing under the means of grace many who for years have not stepped their foot over the threshold of God's sanctuary."

II. Sabbath schools assist the church in *gaining access to the hearts of parents.*

The whole tendency of this institution — of its lessons, its instructions, all its exercises and its library books — is to produce in the minds of the pupils reflection, and lead to serious inquiry. The questions elicited by this state of mind have often come home to the bosom of parents with a power that has melted into contrition hearts that have long resisted the impressive appeals of the pulpit, and all other efforts of the church. Many parents, who never honor God by their presence in his sanctuary, will grant their children the privileges of this institution. These parents are usually inaccessible by the direct influence of the church, whether exerted by her ministry or her private members. The only medium of access to them seems to be through their children. There are, indeed, chords in their hearts, but they will vibrate to no human touch except the soft yet irresistible touch of an affectionate child. O, what parent can resist such an influence? How often has almost an infant one carried home from its loved Sabbath school the first message of mercy that has ever fallen upon the consciences, and reached the hearts of such parents! They have been melted into godly sorrow, and praise has been perfected out of the mouth of infancy. Says Baxter: —

"My first and greatest success was among the young; and so it was that when God had touched the hearts of the young with love and goodness, in various instances their friends — their fathers and their grandfathers, who had lived in ignorance before — became religious, induced by their love to their children, who now appeared so much wiser, and better, and more dutiful than before. In a little time, religion spread through many families, and after a few years there was scarcely a house in which the worship of God was not maintained."

What exhortations have ungodly parents often received, and what prayers and songs have they heard around the dying-beds of pious Sabbath school children! How often, too, have parents blessed God on their own dying-beds for the consolation, the support, and the immortal hopes they have received from this institution through a beloved child!

III. This institution greatly aids the church *in her direct efforts for the good of the* YOUNG.

That the church has duties to perform for the good of her own children, and for the good of the young all around, surely no one can question. With the example of the Saviour before us, how can there be any doubt? For no class of persons did he labor, while on earth, with a more tender interest than for the young. And there is every possible motive to lead the church, through her ministry and all her private members, to copy this example of the Great Shepherd, and "feed the lambs" of his flock. Though young, their life is not the less uncertain, as many a broken-hearted parent can testify. Their salvation, too, is as important as that of the mature in age — its purchase cost the same. Indeed, should life be prolonged, — other things being equal, — the salvation of the young is far more important than that of the aged: because they will have a much longer period in which to labor in the vineyard, they will be able to labor, too, with greater efficiency and to far better advantage. The person converted in middle life or old age, must spend much of his time and strength, as a Christian, in counteracting the unhappy influences of the habits and associations and prejudices of his impenitent days; while, on the other hand, most of the habits and associations that a pious child has formed, are of a religious character, so that most of his time and strength may be employed directly in the service of God. "I have not half the fears," said the late Dr. Todd, who labored abundantly for the lambs of his flock, "that a converted child will dishonor religion, that I have that the aged sinner, who has lived in the iron habits of sin for half a century, will do it. With him, it is the work of life and death to break off those old habits. His thoughts, wicked and vile, will, ever and anon, flow back into their old, deep-worn channels. But piety in the child gushes up like the breaking out of a new spring, making its own new channel, growing and widening, and beautifying as it flows."

Again, every effort to persuade the young to seek the Lord early and to consecrate the dew of their youth to God, is full of promise and encouragement. Childhood is the most interesting and favorable period of existence for receiving religious instruction. The impressions then made are like the deep lines of the sculptor's chisel: ages will not efface them. All the wicked propensities, too, are yet in their infancy; indeed, many of those wicked propensities which increasing age will develop, are yet imperceptible.

The fact, too, that the young may be converted, that very young children may become subjects of renewing grace, should encourage the church to labor for their salvation. Some of the most lovely and brightest examples of piety the history of the church has ever afforded, have been among children and youth. They have exhibited all the graces of the Christian, — repentance, faith, hope, joy, meekness, humility, benevolence; love for the Saviour, for prayer, the Bible, the Sabbath, and the people of God; patience and resignation in sickness, and triumph in death.

But I have said that the Sabbath school greatly aids the church in her direct efforts for the good of the young.

In the Sabbath school, any given church, through the pastor, the superintendent and teachers, meets most of the young connected with the congregation. And there, by a short visit, a brief prayer and address, when other duties will permit, by the pastor, and the instructions of an hour by the superintendent and teachers, an influence is exerted upon them which it would cost days of fatiguing labor to exert in any other way. In the Sabbath school we meet the young under very favorable circumstances. They are in the midst of their associates, and the kindness and affectionate familiarity with which they are there regarded by their teachers and other Christian friends, have banished all that reserve and constraint, and almost fear, that children used to feel in presence of a superior, and especially in the presence of a minister.

These labors for the good of the young, and this kindly notice of them, will convince them that the minister, and that Christians generally are their friends, will secure their confidence and respect,—yea, will entwine silken cords around their hearts and bind them to their own. And as they come forward in life, they will be found among the warmest friends of the church, the sharers of the pastor's burdens, and the lighteners of his toils.

O, what a reward does every minister and every Christian receive for all their labors among the young! No smile, no look of affectionate interest with which they regard them, will ever be lost. No attention, however small, though it be but the placing of the hand on the curly head of the little one by his mother's side, will go unrewarded. And that reward may be no less than the unspeakable joy of guiding these lambs of the flock home to the fold of the Great Shepherd above!

IV. Sabbath schools help to *educate the conscience and prepare the hearts of its members for the instructions of the sanctuary.*

One of the great obstacles to success in the labors of the church for the salvation of men, is a hardened, insensible conscience. Such a conscience never gives the truth a self-application. The word preached or addressed to the individual in private may, indeed, be a sharp, two-edged sword, piercing even to the dividing asunder of soul and spirit; but it will fall upon an obdurate conscience as upon a rock of adamant: there will be no impression there.

No conscience will be tender and impressible that is not enlightened by the word of God. But where the mind is imbued with the truth, the conscience will be so full of light that the smallest sin will be perceived; and it will be so tremblingly alive to what is right that it will shrink, as it were instinctively, from the very thought of what is wrong. If we hide the word of God in our hearts, we shall not sin against Him.

Now one great object of the institution of Sabbath schools is to store the mind with truth. The Bible is the text-book, or books or lessons founded upon the Bible; and all connected with the institution are expected to engage in a careful and earnest examination of its important doctrines and precepts. What a knowledge of the sacred oracles is thus obtained! And what a preparation of mind and heart for the instructions of the sanctuary will all this secure! Supposing the subject of discourse is from Paul's Epistle to the Romans, and suppose the school are studying that epistle, what a preparation among the members of that school for hearing a sermon on such a subject! A stranger might almost select from among that congregation every member of the Sabbath school. They would be recognized by the interest which the bare mention of the text would excite among them, and by the intelligent and interested attention with which they would follow the speaker through every stage of his discourse. The subject is one which they have just investigated themselves. It was made the topic of familiar and free discussion at the teachers' meeting and at the Sabbath school, and all will now be eager to see wherein the speaker's views harmonize with or differ from their own. Their minds will thus be all open to receive the full power of the word of God.

Why is it that there are generally such large and very attentive audiences when the people assemble to listen to political speakers? Who ever heard of persons reading books and papers at a political meeting? Who ever heard of persons falling asleep at such a meeting? These speakers seem to have an advantage over the ministers of the gospel. Every eye is fixed upon them, every mind is intent upon what they have to say ; and if they have a soul, they can't help being eloquent under the inspiration of such a waiting, attentive audience. And why is it? Why, it is because, if I may so say, there has been a sort of Sabbath school preparation for the meeting. All the week the people have been reading on the subject, they have discussed it at every corner of the street, and it has been the subject of their daily meditation. No wonder, then, that they come to the political meeting all absorbed in what may be communicated. Now would it not be an encouragement to the ministers of the gospel if they could find their people as well prepared by previous reading, conversation, and meditation as in the case supposed? I know the preacher has some of this encouragement, for, as he looks round upon the members of his Sabbath school, he knows that in every conscience he has an advocate for his doctrine that cannot be resisted. He knows that this portion of his people are intelligent in regard to the Bible, whatever may be the case in regard to all other matters.

If there were, therefore, no other benefit from this institution but this one, that it is preparing the people to listen with more interest and profit to the preaching of the gospel than they otherwise would do, it is worth all it costs, and should be sustained.

V. This institution is an auxiliary to the church, inasmuch as it *enlarges and develops her own energies*, — calls into employment the moral powers of God's people.

The energies of Christians are enlarged or developed in the same way that the energies of any other class of men are, namely, by cultivation, by exercise. And that there is a vast amount of moral power in the church of Christ lying dormant, inoperative, there can be no doubt. And whatever instrumentality shall call forth this power, or shall furnish exercise for those energies that are already in a measure developed, will prove an important auxiliary to the church in her labors for the salvation of men.

That the Sabbath school is often such an instrumentality, almost every church can bear witness. Some of our most efficient male and female Christians were in the habit of doing comparatively little for the cause of Christ till after they enlisted in this enterprise. Here they were placed where they were obliged to be active. Their energies were developed and strengthened. The more they exercised them, the more they were enlarged, just as the intellectual powers are enlarged and strengthened by cultivation.

In some churches, there are more or less members who have never opened their lips in prayer in a social meeting. They have never uttered a word of exhortation or comfort to their fellow-Christians; they are just like an infant child that never took a step without the aid of its mother's finger; all confidence forsakes them, and they begin to tremble and fall the moment they are left unaided. Now, what shall be done with these friends? Why, if they can be placed in circumstances where they will feel a little responsibility, they will find, as others will, that they possess moral power enough, but that it has never been developed. And there is moral power in the church, if it were brought out into active operation, to electrify the land, and give a new and brighter aspect to all our Christian enterprises.

I wish to illustrate this train of remark by a single incident. In the suburbs of one of our cities, some years ago, there resided a man who, though a member of the church, had never prayed in meeting. He and many of his neighbors attended worship in the city, because there was no church where they lived that they wished to attend. One day this man said to himself, Why should there not be such a church here? That very thought greatly stirred and interested him. He conversed with those neighbors, and they all became interested, and soon said among themselves, Why should we not do something to accomplish an object we think so desirable? They at once began the work, and in a year and a half they had organized a small church and society, erected a house of worship, and settled a minister.

At the organization of this church, the man who had never prayed in meeting had become so developed as a Christian that he was chosen one of the officers, and also the superintendent of the Sabbath school; and he at once became one of the leading men in all their social meetings. He was fourfold the man, as well as the Christian, that he was a year and a half before.

As there was a small debt on the chapel, he wished an introduction to a church where he could solicit a little help in meeting this debt. He was asked if they were doing all they could among themselves? He thought they were. "Why," said he, "were you to sell everything I own in the world at auction, — my furniture, my wearing apparel, everything belonging to myself, my wife, and my two little boys, — I don't think it would bring you two hundred dollars. I have just paid eighty dollars towards the chapel, I pay twenty dollars towards the preaching, and I have just paid ten dollars for the benefit of the choir." And that was the man who, a year and a half before, couldn't pray in meeting! He stood up a full-grown man and a Christian; and there was no way of accounting for this change, so marvellous to himself as well as others, but on the ground that he had been placed in circumstances where his moral power had been called into action. And might we not expect like results from like causes in all our churches? What would be the influence of any and of every church, supposing all its members were actively enlisted as teachers or scholars in the Sabbath school? Not a dwelling in the most obscure corner of the parish would be left one week unvisited. No child or youth — if repeated and pressing invitations, and every variety of persuasive argument and motive, could secure his attendance, or for want of suitable clothing or books — would be found out of this sacred enclosure, strolling the streets or the fields on God's holy day.

VI. I remark, once more, that the Sabbath school renders important aid to the church, *in at least promoting the conversion of souls.*

This point is surely too obvious to need extended consideration. There is hardly a town in this part of the land, where there are not more or less to rise up and call this institution blessed, and acknowledge it, with heartfelt gratitude, as the instrument of at least promoting their salvation. And there is hardly a church in the country that does not regard the Sabbath school as her nursery, from which she is to obtain her most thrifty, fruitful plants. Revivals have been intimately connected with this institution; frequently they have originated in it; and sometimes they have been confined exclusively within its limits. This sacred enclosure, under the influence of the showers of divine grace, has often appeared verdant as the garden of the Lord, in the midst of surrounding drought and sterility. Not unfrequently, from fifty to more than one hundred members of a single school have been hopefully converted in a single season. In our visits to ecclesiastical bodies in all parts of the country, it is a common thing to hear the declaration, in the report on the state of religion, that most of the conversions have been among the young, and especially among the members of the Sabbath schools. The pastors generally are finding the members of this institution the most hopeful part of their people for their own labors.

It should not be supposed, however, that all who are reported as having been converted in our Sabbath schools were converted through the instrumentality of this institution alone. A great variety of influences — parental instruction, where it is right, the preaching, of the gospel, &c. — has no doubt been usually connected with the influence of this institution in the conversion of these individuals. All we can say in relation to the influence of Sabbath schools generally, in the conversion of sinners, is this: that those who are connected with this institution are much more likely to be converted, through the combined good influences that are brought to bear upon them, than any other class of persons. And why should it not be so? There is usually more truth in the minds of such, on which the Spirit of God can operate; and they seem, too, more directly within the sphere of the Spirit's influence.

Many years ago we had the pleasure of being connected with the superintendence of a Sabbath school in which, on one Sabbath, there were present six hundred and seven members, including all ages, from those of three or four to those of almost ninety years. Most of the females in the parish were in the school, and in the galleries, sweeping round three sides of the great church, were the young men. And what was the result of such an attention to the Scriptures among that people? Why, blessing after blessing, rich as could come from the throne of God, was constantly showering down upon them.

At length most of the young men, for some reason, left the school. The same season there was an extensive outpouring of the Holy Spirit, and quite a number of the school were hopefully converted. But that class of young men — they were just like that field we sometimes see, all parched and desolate, while every other field around is verdant as the paradise of God. Not one of them was converted. They had placed themselves beyond the limits of that rain of grace.

A year or two subsequent to this, and sixty of those young men were brought back into a Bible class. And the pastor said, one day, "I now have great hopes of all these young men." And are there not hopes for those who are willing to break away from the power of shame and pride, and come and sit down together in the study of the Word of God? Here is the ground of encouragement in regard to the religious influence of the Sabbath schools, we are bringing the people together under circumstances where the Spirit of God is most likely to operate.

We are in danger of limiting the means which may, in any given case, be employed in the conversion of a soul. Every influence felt in urging one towards the cross has its part in this work.

Abbott, in one of his works, illustrates this point, in substance, in this way. Here is a large rock to be cleft asunder. It will take a thousand blows to cleave it. A thousand persons pass along and give a blow. Now, to a careless observer, much of this labor seems unnecessary. The rock seemed to cleave asunder under the influence of a few of the later blows. But if it required a thousand blows, of course the first blow and every intermediate blow were just as important as the last, under which it cleft asunder. How encouraging this thought is to every pastor, parent, teacher, Christian! No word of truth shall fall from the lips of any one, and no right effort be put forth, but it may be one in the series of influences which shall bring some soul to repentance.

With this qualification, however, all that is claimed for this institution is true. Though an humble, it is a mighty instrumentality in promoting the salvation of men, and especially of the young. The rising generation will yet see Sabbath schools more or less instrumental in filling heaven with joy and earth with rejoicing. Multitudes through this means have already learned their way to the new Jerusalem, and other multitudes are fast treading in their footsteps.

But Sabbath schools are not only often instrumental in making Christians, but also in making the best kind of Christians, and Christians with large and liberal hearts. In examining young persons for admission to the church, it has usually been an easy matter to select those who have enjoyed the instructions of this institution. They exhibit a better knowledge of the Scriptures, clearer views respecting the doctrines, and can give a more satisfactory reason for the hope that is in them. Should the church look on the Sabbath school as an auxiliary, and should she watch over it and use it as such, all that is accomplished through it she may be said herself to have been instrumental in accomplishing. Should she give it the place it deserves among the instrumentalities that are to bless and save men, she may hope here to polish many a precious gem to adorn and beautify the diadem of her Saviour.

I have now mentioned a few of the more obvious ways in which the institution of Sabbath schools aids the church in her labors for the salvation of men. And how forcibly does this view of the subject, if it be a correct view, lead us to this conclusion, that *the church is under the most solemn obligations to see that this institution is sustained..*

There need be no express command in the Scriptures to prove this obligation. The providence of God, in a voice so clear and intelligible that no one can have misapprehended it, has been proclaiming this institution to be an approved means of grace; an institution of peculiar importance to the church; an auxiliary to her ministry and to all her labors for the promotion of her own prosperity and the redemption of the world. Thousands on earth and thousands in heaven are rejoicing over this institution as the instrument of their salvation.

The materials which constitute the frame-work of the church are perishable, and they are fast dropping into decay and crumbling into dust. This institution is furnishing the materials for repairing these wastes of time, and for enlarging and beautifying this building of God, the church. Here we are to find those living stones and polished pillars which are to give strength and proportion and adornment to this glorious temple.

Here, then, is the ground of the obligation resting on the church to sustain this institution, — the voice of Providence.

If the church consult her own interests, or the good of others, she cannot resist the obligation to bestow on this institution her most watchful care and encouragement, and to see that it is vigorously sustained. As the church is composed of various members, this obligation rests on each and every member. No one has a right to free himself from responsibility in this matter. Every Christian, unless imperious circumstances prevent, should give the influence of his personal labors in sustaining this institution. There can be no reason why one class of Christians more than another, except so far as their qualifications for the work are better, or their circumstances more favorable, should forego the rest and retirement of home on the Sabbath to engage in the toils and anxieties of teachers.

But some one may say, " There are few places where the services of the whole church, as teachers, are required." True ; but this cannot justify any one member of a church in the conclusion that his or her services are not needed till the fact has been ascertained by personal inquiry.

But the truth is, there is scarcely a Sabbath school in the country that is not this moment more or less embarrassed for want of teachers ; not because there are no Christians in the place who are competent to fill this office, or who might easily render themselves competent, but because they are so unwilling to do it. There is no one thing of which superintendents so often complain, and which so breaks down their spirits and disheartens them in their arduous work, as the unwillingness of Christians to enter this field of labor. Were it the very field of death, they could hardly avoid it more anxiously than some do.

But supposing all the classes are supplied with teachers, may there not be room for more classes? And would not a little self-denying labor persuade or " compel " others " to come in," till all might be gathered into the fold of the Sabbath school, and the house be filled, so that the whole church might be enlisted in this holy enterprise ?

But if all may not be employed as teachers, there surely is room enough and to spare, or it may easily be obtained, for them as scholars. And in this capacity the church may exert a powerful influence in sustaining the school, in giving to it interest and efficiency, while at the same time every Christian will derive great personal benefit from the social study of the Scriptures.

Finally, those members of the church who are engaged in sustaining this institution have much to encourage them. They are co-workers with the ministers of the gospel. Without a tithe of the dreadful responsibleness and anxiety that often crush, with a mountain's weight, those at the altar, the faithful teacher and superintendent can participate in much of their sweetest pleasure. O what pleasure, compared with that which thrills the bosom of him who has just guided a soul to the Lamb of God, or who is faithfully giving instruction with reference to a result so glorious! In that pleasure teachers may participate. And, if faithful to the end, they will hereafter share in the reward of those who have turned many to righteousness, saved souls from death, and hid a multitude of sins; yea, they will hear that blessed welcome from their Saviour, "Well done, good and faithful servants; enter ye into the joy of your Lord!"

www.ingramcontent.com/pod-product-compliance
Lightning Source LLC
Chambersburg PA
CBHW021153230426
43667CB00006B/377